Mad Dogs
and
Englishwomen

Also by Pete Davies

Mad Dogs and Englishwomen

The Story of England
at the
6th Women's Cricket
World Cup in India

PETE DAVIES

An *Abacus* Book

First published in Great Britain by Abacus 1998

Map © Neil Hyslop
Photographs © Craig Prentis, Allsport UK Ltd

A CIP catalogue record for this book is available
from the British Library.

ISBN 0 349 11009 3

Typeset in Caslon 540 by M Rules
Printed and bound in Great Britain by Clays Ltd, St Ives plc

Abacus
A Division of
Little, Brown and Company (UK)
Brettenham House
Lancaster Place
London WC2E 7EN

For everyone who was there

Contents

Dramatis Personæ

[England in India, December 1997]

Skip – Karen Smithies OBE, 28, all-rounder; assistant
    manager, Coral Racing

JB – Jan Brittin, 38, top order bat; British Airways systems
    manager

Smigs – Jane Cassar, turned 25 in India, keeper & top order
    bat; secretary

Connie – Clare Connor, 21, all-rounder; student

BB – Barbara Daniels, turned 33 in India, top order bat;
    Executive Director of the Women's Cricket Association

Lottie – Charlotte Edwards, turned 18 in India, opening bat
    & leg spinner; works for Hunts County Bats

The Lengster – Kathryn Leng, 24, all-rounder; Yorkshire
    Bank clerk

Laura MacLeod, 20, opening bowler; cricket coach

Sue Metcalfe, 32, top order bat, vice captain; blood
    coagulation specialist

Bev Nicholson, 22, seam bowler; service station attendant

H – Helen Plimmer, 32, opening bat; head of high school PE
    department

Fresher – Sue Redfern, 20, seam bowler; sports coach

Liss – Melissa Reynard, 25, all-rounder; technical assistant at Yorkshire Water

Romps – Clare Taylor, 32, opening bowler; drives a van for the Royal Mail

Megan Lear – coach
Peter Moralee – assistant coach
Shirley Taylor – manager
Steve Bull – sports psychologist
Jocelyn (Joce) Brooks – sports scientist
Karen (Fizz) Giles – physiotherapist
Cath Harris – WCA press officer
Selena (From Kensington) Colmer – Craigie Taylor PR for Vodafone
Craig Prentis – Allsport photographer
Thrasy Petropoulos & Pete Davies – rodents

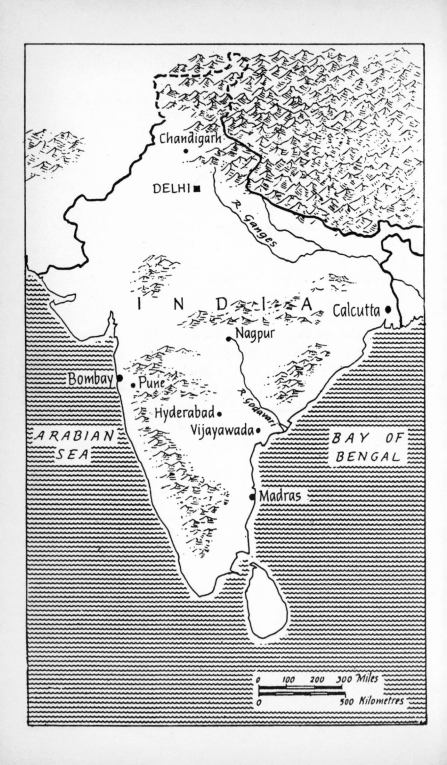

Author's Note

Women's cricket is not a politically correct environment. Consequently there is rarely, if ever, such a thing as a batswoman. As English coach Megan Lear said, 'You don't call third man third woman, do you? It's a fielding position, and it's called third man, and a person with a bat in her hand's a batsman.' I have, therefore, variously referred to them – as the women do themselves – as batsmen, bats, or batters.

Steve Waugh's three rules
for touring India.

1. Be Patient
2. Be Patient
3. Be Patient

1

Minging

Heat, smog, squalor, chaos, dirt, dust, diarrhoea . . . Eleven of the fourteen women who played for England at the 6th Women's Cricket World Cup had been to India before; as the tournament approached, they left me in no doubt about what lay before us. On tour two years earlier they'd endured dismal hotels, eternal train journeys, gut-draining illnesses, and a minor riot in Patna; they'd left the field under a hail of missiles after opening bowler Clare Taylor got bricked in the back of the head on the boundary.

And yet, to a woman, they'd thoroughly enjoyed it. Derbyshire seamer Sue Redfern, despite a bout of gastro-enteritis, said she liked it so much she hadn't wanted to leave. Barbara Daniels, an elegant top order bat from the West Midlands, said, 'India's an amazing place. I don't want to sound pretentious about it, but it really gets in your soul.'

All the same, they said, be prepared. It's heaving with people, it stinks, it's filthy, there's folk lying in the street with no legs on, and nothing works. So I landed at three in the morning expecting mayhem, and there wasn't any. Once the migrant workers from the Gulf had offloaded their new TV sets from the baggage reclaim and disappeared into the night, Delhi's Indira Gandhi International was no more heaving with people than an island in the Outer Hebrides.

It was about that cold too. I went into the chilly dark, and found two cheerful lads with a tatty Jeep waiting to take me to the team hotel – and we'd barely set off when the guy in the passenger seat started launching into cricket. Tendulkar, he said firmly, was too young to be captain; Azhar, he'd been the man for it. Like Graham Gooch, he said, now Gooch was a strong man, a very strong man, a disciplined man . . .

Great. The first bloke I meet in India's a gofer from a suburban hotel, and already the possibility looms that he'll know more about English cricket than I do.

David Gower, he said, now Gower was a strong man, a very strong man, a disciplined man . . .

Maybe he didn't know so much after all. I asked what he thought would happen with the women and he said, 'Oh, England's women will win. Won't they?'

The empty night smelt of diesel and sewage. It was, to apply a term much used by our lady cricketers, 'minging'. The strength of this rancid pollutant pong waxed and waned, but it was impossible to tell what kind of urban cesspit was producing it; the city was wreathed in fog so dense that sometimes the headlights penetrated barely three yards ahead of us. When I finally hit my bed at five in the morning, I still had no idea what I'd landed in.

The view from my room four hours later was of empty lots and building sites shrouded in an eye-stinging, yellow-grey smog. Out of this bilious murk, somewhat miraculously, three dazzling green parrots fluttered down to settle on my windowsill. I was looking at Ghaziabad, a dun industrial town of the most relentless shabbiness. It was an hour's drive from central Delhi – an hour's drive when the traffic's good, which is virtually never – and it seemed quite the most impractical place to deposit a bunch of cricket teams on the brink of an international competition.

The Women's Cricket Association of India, however, isn't a body overflowing with funds, and laying on a tournament this big they had to take all the help they could get – so if the local magnate in Ghaziabad offered munificent assistance in putting up their guests, off to Ghaziabad you went. The local magnate in question was the man behind Mohan Mekin, a conglomerate producing beer, breakfast cereals, and sandpaper; he was on the board of Ghaziabad's Mela Plaza Hotel, an incongruously swank institution in these unpromising surrounds, and a place which summed up one of the everyday contrasts of India.

Basically, you're staying in the middle of a rubbish tip – and yet the people you're staying with just can't do enough for you. Amid infernal wretchedness and catastrophic malfunction, kindness and courtesy thrive. It's as miraculous as the emerald parrots spiralling from the smog, and it goes on daily against a background of ceaseless violence, corruption, and disorder.

It was Tuesday 2 December. On Sunday night, three people had died and seventy more had been injured in a double bomb blast at Chandri Chowk in northern Delhi; the latest of twenty-four such bombings in the year. Sixteen more had perished during riots in Coimbatore in Tamil Nadu; another forty-four had lost their lives to hailstorms in Uttar Pradesh. On the roads of the capital, meanwhile – just the capital alone – the death toll for the year to date had passed well above 2,000. I took a cab into the city, and it wasn't hard to see why.

The unpeopled and foggy blank of the night was transformed into automotive anarchy. Bicycles and scooters, rickshaws pedalled and motorised, carts drawn by hump-necked oxen and stocky, massive-shouldered buffalo, filth-smeared trucks and buses belching foul blasts of black fumes – incessantly parping and honking, all these and many more careered around each other in a frantic morass of dented and rusting metal. It was a tumult from which the concept of lane discipline was entirely absent, and in which the only rule of the road appeared to be that whoever made it through the gap first was the winner. On the face of it, it was ghastly – nakedly lethal, and environmentally disastrous – but it was also enthralling, energising, teemingly vivid.

We passed roadside racks selling crash helmets; self evidently a good investment but one ignored by all too many people, among them families as large as five wedged implausibly on to mopeds. We jolted over potholes the size of medium-sized meteor strikes. We dodged cows milling about in the middle of snarled and manic junctions – and we crossed rank rivers and canals that were truly and absolutely minging, so bad that I'd glue my hands over my nose as I gawped at all the people washing their clothes in them.

Sometimes I had to look away; on the first morning, it was too much to absorb. So then, ensconced in the rattling, bouncing, squashy comfort of a splendidly rotund cream Humber Ambassador, I'd scan the *Times of India* and the *Pioneer*. 'In recent interaction with newspersons', said one of these august organs, Police Commissioner T. R. Kakkar claimed that the Chandri Chowk bombers 'are about to be nabbed'. The *Pioneer* didn't believe him: 'Investigators are yet to have any clue whatsoever in the matter.'

The coalition government of the United Front, meanwhile, was falling to bits after the withdrawal of support by the Nehru dynasty's Congress (I) Party, this move occasioned by the implication of one of the Front's member parties in the assassination of Rajiv Gandhi. The manoeuvring of the politicians, said the *Times*, was a 'sordid and cynical spectacle' in which India was 'held to ransom by the giant-sized egos of petty men'.

Against this background, working to stay calm in the face of many trials (and usually succeeding), England's manager

Shirley Taylor would later say that you always had to remember, 'Trying to organise anything here – it's bows and arrows against the sun.'

The woman principally responsible for organising the 6th Women's Cricket World Cup was Anuradha Dutt, the Honorary Secretary of the Women's Cricket Association of India. It wasn't a full-time job; to make her living, she was a partner in the law firm of Menon and Dutt, with tidy offices over an optician's shop in a quiet Delhi backstreet. But, she said, 'I haven't been to court for a month. I have,' she smiled, 'a lot of clients giving me ultimatums.'

Never mind court, she hadn't been to sleep much lately either. Without help either from government or from the Indian men's cricket authorities – with whom she didn't wish to be involved anyway, preferring to avoid their deranged internal politics – this short, stoutly built and impressively forceful woman was putting together the biggest Women's World Cup there'd ever been. Eleven teams would take part, and the budget was a shade over £600,000; to put that in perspective, the previous tournament in England in 1993 had eight teams, and the cash injection from the Foundation for Sport and the Arts that saved it when it looked like folding was (in a far more costly country) just £90,000.

The eleven countries involved were Australia, Denmark, England, Holland, India, Ireland, New Zealand, Pakistan, South Africa, Sri Lanka, and the West Indies. It should have been twelve; when I started looking into this, Japan were also slated to take part. Sadly, they faded from the scene – a shame, as a Japanese women's cricket team would surely have been a most original sight to behold. They were replaced by Canada, who then withdrew as well, leaving Dutt scrambling at the last minute to persuade Bangladesh to take part. She offered them playing kit, she offered to pay half their travel to India and back – but they couldn't muster a squad, and Dutt was left with a problem.

Only a few weeks earlier, some degree of financial stability had been secured with the arrival of scooter manufacturers Hero Honda as tournament sponsors. The first round of the tournament, however, involved two groups of six teams each, and during these group games Doordarshan (the Indian equivalent of the BBC) meant naturally to concentrate on screening the home team's games. But Canada had been in India's group – so now all the teams in that group had a bye, India had one fewer match on the box, and the sponsors had that much less exposure.

If the sponsors were discontented, everyone else was too. In the weeks leading up to the competition, visiting teams had been pleading down India's sporadically functioning phone and fax lines for some semblance, any semblance of a fixed itinerary; the Australians apparently threatened to withdraw at one point if Dutt couldn't tell them where they were going. For their part, the English were in an understandable lather about plans that had them travelling overnight on a train to their second game, getting off the train at six in the morning, then starting play at nine-thirty. Everyone in England's group, meanwhile, was miffed about the fact that their itineraries (whatever their final form) had them hauling butt and baggage round half the sub-continent, while India sat tight and played all bar one of their group games in and around Delhi.

Aussie coach John Harmer said bluntly, 'It isn't fair' – but the International Women's Cricket Council was a toothless, penniless body consisting principally of three women in New Zealand who could do little but yelp ineffectually down the long-distance line, while Dutt laid the show on as she pleased. Or, according to your point of view, as best she could in the circumstances.

Those circumstances were hardly propitious. Though India had one of the best teams taking part – one of the four thought most likely to make the semi-finals – Dutt reckoned that there weren't many more than 2,000 women playing cricket in her country at a decent level. 'Cricket', she said, 'is not yet accepted as a woman's game, not here. We have a very conservative society, and the middle and lower classes especially don't see a place for women in sport. It's a boy's thing, and they don't like it.'

This is a country, remember, where some men, if they don't like the wife they land up with in the arranged marriage game, they set fire to her; they're called 'kitchen fires', and one such case was going through Delhi's courts as we spoke, with the man involved looking more than likely to get off. In that context, for a woman to find any form of greater freedom has to be a blessing, and playing cricket might well be such a liberating thing.

Dutt said, if the tournament was successful, 'I wouldn't say it would have an impact for women in India generally. But as a way of getting more women to play, as a way of encouraging self-expression, yes – if a girl goes to play, then she's expressing herself. There are so many restrictions on girls, even on how they're to think – but with cricket it's a chance to be by yourself, to concentrate on something and try to do it well, and for a girl in India that's very, very important.'

With that perspective as a backdrop, it's ultimately futile for visitors to complain. They did, and so shall I, because England's travel arrangements would turn out to be completely insane. But at least if a woman plays cricket in England, it's not likely that anyone will set fire to her – whereas what Dutt was trying to do was get as many games as possible played in as many places as possible, just to spread the word that women could play. Certainly, there was a political element of making sure that different states all got their piece of the action, and there were also financial considerations involved in taking games to any place where the locals would shell out to help meet the competition's costs – but the missionary idea was in there too, and it cannot be gainsaid.

As for India playing their games around Delhi and not

travelling much, well, OK, it did ming a bit. But if England host a football tournament, where do they play all their games? I think they play them at Wembley, don't you?

Stern but congenial, Anuradha Dutt gave me more of her time to discuss these things than she needed to, while her office heaved and toiled all about us. Feeling I should leave her to it, I asked how I should get from there to the centre of the city, and got out my *Lonely Planet* so she could show me where we were on a map. She smiled and said, 'We Indians aren't used to reading maps.'

'Very much traffic,' said my rickshaw driver, 'very pollution.'

No kidding – and auto-rickshaws are absolutely the best way to see it. In essence, they're three-wheeler mopeds with a fairing on the front, a two-person bench seat on the back (regularly occupied by entire extended families), a canopy over the top, and no sides. The back end of the canopy's often painted with a bright dream of beaches and palm trees, and always carries the wholly redundant request, 'Horn Please'. As for having no sides, that means you're travelling at exhaust pipe level among the rattletrap buses and trucks, toking regular lungfuls of gross blue-black filth.

Maybe it's the constant exposure to this muck that does their heads in, but the fact that my rickshaw driver from Dutt's place uptown was a decent bloke gave me a totally misleading first impression of his trade. With all too few exceptions, India's rickshaw drivers are incompetents, thieves, or outright maniacs. They never know where your hotel is – or they do know, but feel entirely within their rights giving you a lengthy tour of the ring road before you get there while the meter heads off into the economic stratosphere. This, of course, assumes that they've agreed to put on the meter in the first place; one of the many daily battles of life in India involves standing by the roadside laughing at preposterous fares proposed by larcenous little buggers claiming their meter's broken.

Still, my first driver was a good one; he took me directly where I wanted to go (the Red Fort via Connaught Place), yelling inaudibly against the constant roar and grind of the traffic about whatever landmarks we passed along the way. Apart from seeing Dutt, my purpose in arriving a day ahead of the England squad was to try and acclimatise in this way, at least a tiny bit – which turned out to involve wandering around in slack-jawed astonishment, ticking off my mental list of items variously horrid and bizarre that you're going to have to get used to.

So here are two painted elephants meandering down the road amid six lanes of traffic. Here's a bloke with no legs. Here's a grime-smeared child toting a gummy-eyed baby, pawing at my forearm saying, 'No money, no Papa.' And, at the spectacular if slightly dishevelled Red Fort, here's a backpacker with spiky hair and a stud in his nose being pursued by a scrawny boy. 'Need chapati,' says the boy.

'Fuck off.'

'Need chapati, hello, need chapati.'

'I don't give a shit. Fuck off.'

Makes you proud to be English, eh?

My cab ride back to Ghaziabad was somewhat unnerving. We had a co-driver and at first I figured, after we'd had a garage stop and he'd got out at a few red lights to check the tyres or the petrol tank, that he was our in-flight mechanic. Then he took over the steering while the old guy in the turban at the wheel spent a kilometre or so cleaning his spectacles. Then the old guy had a monstrous coughing fit for another kilometre or two, while the co-driver thoughtfully kneaded his back. So maybe he was just there to take over if the old guy died. Still, at least the brakes worked. Good thing, really, because otherwise we'd definitely have ploughed into that jaywalking cow.

We passed people living along the roadside in squares of waist-high mud wall roofed with sheets of black plastic. We passed pigs rooting in black puddles in front of a dingy line of body shops. Lorry tyres stood in piles on the oil-streaked, litter-strewn earth; a guy squatted on his haunches hammering at a fender. A buffalo pulled a cart laden with a mountain of rags, and another hauled a huge chunk of engineered steel. The crumbling kerb all the way was a thronged array of inventive toil in the face of crushing odds. I especially liked the shop that was 'Closed For Renewation'. Above it all, gigantic hand-painted billboards sold suits, shirts, televisions, fridges, washing machines and, oddly, a film called *Virgins From Hell*.

As dusk fell back at the Mela Plaza, I went out for a walk. A broken pipe gushed in a muddy drain; two men were washing in it, and drinking from it too. A line of metal tables on the dirt verge stood ready with one-ring gas burners to boil or fry you an egg. Teenage boys sat bashing at bicycle parts. People swathed in ragged blankets huddled round pathetically small fires. The road heaved with rickshaws and scooters, and scooter garages the size of garden sheds stayed open into the night in the hope of another disintegrating moped to patch up, another few rupees' worth of trade. Among them was a shop front barely wider than the glass door by which you entered; the door offered 'Travels (Now Computerised)'.

Somewhere in another world far away, the England women's cricket squad was getting on a plane.

2

Original English Lady Cricketers

What is life but a game of cricket? And if so,
why should not the ladies play it as well as
we?

– John Frederick Sackville,
3rd Duke of Dorset, 1777

Nancy Joy, a member of the England side that toured
Australia in 1948–49, subsequently published a
sprightly little tome titled *Maiden Over* – principally a
diary of the tour, with a short history of women's cricket thrown
in. According to Joy, the first recorded game of women's cricket
was held on 26 July 1745 on Gosden Common near Guildford.
Played between 'eleven maids of Bramley and eleven maids of
Hambleton, dressed all in white' – as reported by the *Reading
Mercury* – 'the girls bowled, batted, ran and catched as well as
most men could do'. For the record, Hambleton won by eight
notches.

Early reports of the women's game appear interested at least
as much in what the players wore as in how they played – a trait
also shared with early coverage of women's football – but such
reports are none the less sufficiently numerous to suggest that
in the second half of the eighteenth century, women played

cricket with some regularity. One game in 1747 was abandoned after a pitch invasion by *hoi polloi* – but this appears to have been standard English rowdiness, as opposed to an affronted male revolt on specific grounds of gender grievance.

When the national habit of starting out with a sporting event and ending up with a riot didn't intervene, women's games proceeded in good order either between villages, or between teams of married players and single players from within one village. A match of the latter kind became an annual event at Upham in Hampshire, where the prize played for was 'a large plumcake, a barrel of ale and regale of tea'.

In 1768, a three-game series in Sussex between Harting and Rogate Common drew a crowd for the third game not far short of 3,000. Substantial betting was, of course, very often involved, especially when the posh played at their country houses. In 1777, when the Countess of Derby held a match, the batting of one Elizabeth Ann Burrell so caught the eye of the 8th Duke of Hamilton that he promptly fell in love and married her.

The women's most famous claim in the early days, however, is that they were the first to bowl overarm. This innovation is attributed to Christina Willes; bowling to her brother John when he wanted practice at his home near Canterbury, she delivered the ball over her shoulder to avoid her hoops and bustles, and it's a straight line and length from there to Dennis Lillee. Willes took his sister's new method to Lord's in 1822, playing for Kent against the MCC; he was immediately no-balled by an umpire named Noah Mann. In a fine fury of dissent, Willes leapt on his horse and rode out of Lord's, proclaiming that he'd never play again – and he didn't, though overarm bowling became law only six years later.

For all that, reports of women playing cricket in the Victorian era are less common than in the previous century. Several noted players, including W. G. Grace, were said to have learnt much of their game from knowledgeable mothers – but, perhaps because the times were more prim, it appears that if women could bring up good players, they were less encouraged to play themselves. Consequently, the first women's clubs didn't appear until the end of the nineteenth century.

The first was an aristocratic outfit called White Heather, founded in 1887. Some years later, the club's top bat Lucy Ridsdale would marry Stanley Baldwin; she attributed a batting average of 62 that season to the calming effect of her nuptials. With that fine disregard of the posh – especially the sporting posh – for matters of historical import, Lady Baldwin would also hold a General Meeting of White Heather at Number 10 bang in the middle of the General Strike.

Other early clubs were Severn Valley, Derbyshire Ladies (the Dragonflies), and Clifton Ladies, for whom W. G.'s daughter Bessie played. Also roaming the land were the Original English Lady Cricketers, two professional sides who put on exhibition games, and whose first match at the Police Athletic Ground in Liverpool in 1890 drew a crowd of 15,000. The *Liverpool Post* reported that they 'came to scoff, and remained to praise'. According to Nancy Joy, less generous observers said of these women that 'they might be Original and English, but they were neither Ladies nor cricketers'. Any hope that they might successfully proselytise for the women's game, however, went up in smoke in 1892 when their manager did a runner with the profits.

Overall, it doesn't seem that many women played, or that many men took them seriously when they did. A tenderly solicitous proposal was once put forward that women should play on a shorter pitch, with a smaller bat and a lighter ball – and the name of this proposal's originator says it all. He was called Richard Daft.

The Women's Cricket Association was founded in 1926 by a group of friends, mostly hockey and lacrosse internationals, who wanted a permanent organisation adding regular cricket to their other pursuits. The following season they organised forty-nine matches, and had ten clubs as members. The games at first were private, unheralded affairs played on school and village pitches, but at Beckenham in 1929, the first representative match was held between London and the Rest of England. In the next few years the WCA grew fast, to a membership of eighty clubs by 1934.

The first chair of the WCA was Mrs Patrick Heron-Maxwell MBE. With a record of good works and civic duties on top of her sporting prowess – she fenced, climbed, and played hockey and tennis as well as cricket – the grand sound of this good lady sets the tone for the early days of the WCA. From Joy's account, it seems in the main to have been a southern and slightly snooty outfit; she writes of two players 'emerging at intervals from their northern mists', and of the industrial north in general as if it were another country altogether. Indeed, the north had its own English Women's Cricket Federation, thanks to which 'many a factory and business girl was enabled to enjoy a game of cricket'. Reading between the lines here, it appears that the women had their own version of 'gentlemen and players'.

But to play any serious amount of cricket at all, most early players would have needed their share of money and leisure. How else could they have afforded to mount a tour Down Under? In 1934, that's exactly what they did, setting sail for Australia and New Zealand to play the first Test series in the history of women's cricket.

They left Tilbury in October. Joy reports that they weren't a fully representative side – they were a squad whose members could afford the time and money to go, basically – but they were still too good for their hosts. At the Exhibition Ground in Brisbane in December, they won the first Test by nine wickets; at the Sydney Cricket Ground in January they won the second by eight wickets, while the third game in Melbourne was drawn. A month later in Christchurch, England wrapped up their first international excursion with a comprehensive demolition of a Kiwi side; they won by an innings and 337 runs.

The honour of the first century in women's international cricket goes to England's Scottish opener Myrtle MacLagan, who got 119 in Sydney. Australians being Australians, however, and disinclined to be outfaced by the English at anything, least of all cricket, they rapidly got better – improving enough that when they came to England for a return tour in 1937, they won the first Test at Northampton by 31 runs. The series ended drawn – and with the principle of international women's cricket firmly established.

England toured the Antipodes a second time in 1948–49, and again in 1957–58; the Australians came here in 1951, and the New Zealanders in 1954. England went to South Africa in 1960–61 – one of the players apparently opting to forgo buying a new car so she could go on the tour – and Rachael Heyhoe (who would go on to accumulate the current Test record of 1,594 runs) made her first Test appearance at Port Elizabeth that winter.

The West Indies put out their first women's Test side against Australia in 1976; in the same year, India played their first Test in New Zealand. In all, there have now been 99 women's Test matches; the 99th was between England and New Zealand at Guildford in July 1996. England have played in 68 of those games, and the world's cricketing women will hit their Test ton in the summer of 1998 when the Australians come to England on tour.

It has, naturally, been a patchy history, an unsung amateur tale of the game privately pursued by hockey players and PE teachers – eight of the seventeen who toured Australia after the war were teachers – and if some of those involved in the early days were rather grand, many others then and since are people who've made considerable sacrifices to play cricket for their country.

Like many of those who went before her, Helen Plimmer,

one of England's squad for the World Cup in India, was a PE teacher – while men can make money playing games, many women have to make theirs from teaching them – and Plimmer reckoned England's tour to India in the winter of '95 would have cost her around £3,000 in air fares, spending money, and lost wages. But faced with this price tag she said simply, 'If you love the game, and you want to go there and play for your country, you take that on board, don't you?'

Nor should anyone think that because these women don't get paid, they aren't serious about it. England's coach Megan Lear said sternly, 'Given that we're amateurs, our preparation for this World Cup has been as professional as it's possible to be. We want to enjoy our cricket, of course. But we want to win.'

The first women's World Cup was held in England in 1973, two years ahead of the men's first tournament – allowing the women to claim that they thought of that first too, as well as overarm bowling. It was the fruit of discussions between Rachael Heyhoe Flint and Jack Hayward (now Wolves' bene-factor), after Hayward had sponsored two tours to the Caribbean. Hayward financed the entire project, and seven teams took part – England, Young England, New Zealand, Australia, Jamaica, Trinidad & Tobago, and an International XI – and England won it, beating Australia by 92 runs at Edgbaston.

The next three tournaments were held in India, New Zealand, and Australia; the Australians won all three of them, with Denmark, Holland, and Ireland joining in along the way. In 1993, the competition returned to England; the hosts took their second title, beating New Zealand in the final at Lord's by 67 runs before a crowd of 4,500.

In the wake of that victory, the WCA were criticised for not capitalising on it – for failing to follow through and spread the word, for failing to lay on matches, or a winter tour, where the media could pay attention to an English cricket side who (unimaginable, if you think about the state of the men in recent times) were champions of the world. The trouble was, however, that hosting the tournament had all but broken them financially. This, remember, was a national body running on such a shoestring that its players had to contribute to their own air fares when they went overseas.

None the less, by the time England left for the World Cup in India, circumstances had significantly improved – enough for manager Shirley Taylor to say simply, 'Things are better than they've ever been.' Preparations had been thorough, starting with the tour to India two winters before. England won a three-match Test series 1–0, lost a one-day series 3–2, and got thoroughly acclimatised.

'It had its trials and tribulations,' said Taylor. 'Transport and communication are difficult; sights and sounds and smells can be disheartening. But the vibrancy of India is indescribable, I'd recommend anyone to go. And they're so passionate about cricket, we were treated so well. It was like being an FA Cup Final team; we had crowds watching us just get on the bus.'

They had armed guards everywhere they went, too – not that that did Clare Taylor much good in Patna. The Yorkshire bowler was fielding on the boundary, in front of a crowd of 15,000; England were on top of the game, the crowd got crotchety, missiles started flying, and Taylor was hit in the back of the head. The general concensus in the squad was that her head was hard enough to take it – one of her team-mates said, 'I think it bounced back further than it was thrown from.'

Manager Shirley Taylor (no relation) took the incident with classic English *sang froid*. She said, 'We had them in trouble, and it's what they do with the men. So they were doing us the honour of treating us as real cricketers, weren't they?'

It was an isolated incident in a happy tour; the outfielders, said the players, got more proposals of marriage than they ever did missiles. Moreover, with all but three of the World Cup squad going on that tour, Lear and Taylor felt the experience was priceless.

The scale of the challenge in retaining their title, however, became clear the following summer, when the Kiwis came to England on tour. Since their defeat at Lord's, the women's game in New Zealand had merged with the men's game – most top clubs in the land of the long white cloud now had a women's section – and on top of the better coaching this move had brought to their game, the Kiwis also had a sponsor, a telecoms company whose backing meant their players weren't putting their hands in their own pockets any more.

In a three-game one-day series, the Kiwis won all three. Admittedly, they'd been together in training for over a week from their arrival before the first game, while the English – still broke – could only meet up the evening before the first game. Once they'd got together, the margin of defeat was smaller in each game, and the subsequent Test series was drawn – but Megan Lear saw it as a useful wake-up call as to the size of the task before them. Three Englishwomen were painfully alerted to the situation in another way; they all had fingers broken by the ferocious batting of New Zealand's Debbie Hockley.

During the following winter, some thirty players attended regular training weekends – at Headingley for those in the north, at Lord's for the southerners. In the background, meanwhile, plans to integrate women's cricket with the men's game were firming up inside the new England Cricket Board. They'd already given the women £50,000 towards the cost of hosting New Zealand; now they started sending in senior players like Mike Gatting and Dermot Reeve to help with the coaching. Then, in the summer of 1997, the national side were brought into the new sponsorship deal with Vodafone. After years of penny-pinching, the women at last wouldn't have to spend their own money to buy their kit when they played for England.

The Vodafone people said with genuine enthusiasm that it was a delight to work with the women, that they were so much fun to be around, and that they couldn't do enough for you. But as one of the squad said wryly, 'They probably don't realise how pathetically grateful we are for any help we get at all.'

In the early days of the WCA, the main event of the domestic season was Cricket Week in the village of Colwell in Worcestershire. This still goes on, but more important nowadays is the WCA's Area Championship in Cambridge in late July. In 1997, this involved sixteen sides in three divisions playing for five days on ten college pitches – and of these sixteen, Yorkshire in recent years have been streets ahead of the rest.

But if these were the top ten per cent of the 1,500 women known to be playing with the ninety clubs now affiliated to the WCA, just how good were they? England's coach Megan Lear was a PE teacher from Kent who played for England in two World Cups; she said, 'Our top thirty are extremely talented. The problem is getting the standard of game to prepare them. We'll be playing the Kent and Middlesex Under-17 boys' teams, and that's about the right level. They've already been bowling at us in the nets at Lord's – and the lads have been a bit surprised at how good the women are. Of course, we've still got lots we can learn – but the best women are a lot better than most people realise. Obviously, the game will never equate to the men's game in terms of strength or speed – but women's tennis doesn't either, and that's equally good to watch, isn't it?'

Some would say it's better. But Lear, like all those involved, doesn't want the women's game compared to the men's; she'd simply like it to be watched and reported on its own merits. So I can report that if the bowling's not as quick, the best make up in guile and accuracy what they lack in pace. Otherwise, the top players' batting is technically excellent, intelligent and stylish, while their fielding is quick and aggressive. Wandering round Cambridge, you'll see plenty of players who haven't got that much of a throw on them – but again, the best of them can really sling it in.

The event's a treat – heaps of cricket all over the place, and corking bacon rolls in the Venn Pavilion at the Queen's pitch – but for players hoping to go to India, the 1997 championship was nerve-racking. On the evening of the final day, a squad would be named for a one-day series against South Africa in August; if you didn't get in that, your chances of a place in the World Cup fourteen were slender to vanishing.

I concentrated on watching Yorkshire; they'd been champions for five years running, and they notched up comfortable wins against Kent, East Anglia, Surrey, and the West. On the last day, they faced the West Midlands – and with a bit of rain on the wicket the night before to help the bowlers, when West Mids won the toss they put Yorkshire in, rattled through their top order, and held them to 156 for 7.

What followed was enthralling. Yorkshire have good bowlers – Clare Taylor, Melissa Reynard, Kathryn Leng, Bev Nicholson and Julie Mann had all been training with England through the winter, and Jet van Noortwijk plays for Holland – but what really impressed was the tightness of the fielding, the pace and aggression of it. It wasn't just that the bowlers were good, it was at least as much that the batsmen had nowhere to hit it – and all the while around them the fielders were calling out to each other, encouraging and applauding, urging on the bowlers. I'm not sure I'd say it was intimidating, but it was very definitely professional. It was, as they say, focused.

Still, West Mids got off pretty well, making 56 in the first 20 overs before they lost their first wicket to a run out – so their captain Barbara Daniels went in. Before she did she said grimly, 'I think there's fourteen other counties willing us to beat them. Someone's got to do it eventually, haven't they?'

Thirty-two years old, as Executive Director the only full-time paid officer of the WCA, Daniels was a slim, spry, sharply perceptive woman who batted with a piratical dash, and a scurrying rapidity between the wickets. The previous summer at Scarborough, I'd seen her make a flawlessly elegant 160 against the Kiwis – sharing a Test record sixth-wicket partnership of 132 with Kathryn Leng in the process – and now, the balance of this game clearly hung on her performance.

Julie Mann was bowling to her. Mann had quite the most extraordinary run-up I've ever seen; she herself described it afterwards with a self-deprecating laugh as, 'My Little Pony.' One England coach wondered if she was a pentathlete; by the time she actually bowled, he said, she'd hopped over several hurdles, thrown the javelin and the discus, done the high jump, and if it hadn't been for the necessity of delivering the ball when she got to the crease, she'd have been away down the wicket doing the triple jump into the bargain. But whatever it looked like, she was serving up trim and tidy material; three of her first four overs were maidens.

Daniels watched Mann's first ball zip by outside off. The second and third balls she looked uneasy, trying to cut square, but misreading the flight and swiping air. The fourth ball, cutting again, she got an edge, and the ball looped to gully for a simple catch. She came off absolutely furious; she said bitterly of the chance she'd had to help her side finally beat Yorkshire, 'It's a moment I've been waiting for for years. And I've thrown it away.' She paused a long while, then said, 'Still, we've a lot of batting yet. We can still do this.' Then she laughed and said of Mann's mesmerisingly weird approach to the wicket, 'I remember the first time I faced her, I couldn't hit the ball. I was looking at her thinking, What is *this*?'

Yorkshire won. The West Mids needed only 101 off the last 30 overs, with eight wickets still standing, but they never got close. Yorkshire's bowling and fielding was remorselessly tight, West Mids finished all out for 106 in the 48th over, Julie Mann recorded figures of 2 for 4 in 8.5 overs, 6 of them maidens – and still she didn't get picked for England.

As the players from all the other pitches gathered at the Queen's pavilion, those on the fringe who hadn't made it were told before the announcement, the selectors breaking it to them privately. Shirley Taylor paced about in the crowd, visibly uneasy. She said, 'I don't like it. You're trying to avoid people's eyes. They're trying to have a private word with those who'll be most disappointed, but there's no easy way to do it. It's like the CO writing the letter to the dead soldier's wife. You know any way you do it, you're going to break a heart.'

Yorkshire's Clare Taylor said, 'It's tense. There's eight or nine that are certs, maybe. If I'd got the nod and the wink myself I'd be gutted, it'd really hurt. You might put on a brave face, you might be the *c'est la vie* type – but I'd be hurting.'

Julie Mann was definitely hurting. She said, 'I didn't think I was in contention, but to be told . . . I was disappointed. I thought I might have got in. Realistically, I was borderline . . . well, I'm quite upset. It's a bit public. Those that aren't in, the eyes are on you.'

Throughout the five days, and most especially now as the WCA's President Norma Izard announced the squad, it was abundantly plain how much their cricket meant to these people, and how badly they wanted to play for their country. Yet – because they're only women – no one watched them play at Cambridge bar their friends and relatives and, with the exception of former England player Sarah Potter in *The Times*, no one reported it.

Ask those involved what they'd say to anyone who remains sceptical about the idea of women playing, and the answer's the same every time. Come and watch, they say, just come and watch. ECB coach Paul Farbrace had been working with the women through the winter; he said, 'I've found them thoroughly good to work with. It's been an enlightening experience. I'd coach anybody, I'd coach Martians if they want to play cricket – but it's not hard with these because they're so keen, they're so dedicated. And the technique, some of it's fantastic; there are some very, very gifted players. Really, people should just come and watch.'

Of the squad named to play South Africa, six came from Yorkshire. They'd won the Area Championship for the sixth year running; Wakefield, North Riding, and City of Leeds are among the country's top club sides.

Yorkshire's captain Sue Metcalfe was 32 years old, a coagulation specialist with the National Blood Authority who played for North Riding. She attributed Yorkshire's success to a strength in depth built up with the active support of the men at Headingley; they had a centre of excellence there, and ran coaching sessions all winter at Sheffield, Bradford, and Northallerton. But then, whether you were a man or a woman, cricket in Yorkshire was something else anyway, wasn't it?

She said, 'To play for Yorkshire and win, it means so much. In Yorkshire, there isn't any kind of cricket but serious cricket. I play in a night league, and there's little villages up there that'll probably only have eleven women in them to start with – but they'll get a team out, and the competition's fierce. The standard'll vary, sure, but everyone wants to play, everyone. So the men in Yorkshire know how serious we are. I don't know about the rest of the country, but they know in Yorkshire.'

They say, of course, that when Yorkshire are strong, England are strong. Eric Chapman, chairman of selectors for the women, was himself a Yorkshireman, and immensely proud of his players. He said, 'They're grand lasses, they really work hard. But,' he sighed, 'it's still hard to get it in the papers. It's like knocking your head against a brick wall.'

Actually, things are getting better. It's become fairly generally recognised that women don't just play tennis or golf, and that the best of those who play the traditionally male team games do so with much skill and dedication. Sports editors on the broadsheets are increasingly willing to give them space – maybe not much, not often, but some – and to use that space for duly serious reporting. It is, in other words, not a freakshow any more – and the one-day series against South Africa in August attracted coverage in a healthy number of the papers. Five Live showed up too, the local media pitched in, the BBC put an hour's programme together on it, and Sky broadcast one of the games live in its entirety – which, happily, turned out to be the best of the lot.

The first game was at the Gloucester County Cricket Ground in Bristol. A crowd of 400 on a Friday was, locals said, better than the men might have managed; the catering staff were caught out, not expecting so many, and the refreshing exuberance of the England players calling out to support their batsmen from the balcony was much remarked on as well. It all looked a bit too much for the South Africans; it was their first time abroad and the women's game there, though lately resurgent, had long been dormant in the dead years of apartheid. Though indoor cricket's big there, many of their side had only been playing the outdoor variety for a couple of years – and it showed.

Batting first, England's openers Charlotte Edwards and Helen Plimmer scored 45 and 47, Sue Metcalfe made her half-century off the last ball, and a total of 227 for 6 was then defended with some clinically sharp bowling. Captain Karen Smithies took 1 for 12 in 10 overs, 5 of them maidens; player of the match Sue Redfern picked up 4 for 21. South Africa struggled to 148 for 9, and lost by 79 runs.

But no one in the England camp was underestimating them. Megan Lear said, 'They'll be intensely competitive, and very proud. That mental toughness will certainly be there.' So it proved at Taunton two days later, before a crowd of 1,000 and the cameras from Sky.

South Africa's coach was Conrad Hunte from Barbados; an entirely charming man now 64 years old, he'd played 44 Tests for the West Indies, and scored 3,245 runs. He went to South Africa to work for the United Cricket Board after Mandela was released, overseeing the women's game, and travelling as a cricket missionary to develop the sport in countries like Uganda and Tanzania. He judged that his women's side stood fifth in the world – after England, New Zealand, Australia and India – and he felt happily confirmed in that ranking after three solid wins over Ireland, in Belfast and Dublin, before they came on to England. Now he told me, with an infectious laugh, 'We don't aim to stay fifth all the time, y'know?'

To begin with, England at Taunton didn't look as if they meant to give the South Africans any chance at all of revising their ranking upwards. They batted first again, and Charlotte Edwards – seventeen years old, winning her third cap – struck a delicious 102. When she passed the ton and held up her bat, she was literally dancing for joy between the wickets; it was a wonderful sight. Overexcited, she promptly got herself stumped – but with Sue Metcalfe coming in to hit 44 off 47 balls, and wicketkeeper Jane Cassar crashing an unbeaten 50 off 36, England's total of 253 for 5 looked uncatchable.

What followed was probably the most exciting run chase Sky broadcast all season. Hunte sent out his No.11 bat Denise Reid to open as a pinch-hitter; with England playing as if they thought all they had to do was turn up – and dropping Reid three times – she belted 56 off 44 balls. With the other opener Linda Olivier hitting 60 before she fell, South Africa were off like a train. England managed to slow them a bit; with ten overs remaining they were 202 for 4, still needing 52.

The finish was breathless. In the 43rd over, a stunning direct hit from Edwards in the covers ran out South Africa's captain Kim Price; their strongest bat Helen Davies came in, and promptly struck three fours off the next four balls. In the next over, Clare Connor had Davies brilliantly caught and bowled. Four wickets remained, with 28 required from 6 overs.

There was a run-out in the 45th over, Connor bowled a maiden in the 46th, Sue Redfern gave away just one single in the 47th. Then the South Africans got four off the 48th, five and a no ball off the 49th, and lost another player run out in the process. In the last over, they needed nine runs; on the second ball, the tension by now electric, the crowd hushed to absolute stillness, Smithies dropped a catch at mid off. It was England's sixth spilt catch, and it probably cost them the game. Needing seven off the last four balls, two off the final delivery, Anina Burger and Alta Kotze – batting 7 and 10 respectively – nurdled, slogged, and swept their way to a remarkable last-ball win.

'It was,' said Shirley Taylor, 'such a thrilling game of cricket that I can almost forgive them for losing it. Almost.'

Kim Price said, 'There was aggression all through the batting. We've come here not knowing what to expect, it's a learning curve for us – but we've come here to win, too. All sporting people are the same, aren't they? We don't want to let our country down. So England relaxed, they had that big total – and that's where you can't give us an opportunity. Because,' she laughed, 'we're too stupid to know when we're beat.'

On Wednesday 20 August at Lord's, before a crowd near 3,000 and John Major among them, the third game went back to the form book. To say that England were stung would be putting it mildly; they were furious with themselves. Fielding first, they skittled South Africa out for 134 in the 47th over; they passed that total serenely with ten overs and seven wickets to spare.

The last two games were rained off; the one at Milton Keynes completely, the other at Hinckley when England had once more ruthlessly filleted South Africa's top order, and had them buckled and wheezing on 57 for 5 after 27 overs. They were worthy 2–1 winners of the series; as Kim Price put it, 'They don't play bad shots, they don't give their wickets away. You have to work really hard for every single one. They're a very professional side, a very good side all round.'

All the same, she said, 'We've gained a lot of experience, and we'll put it in the memory bank. The girls are thinking the game now, they're not just going out and hitting it. It's not been easy for us to come here – there's been a few sacrifices, one of us had to give up her job – but it's been fantastic. We've been royally treated, and to play at Lord's was awesome. I'll tell you though,' she laughed, 'it's a real long walk from that dressing room.'

Conrad Hunte was happy too. 'We need to get our bowling more consistent, and we need to learn to build partnerships. We need to get trust and confidence between the players; we had too many silly run-outs. But the experience has been invaluable, and the win at Taunton shows we can get a big score against the best. So it's been a success – and England deserved to win. They're a much better disciplined side, they're very well coached, well drilled, and they're very athletic. Even though some of the girls are big, they're quick; their running between the wickets has been exemplary, and their fielding's very alert. I don't know about Australia yet, but having seen New Zealand on video, I'd put them and England as co-favourites in India.'

We were talking on the boundary at Milton Keynes, after it had finally been decided that the pitch was unplayable. Waiting on the umpires to make that decision, the South Africans had been teaching the English women dance routines to African tunes on their boom box. Now they were all spilling on to the outfield for an impromptu game of football, one of the Yorkshire players grinning sternly that big beer money was at stake. Around us, the last smatterings of a small crowd were drifting away.

'Any women's sport,' said Megan Lear, 'is always going to struggle for attention, and we just have to live with that. But to be fair, we're making progress. So we have to carry on going out and playing good stuff – and hopefully, over time, people will come and have a look. And, hey – we won, didn't we?'

3

Skip

Coalville in Leicestershire's a worn and unprepossessing place. Closed shops dot the High Street past the Argos car park, their windows painted or papered over. Once there were six pits within a few miles' radius, but they've all been shut. You can see the winding gear of one of them, Snibston Colliery, just down the road from the crossroads by the plain brick clocktower of the war memorial; it's a Discovery Park now, with a museum, nature trails, a golf and leisure club. Before we wrought this post-industrial progress, on Fridays and Saturdays when the miners knocked off, the two pubs on the crossroads used to heave with life, and all afternoon they'd trickle in and out of Coral the bookies a few doors down. Once the redundancy money was gone, of course, business in the bookies took a bit of a dive.

It wouldn't be unnatural to find an English cricketer in there, dropping a few quid on the nags; Karen Smithies, however, earned her money in Coral rather than spending it there.

Twenty-eight years old, five feet two inches tall, Smithies had short, pale ginger hair, a ready smile, and a friendly, dry, quick-witted manner. She'd worked for Coral eight years, she knew all her punters – she had one called William Shakespeare, another called Albert Hall – and the banter flew as she took their money. But then, she knew these people; her grandad Charlie Spouge was a miner, and she played her first cricket at Snibston Colliery.

She was born in Ashby-de-la-Zouche; her dad was a designer at an electrical machine firm until he retired, and her mum still worked in a factory making rubber components for cars. They lived in Ennistown, and then Coalville; Karen married Dean when she was twenty-one, and they went to live in Ravenstone just a mile down the road. Dean was a plate welder in a quarry firm; they had a neat, tan brick semi on a tidy little modern estate. Over the clock on the mantelpiece in the sitting room, a framed photograph showed her running with clenched fists and a wild smile of triumph across the pitch at Lord's in '93.

If she was a man, and victorious in a cricket World Cup – something no Englishman has ever been – she'd be wealthy and well renowned. She was, instead, the assistant manager of a betting shop – and she was refreshingly unbothered about it. She'd played cricket for fourteen years, and she'd always known it'd never make her rich. It might not be just, but it really wasn't the point.

She said, 'Money's not everything, is it? I'm the captain of an England side that's won the World Cup, and that's good enough for me. Besides, I've had recognition for it. I'm an OBE, I'm a Lady Taverner, and [here she pointed at the picture over the mantelpiece] it's all come from that. I mean, who'd have thought I'd get an OBE? I certainly didn't, it never entered my mind, it was a big shock. And it was wonderful going to the palace – not because of who else was there, or Prince Charles doing the investiture, but because of those words when I walked into the room. "For services to ladies' cricket." That rings out loud and clear. I can remember that all my life.'

Even so, she nearly packed it in after they'd won. At first there was euphoria. In another bad summer for English cricket – we lost the Ashes again, Gooch resigned – the last hour of the women's final was live on *Grandstand*. When Jan Brittin took the winning catch, Smithies fell to her knees to kiss the ground; then she found herself running into the embracing pack of players. She had to hang on to Clare Taylor for a while, her legs were jelly, they'd have given out otherwise – but they were the best team in the world, weren't they?

All the papers ran with it, local and national. Back in Coalville everyone was high on it, including even those among the older ex-miners in the bookies who'd never taken it seriously before, the idea of a woman playing cricket – but everyone likes a winner from their home town. Only then, of course, it faded. The WCA was broke, there was no winter tour to look forward to, no one coming here the following summer. Three weeks after the final, Smithies was playing in a game at Oxford; 'And it was one of the most awful games I've ever played. Nothing I did was right. If I'd have had fifty fielders, I'd not have got it right. Because all my energy, my whole mind went into the World Cup, and for that to be gone . . . it was like playing in a hole. It was horrendous.'

Steve Bull kept her going, a sports psychologist who'd been with them when they won the Cup. Four more years, he told her, stay with it one more time – because how many can say they've played in three World Cups?

When I asked how much cricket took out of her life she smiled and said, 'It *is* my life.'

Her dad was captain of the Snibston Colliery side and he was treasurer, secretary, he'd get the pitch ready, everything; Karen went with him to every game from when she was four or five. She learnt how to score early on, and started playing at fourteen for the lads' under-18 team; she ended up captain. She started playing for Nottingham Ladies (now Newark & Sherwood) at fourteen as well; she won her first cap three years later, in a one-day match against India at the Gymkhana Club at Osterley in Middlesex. It was a horrible pitch and she didn't get to bat or bowl, but she didn't care – England won, she had a cap, and it was all she'd ever wanted.

School suffered. She got six O-levels, but cricket took over more and more. She started on three A-levels, but dropped one of them; of the other two she passed sociology, but failed English Lit. You would, probably, when you're eighteen and playing for your country against Australia. That summer, she and Jo Chamberlain put on a Test record seventh-wicket stand of 110 at Hove to save the game – that would matter a bit more than Eng Lit – and she remembered it clear as a bell. England were in trouble, 108 for 6, 'And we had to bat out the day. So we had to get over the initial onslaught, they were pinging it in hard and fast, and they were giving us a bit of lip – but we did it.'

Being more of a bowler than a batsman, the partnership was up there for her with the win at Lord's. But of her life altogether she said, 'If I look back now, every memory is cricket. If I feel low, if I have a bad day at work, I'll remember Lord's. I'll remember walking through the Long Room. Or I'll remember that stand at Hove, and touring India, and all the people I've met, all the people I still write to, Lena in Denmark, Linda in South Africa – because it's not just the game. It's the people that make it special.'

I asked how she could even think about packing it in, and she laughed. She said, 'It's a big issue. But I've got other things. I'm married, maybe I want a family soon, and Dean's not a cricket man – well, he is now, he knows there are six balls in an over – but as time goes on and the game gets better and we play more and more, and we train harder, and he's got another winter coming up on his own . . . I think he's getting to the end of his tether. I'm sure that's how he's feeling. But I can't leave the game alone, can I? So I've talked it over with Clare, and I've said that come the day I do it, it won't just be England. It'll be club, country, the lot – and I'll feel awful, I know that. It'll be like someone wrenching both me arms off.'

As a batsman, she was a bit of a prodder. Her strength was her bowling, right arm slow-to-medium outswing with a canny, deceptive flight. Megan Lear's assistant Peter Moralee compared her to New Zealand's Chris Harris, because of the way she mixed it; she'd throw in an off-cutter, try a leggie, put in one slower than slow, keep 'em thinking all the while. And then she was captain, starting from the tournament in '93 – a job she laughingly described as, 'Looking as if you know what you're on about, when sometimes maybe you don't.'

It was the end of September; one of her biggest concerns was how she and the other older members of the squad should look after the younger ones in India, especially the three who'd not been out there before. Charlotte Edwards would turn 18 while they were there, Laura MacLeod would be 20, Bev Nicholson 22, and they were in for a shock.

She said, 'That first journey when we got on the coach – I've never seen a women's squad so quiet. Cows wandering about, people on elephants, thirteen on a moped, you go past a train and they're dangling out the windows and off the roof – but it's their way of life, isn't it? I think the most harrowing thing we saw was a leper in a subway in Delhi, no arms, no legs – you have to look the other way sometimes. But it's a weird and wonderful place, I'd suggest anybody should go and see it, it's great. I love playing out there, because they're so enthusiastic for cricket – and playing in front of a crowd's no problem for me, it raises my game. OK, 15,000 in Patna, that was a bit daunting – but,' and here she grinned, puckish, 'if you're the captain you can choose who goes on the boundary, can't you? You can stay slip to slip.'

Apart from the odd flying brick, there are the culinary perils too. Last time, Clare Connor ended up three days in hospital – but Smithies was fine. An old miner who'd been out there in the army told her to take some brandy, have a tot every night and she'd be fine – so she did, and she was, and never mind all that anyway because she was going back to India to win. It was one-day cricket and anything could happen but, she said, 'We're good enough to beat anybody.'

I said, when our men had been in India in '96 they were getting beat, they looked so miserable all the time . . .

She snorted, 'You might as well have sent us. It drives me crackers watching them sometimes. They look like they're just going through the motions. OK, I can see how they must feel at times – but I'd have thought playing for your country, there's so much prestige in that, and doesn't that outweigh everything? Maybe it's because it's their job, I don't know – but women's cricketers tend to be more vibrant, more enthusiastic, more committed, because they've given such a lot to play. You've got to want it desperately to be there. I've always said, between me and my parents, cricket's probably cost us fifteen or twenty thousand pounds in lost wages, travelling, kit – but I'd give it all again. And this now, we'll love it. When we get to that first game in Hyderabad, I'll be telling those youngsters to enjoy it, just to live in that moment. Because whatever happens, they'll have it for all the rest of their lives.'

4

Give an Indian a Microphone

In a remote village in the impoverished state of Bihar, some seventy people – half of them women and children – were massacred by the Ranvir Sena, a private army put together by upper caste landlords. Borders were sealed 'to nab the ultras', and senior police 'rushed to the scene'. In the Indian papers, senior police always rush to the scene – but they don't rush very quickly, because by the time they get there the mayhem's always long over.

Meanwhile in Delhi, Sahib Singh, the Chief Minister of the city government, faced embarrassing allegations in the newspapers that his nephews Pawan and Neeraj were involved in the murder of a property dealer. Mind you, if the papers were to be believed, these guys had been embarrassing for years. In 1991, there'd reportedly been a case of assault on a woman 'with intent to outrage her modesty'; two years later, Neeraj supposedly threatened a crowd with a revolver during an election campaign. Since then, there'd been three further allegations of attempted murder, and another of involvement in a shooting outside a school where (said the paper breathlessly, as if this made it so much worse) 'an examination was in progress'.

So if the Honourable Mr Singh could just bring these evidently charming family members along to the World Cup's opening ceremony, he could liven up proceedings no end . . .

I downed another breakfast dose of bus crashes, scandals, forest brigands, and the National Liberation Front of Bodoland, then Prasoon Tripathi took me off in the Mela Plaza's tinfoil 4×4 to meet England at the airport. Prasoon was the Mela Plaza's marketing manager, a genial and extraordinarily hardworking young man who'd recently got married to a woman he'd never previously met. He hadn't known, he said, 'If she was tall or dwarf, slim or a fatty.' Now she was marooned upstairs in a hotel room where, on one of his infrequent visits, she'd told him to go on a diet. She was, said Prasoon, 'A lovely girl' – but how did he know?

We set off through air like mustard soup, past the standard gallimaufry of the half built and the half collapsed. At one point we came on a truck rolled on its side across both lanes of the carriageway, with a bus splayed off the road beside it into a thicket of trees. A crowd stood about in the road, staring at the wreckage. We avoided this by the simple expedient of driving around it into the oncoming traffic on the other carriageway – you know it makes sense – and Prasoon's pager was blipping all the while. He was annoyed because he'd forgotten his mobile. First world, third world, different world entirely.

We passed two auto-rickshaws. The first one was broken down, so the guy driving the second one was giving his mate a shunt down the road to the rickshaw clinic by sticking out his right leg, wedging his foot onto the other guy's rear fender, then using his leg as a push-rod. 'Strange things to see in India,' said Prasoon contentedly.

We passed appalling shanties huddled under damp-blotched

tower blocks. Signs carried absurd injunctions urging Delhi's citizens to Keep The City Clean & Tidy, and to Keep In Your Lane. I thought, this place doesn't capture the imagination – it blitzes it.

On the importance of cricket in India: when the Directorate of Income Tax ran a Voluntary Disclosure of Income scheme – offering amnesty for payment – who did it use to head up the ads? Kapil Dev. 'To me,' said Kapil's copywriter, 'paying taxes is like having a sound technique in cricket. It helps you grow and stay in the game for a longer time.'

I tried to imagine Beefy fronting PR for the Inland Revenue, but somehow I couldn't see it. Pakistan's Imzamam-ul-Haq, meanwhile, was acquitted of assaulting a fan after said fan (allegedly) called him a potato. And where did this happen? At the Sahara Cup in Toronto – where the financial muscle of sub-continental cricket was busy exporting the game to its diaspora and beyond in a way the English could neither imagine nor execute.

Cricket was everywhere. It was on every street corner, it was on billboards promoting the Pepsi Series between India and Sri Lanka ('More Cricket, More Pepsi') and it was on Murdoch's Star Sports in the airport lounge. On a chat show called *Gavaskar Beyond The Boundary*, Sachin Tendulkar was gracing us with the news that he always puts his left pad on first.

More seriously, he and G. R. Vishwanath were discussing the ways of the modern world. It's now a regular plaint in India that Test cricket is dying there; that the one-day game is all anyone cares for, fans and sponsors alike. Specifically, Gavaskar and his guests were saying that the seam on the one-day white balls was harder than that on the red ones, so it was tougher on the spinners; if you wanted to give it some fizz, you ended up chewing the skin off your fingers. So in the one-day game you just ping it down, whack it about and rack up the runs, while the crowd bays and the art of spin dies.

Prasoon – who'd played cricket for his university, as a batsman and close fielder – watched these musings, then read in the paper how the public weren't buying tickets for the Test against Sri Lanka in Bombay. He said sadly, 'The heart of cricket is in the five-day game. But life is so fast now, everybody wants to go quickly. So you play fifty overs, and it's gone before you started.'

He tied a banner to the railings around the Meet & Greet zone: Hotel Best Western Mela Plaza Welcomes Teams For The Women's Cricket World Cup '97. Just along from this, a bloke stood on a Meet & Greet desk, dusting off an enormous plywood apple. I don't know why the airport was decorated with an enormous plywood apple, I'm just telling you it was.

Some time past midday, England and Ireland stumbled wearily off the plane – and of the two squads England, now a well-resourced outfit, looked very much the world champion team. They had on uniform sky-blue tracksuit bottoms, white short-sleeved shirts, and sharp new Vodafone baseball caps; they had more support staff than any other side in India, and they even had a PR woman. Once out of the arrivals hall, manager Shirley Taylor gave the trophy they'd held for four years to the appropriate emissary – and now, of course, all they had to do was win it back.

Sports psychologist Steve Bull looked about him and said, 'I was hoping for a dilapidated bus.' They had, in fact, given us a posh new white one, but there was some question whether it was big enough for both the squad and all their baggage. A small army of porters started manhandling things onto the roof rack, dangling off a ladder perilously overladen with giant Gunn & Moore kitbags. Then they started hassling me for tips. The drawback of being a bloke around a women's cricket team in India is that everyone instantly assumes you're in charge – so I ended up tipping for England before they'd even left the airport.

Finally we did, squeezing on board past a mountain of bags, with the younger players reaching for Priority No. 1 – the new boom box, produced to ironical shrieks of 'Spice up your life!' – and as we set off, Shirley Taylor passed out the rooming list.

Wicketkeeper Jane 'Smigs' Cassar from Ilkeston was sharing with Yorkshire's Helen Plimmer – known simply as H, a thoughtful, handsome woman, and a quality opening bat who was privately worried whether she'd get a place in the starting eleven.

Melissa Reynard, a busy little seamer from Harrogate, a quiet and observant character who'd prove invaluable in the coming weeks, went in with captain Smithies.

Bev Nicholson, another Yorkshire seamer who was working just then at a filling station on the A1 near Thirsk, was one of the three younger players who'd not been before – and she was more nervous about it than anyone. She was put with Clare Connor, a composed and intelligent student of English at Manchester University who knew what it was all about, after spending three days in hospital last time watching lizards climb the wall while her belly fell out of her backside. Connor was only twenty-one, but besides India two years earlier she'd also toured Zimbabwe with the boys' side from her school, and she'd been to Romania to work in orphanages; she'd be calm company for the fretful.

Vice-captain Sue Metcalfe, thirty-two years old, a tough, stern woman from the Dales, got the baby of the pack – Charlotte Edwards, still only seventeen, but as unfazed as Bev Nicholson was uneasy. Previously captain of her county's Under 16 boys' side, Edwards was an opening bat of massive and thrilling promise; rock-solid, placidly confident, she said simply, 'The others'll look after me.'

Barbara 'BB' Daniels was in with Kathryn Leng, a leg-spinner from Leeds who played men's cricket in the Bradford League. Surrey veteran Jan 'JB' Brittin, thirty-eight years old and now at her fourth World Cup, shared with Laura MacLeod, a promising medium pacer from Cheshire, and the third one new to India. As for Derby's young seamer Sue 'Fresh' Redfern, she got Clare 'Romper' Taylor – one of the outstanding sportswomen of our time.

Who else, after all, has represented their country at World Cups in both football and cricket? As women's sport becomes more professional and demanding, who else ever will? Thirty-two years old, a centre-half for Liverpool and England, an opening bowler for Yorkshire and England, Taylor lived in Huddersfield, and drove a van for the Royal Mail in Bradford. Tall, lean, strong and big-boned, she had character by the boat-load, and was the kind of squad member you can't put a price on. She often looked to see how others were getting on; she knew when to gee people up, and she knew when to leave them alone. But all she said now, watching the grubby vivid-ness of India stream past the window, was, 'It feels like I've never been away.'

The squad were greeted at the Mela Plaza with garlands of orange flowers, and had dots of vermilion paste set on their foreheads. A table of tea and coffee was laid out; porters hauled in the baggage. Mary Brito was there, a Yorkshirewoman now resident in New Zealand, and President of the International Women's Cricket Council; she and English coach Megan Lear went immediately into confab.

Brito said she'd spent NZ$3,500 on faxes trying to get India to listen to her. When Megan asked whether they'd listened Brito laughed and said, 'The only way I could get through to them was to put my foot down and threaten to cancel.' The two women talked urgently about how they needed to iron out all manner of rules and arrangements, while jet-lagged players lurched past them and off to their rooms.

They had two hours' rest, then re-emerged for chicken and rice. Sports scientist Joce Brooks gave a pep talk; she told them, 'Stay up as long as you can. We'll have a warm-up at nine-thirty tomorrow – white shirts, blue shorts – and remember to look after each other. Check the seals on every water bottle, don't eat anything that's not peeled, and make sure everyone around you does the same. And don't bite your nails. OK?'

There was much discussion of what was most likely to fend off a rotten gut. Whisky and coke? Brandy? The BA purser on their flight had recommended port and given them a bottle of it, along with four bottles of champagne as well. Romper wasn't sure what that was meant to cure, but she figured someone would enjoy it.

In the morning, the papers said that the dissolution of India's eleventh Parliament, the Lok Sabha, was imminent. Delhi's city government, meanwhile, was preparing to celebrate its fourth anniversary, a spectacle described by the *Hindustan Times* as 'a nauseating civic scene'.

In Ghaziabad, Megan Lear and Shirley Taylor had their own kinds of chaos to cope with. They'd managed to get the players out of dragging into Delhi and back to rehearse the opening ceremony; efforts to find a better way of getting from Hyderabad to Vijayawada and back than two overnight trains were proving less successful. 'I'm assured it's first class,' Megan muttered. 'I'm not convinced, but I am assured. So,' she grinned, 'it'll be the Orient Express, right?'

They set off to practice. Skeins of cool mist lay across the road; impassive men sat on their haunches amid food stalls and crash helmet vendors. We passed an impromptu kids' game on a dirt patch fringed by a bog; they had one stump, one bat, one pad, and were watched by stolid buffalo ankle-deep in sodden weeds. On the bus the Spice Girls sang, 'Whooo-oo-ooh . . . do you think you are?', and were abruptly cut off as we turned into the practice ground.

'England,' said a quiet voice. 'That's who we are.'

We were at the Mohan Sports Stadium, part of our benefactor's Mohan Mekin Brewery complex. Pakistan, also staying at the Mela Plaza, were finishing their session on the far side of the pitch. England got in a huddle and Megan told them how they were off rehearsal duty, 'So I want two hours of hard work and quality now, 'cause you can rest up after.'

There was only one net; Lottie padded up and Laura, Bev, Fresh and the Lengster went to bowl to her. Peter Moralee pinged high balls and ground balls out to the others to field and return to Smigs. A growing clutch of men watched attentively by the gate, quietly approving good catches or throws; in the background, puffs of smoke plumed against the sky, and the road was a permanent soundtrack of parping horns. Moralee got the players in a semicircle for some rapid-fire close catching; Shirley spoke with a local journalist, then we wandered off to have a look at the dressing rooms.

They were getting a new coat of paint; Holland would play the Indians and the Kiwis here in Group B, the group where no one had to travel much. Shirley, by contrast, was wrapping her head round a travel schedule that looked more ghastly every time you thought about it. We had five group games in nine days, from 10 December to 18 December; we had the South Africans in Hyderabad, Pakistan in Vijayawada, Denmark back in Hyderabad, Ireland in Pune, and Australia in Nagpur. Then, beyond all that at the end of the track, there was the alarming fact that the date of the final had been changed.

For months it had been set for 28 December. Only weeks before the tournament, however, the Indian men's authorities announced with an oblivious disregard that India were playing a one-dayer against Sri Lanka that day. Dutt had no choice but to move her final back to 29 December, since otherwise it wouldn't get on TV – which, apart from having the whole thing end pointlessly unheeded, wouldn't leave the folks at Hero Honda too happy. Only trouble was, of course, that by then England had booked their plane tickets – and were due to leave Calcutta for their connection home that evening of 29 December. So if it rained that day and the final was held on 30

December, and if England were in it, well – they wouldn't be, would they? They'd be gone – because at that time of year it's a nightmare getting one ticket in and out of India at short notice, never mind getting twenty-odd.

Shirley stood in the empty dressing room, watching the players work on their catching through the doorway. She sighed, 'There's nothing we can do about it. We just have to pray it doesn't rain. And, of course, that we reach the final in the first place.'

The players were slinging the ball at each other in pairs, back and forth hard and fast, fifty catches left hand, fifty catches right – and one jerked her head back sharply as she took it in front of her chin, then stopped. Megan was on her quick and stern, calling out, 'Don't stop, eh? It's going to come at you that hard in a game. And it won't hit your face if you catch it, will it?'

When they were done she told them, 'Well done, girls. It's really important that we came here this morning and got some practice in. I know we're a little tired from the journey and it's showed a bit, but there's been a lot of effort and that's showed too. Now the thing that matters – I don't mind if you make mistakes, 'cause we're all human. But what I do mind is if you don't work to recover a mistake. So put mistakes out of your mind the minute they happen, and stay with it. Because in practice and in a game, it's the body language that says it all.'

Her own body language was a mix of warm, fierce humour with, sometimes, an uptight tautness. The latter would become more evident as the days and weeks went by; it was born from a blend of fatigue, a deep-seated fear of flying (in light of which, it was extraordinarily brave of her to go through all the travel as she did), together with an intense protectiveness of her players and, above all, an absolute and undimmable passion for cricket. She'd played in nine Tests for England, and in two World Cups; at the second World Cup in India in 1978, she'd scored 96 not out against the hosts at Eden Gardens in

Calcutta. Her playing days were cut off when a serious car accident left her eyesight damaged; now, coaching England since
the spring of '96 towards this sixth World Cup, the freight of
responsibility she felt in that job sometimes plainly weighed on
her.

But for all that, and for all that the disorder of the tour sometimes enraged her, she loved India. It was, she would
repeatedly say, 'A life experience'. Now, walking away from
practice to a neat little garden for tea and biscuits ('50–50
Tasty-Tasty – Eat Healthy, Think Better') she said happily,
'They love their cricket, don't they? We get a bigger crowd to
watch us training than we do in England when we play.'

The central dictum laid down by Steve Bull as he sought to get
the squad's heads right in the run-up to India was, 'Control
the controllables'. He said, 'You want to avoid them whining
and moaning about the pitch, bad luck, umpires, weather,
hotels, all that. You concentrate on what you can control – your
kit, your bedtime, your diet, your fitness and your mental attitude – and the rest you put out of your mind.'

One of the controllables which Megan meant firmly to avoid
was the prospect of endless show-your-face-and-be-polite dinners after matches. Scrums of local bigwigs scoring kudos
points by throwing bashes at which England's women were the
star attraction might be all very well on a two-month tour, when
you had time enough for rest days – but at a World Cup requir-
ing you to play and travel on alternate days, she wasn't having
it.

Still, with six days to go before the opening game, there was
no harm in going out tonight. We drove into Delhi through the
smog-murked dark listening to David Bowie and the Human
League, and on the journey I sat with Steve Bull. Thirty-eight
years old, he'd been working with athletes and cricket teams
for a dozen years; one of his early projects, funnily enough,
was helping an ultra-distance runner do twenty marathons in

twenty days in the deserts of California and Nevada, an adventure about which QED made a documentary called *Mad Dogs and an Englishman*.

He'd been working with the women since the late eighties. Using Sports Council grants, women's cricket had been one of the first English sports to make use of the new-fangled arts of visualisation, of mental preparation and organisational psychology; they were reaching for what Bull called 'the two per cent zone', that marginal edge upstairs that took you past your opponents – and come '93, these disciplines had plainly played their part. Bull told me, 'I remember standing on the left-hand side of the balcony at Lord's, watching JB throw up the ball under the scoreboard. I know Karen's got that picture on her mantelpiece; I've got it on slide myself. I've used that in so many lectures to show what a positive attitude is.'

And what if someone puts a corker through the gate and sends your middle stump spinning? What do you tell the player who's been done by an absolute Jaffa?

'You tell them,' he grinned, 'shit happens. It's a very useful phrase in sports psychology, that.'

It's a useful phrase for matters Indian, too. We'd come to a roundabout so densely clogged with traffic that the gridlock was absolute; for twenty minutes we sat motionless amid what felt like every vehicle ever built, rebuilt, customised or otherwise cobbled together in this tangled, honking, discombobulated corner of the world. We didn't know it, but the Indian government had fallen; assorted folks were out protesting or celebrating or both, and Delhi was seized, seized utterly.

Somehow – unlike several other teams who sat in this stuff for hours, then turned round in despair and went back to their hotels – we did finally make it to the smart private school at which a dinner was being laid on to welcome us all. We walked in to be greeted by smiling, immensely well-mannered pupils in red blazers and ties; we were given necklaces of flowers and dabs on the forehead and Romper said quietly, 'Can you imagine kids in our schools ever being this polite?'

We were led to a circular arena laid out with groups of seats for each squad, under trees hung with white drapes and brightly decorated with sparkling strands of lights. Eleven flags flew over a picket fence behind a lectern with a microphone; a voice softly announced, 'The England cricket team are now here,' prompting quiet scatters of applause.

Amid all this courtesy, the gents was guarded by a soldier with a sub-machine-gun. The High Commissioner of Pakistan rolled up in a silver-grey Mercedes; on stage, groups of children of different ages sang a frantically cheerful ditty about 'having a ball and a jolly good time'.

Welcome senorita
Welcome mi amor
Welcome all the dear ones
Welcome all whom we adore

Enchanted, Connie got an English clapalong going; the children were whooped and cheered off the stage. Holland arrived, along with a Health and Education Minister, the High Commissioner of South Africa, and a councillor from the British High Commission. An interminable round of speeches then ensued, with all the usual stuff about how international sport brings us all together. The Health Minister gave out about a billion prizes to assorted young cricketers, swimmers, high jumpers, judo and tae kwando exponents. South Africa arrived, and Sri Lanka. The English passed round a tube of mosquito repellent, and tried not to fidget. We were all tremendously respected, esteemed, distinguished, and honoured. We were also hungry.

'Sport,' said the Minister, 'is a strong and solid mechanism which binds the whole world in a filial bond. I've got great regard and great love for anybody who is a sportsman. They are very committed, very sincere, very dedicated souls, full of love for others.'

He'd obviously not met Maradona then. Meanwhile, more children were bundling on stage and singing something that sounded oddly like a sea shanty, then there was some of that rather wonderful dancing, the jittery, bendy-twisty, multi-coloured ant-stamping routine. Steve and Joce got hold of Prasoon and told him, Look. We have to leave the hotel at 8.30 tomorrow morning, with everything packed. We haven't eaten yet and even if we leave now without eating, we'll not be back there 'til well after ten. So can we shake a leg here?

There was, meanwhile, no sign of Skip, Megan, or Shirley, who'd gone to a captains' and managers' meeting that had been meant to start at four. We went off to eat while the cultural show meandered on in the background, fled to the bus, and at last bumped into the missing trio – who had, they said, been holed up in Australia and New Zealand's hotel staring aghast at the terminally congealed traffic. So we got to the bus, and then hung about for twenty minutes until the driver showed up.

Amid many entanglements over the rules, the most interesting thing to emerge from the managers' meeting was a recommendation by both the Australian and New Zealand High Commissions that if their teams were drawn in a semifinal in Guwahati, they shouldn't go there. Guwahati's the capital of Assam, where assorted forest brigands and 'naxalites' (armed militants) have been getting up to no good for years. When England went there two years ago, they enjoyed the interesting experience of being shooed to their rooms while a customer with a gun was seen off from the bar; the local paper inventively reported that they were followed to their rooms and raped, which they weren't, but it was a bit hairy all the same.

Still, Megan's attitude to the Oz and Kiwi demur was blunt: 'Fine, they can go home then. We'll play there.' As to the drawn-out business of this evening she said only, 'You can't blame the organisers. Would you want to organise something here?'

Someone put Aretha Franklin on the boom box, and we set off back to Ghaziabad.

The Lok Sabha was dissolved, but no one was reading the papers the next morning because it took forty-five minutes to check out amid a boggling morass of paperwork. Fresh, meanwhile, had black ankles; moz repellent, it seems, brings out your shoe dye. It also melts plastic, so now my Biros were all sticky. Makes you wonder what it does to your skin.

As we set off, Shirley attempted to brief the squad on their role at the opening ceremony, but no one paid attention; drawing the window curtains on the bus had produced a minor outbreak of dozy mozzies, who were now being systematically splatted. 'Smigs! Overhead! Overhead! Nine o'clock! Bandits one-five! Coming out of the sun!'

An hour and a bit later we arrived at the Sports Authority of India's National Stadium, a fine, double-portalled brick edifice put up for the 1st Asian Games in 1951. We disembarked into the hushed jangling of a hundred girls running past, all dressed in white with golden pendants tinkling as they went. By the main entrance the pillars were wreathed in flowers, and a gaggle of uniformed cricket teams took turns being photographed – by each other, and by a dozen local snappers – before a giant floral World Cup logo, a woman with flowing hair thumping a drive through the off side.

In orange dresses and black blazers, the Dutch seemed giantesses beside the tiny women of Sri Lanka. Pakistan wore khaki trousers and army-green blazers; the English had on cream skirts, white shirts and blue blazers, while the Indians were resplendent in shining aquamarine saris. I looked about me at the mighty arch of India Gate down the road in the haze, and at a cow watching a game of hockey. Conrad Hunte rolled up, and said he and his squad had arrived yesterday; they'd taken twenty-nine hours to get to India, from Jo'burg to Delhi via Durban and Bombay. He didn't look remotely tired, and talked readily and happily to every scribbler who approached him.

We went into a grand entrance hall decorated with black and white pictures of Nehru opening the games in 1951. Beyond this, there was one roofed stand; the rest was an open oval of concrete benches. A running track of yellowing grass ran round an astroturf hockey pitch bizarrely adorned with potted plants by the goals and the corner flags. Sad to say, bar the teams, the officials, their guests, assorted schoolchildren and other participants in the forthcoming cultural show (yup, another one) the stadium was empty.

A disinterested hawk hovered over the void arena in a sky the colour of dishwater. The Honourable Sahib Singh turned up, unfortunately without his interesting nephews – one of them had reportedly just been arrested – and there was much handing over of bouquets. 'On arrival of the chief guests,' warbled the uncertain PA, 'we announce the motorcycles of Hero Honda. The motorcycles of Hero Honda, kindly enter.'

Eleven scooters in unsteady formation puttered exceedingly slowly along the running track, followed for no very clear reason by a bagpipe band, and then the cricket teams emerged with England, as the holders, in the lead. The squads shuffled into an uneven fan below the guests of honour; assorted officials and the Chief Minister then burbled an incomprehensible sequence of speeches through a fog of echo, fade, and feedback, culminating in a woman announcing wistfully, 'Balloons and pigeons.'

After an agonising pause, a solitary pigeon was thrown up from the VIP box, flying fifteen feet to settle cosily in the girders of the roof. The hawk swooped closer, doubtless dreaming of pigeon pie. Somewhere in a far corner, a few desultory bunches of balloons drifted away out of sight. The Hero Honda man, meanwhile, was now muttering at the mike, followed by

Mary Brito, and I have absolutely no idea who else. Accompanied by a brace of heavies toting machine guns, the Chief Minister went to shake the hands of 154 cricketers, prompting the announcer to incoherent ecstasy. 'We are so very glad and happy and very happy to have the Chief Minister among all the girls.' I guess you have to say this kind of stuff, otherwise he sends his nephews round. The bagpipe bunch, meanwhile, set to wailing and skirling again, presumably to while away the time.

Wearying, I saw a bloke with a cup of something hot, so I went for a wander to see what I could see. The bowels of the stadium were a dim-lit litter of ladders, paint buckets, rusting chairs, indeterminate piles of sand and bits of wood. Finally I found a dusty lounge upstairs, with a metal urn of chai parked on the floor in the corner. I was stooped over this when Shirley Taylor came in gasping, after forty minutes stood smiling for England on the hot and airless running track. She grinned and said, 'Give an Indian a microphone, they're on it for ever. When karaoke comes to this country, that's the end.'

Large numbers of children did some very sweet and impressively complicated formation jingling, then we got the creation story in dance. The creation took a fair old while to get going, because no one could get the music to work. Then there were more tots, more dancers, and a rather exciting troupe of madly grinning blokes with beards who pranced about with big sticks and stood on each other's shoulders while someone banged a drum, and someone else howled vaguely into the abyss of the PA. I think someone may have been banging dustbin lids together too; hard to tell, but it was more fun than the speeches.

And I know, it's easy to be snide. In truth the costumes were fabulous, the kids were great, the dancers were intriguing and, if somewhat rickety, it was all very exuberant – but what's any of it got to do with cricket? Why do the organisers of international sporting events have this compulsion to make us sit through all this stuff? Why, especially, if they can't get anyone to turn up and watch it?

There were team photos yet to do, and photos with Mr Hero Honda, and a photo of all eleven squads sat together in the stand – during which the photographer memorably asked 154 women from eleven countries to 'smile while I expose myself'. Then we had to go off for lunch at the exceedingly swanky Meridien with the Minister of something or other, who as far as I'm aware didn't actually turn up – until finally, at last, we could leave for the airport, and start making ready to do what we'd come here to do.

Whereupon I looked at what getting England through an Indian airport was like, I thought of the schedule ahead, and I shuddered to my bones. We were fourteen players, two coaches, one manager, three support staff, one PR woman and me. We had twenty Gunn & Moore bags, seventeen Vodafone bags, four coffins, two suitcases, one kitbag, one rucksack, one pro-sport medibag, and one ultrasound machine in a shiny silver case. We had a bloke trying to dun us for excess baggage, and the bloke who was supposed to be our minder and helper was nowhere to be seen because he was a cricket fan, and he was running round getting the players' autographs and addresses. The security bod, meanwhile, was in a tizz because the sachets of Hi-Five energy drink were apparently impervious to his X-ray machine, while outside Joce Brooks was narrowly avoiding getting run down by some nutter in a cab.

And that's only the beginning.

5

Kind Welcomes,
Inconvenience Is Regretted

The domestic departure lounge was a low-ceilinged, ramshackle place with a distinct air of impermanence. The boarding gates were tatty doors with hand-painted signs on glass panes looking out onto a vista of hissing jet engines under a phlegm-coloured sky. Players huddled in card schools on the floor round their hand baggage, or queued at the long distance phone booth. A sign said, 'Work In Progress. Inconvenience Is Regretted'. This sign could be posted anywhere in India.

Megan was feeling rocky; she'd nearly fainted at the Meridien. She blamed the malaria tabs; the prospect of a two-hour flight to Hyderabad probably wasn't helping either. She had on her lucky BA sweater, a tattered old charm; most of the other players had scrambled into casual clothes on the bus but JB and Melissa hadn't found time, and were still in blazers and skirts. When a passing American asked who we were, H told him, then said JB was the manager and Liss was the coach. Liss was five foot two, twenty-five years old, a puckish little dyed-blonde elf; the American patted her on the head and asked, 'How d'you get to be coach then?'

Liss was mortified that she hadn't thought of a good come-back line. She said quietly, 'Maybe I'll grow into me blazer in a while.'

The flight was uneventful; the players turned down the airline food, so when we landed Joce did a Nutri-Grain hand-out at the baggage carousel. At 8.45, we went five yards into the arrivals hall to find more photographers, and more people with bouquets of flowers. After a fourteen-hour day (and counting) this wasn't a moment when people were mad keen to be photographed, but Skip did her job, and stepped up gamely to smile for the cameras. She could be impressively good at that, considering she viewed the media in general with a wariness that bordered on loathing.

We went outside to a dingy forecourt where a small bus of ropy and inadequate aspect waited, with more mountaineering porters scrambling coffins and kitbags up the ladder at the back in the dark. Steve Bull eyed bus and baggage and said dubiously, 'This'll be the mother of all tests here.'

All the while, a shrunken woman and a faintly mad-looking girl were plucking at our sleeves. 'Sir,' said the girl, 'sir, chocolate, money, bye bye.' Players offloaded their bouquets to other beggar children, who promptly tried to sell them back to us as we wrestled to fit everything on the bus. Of course it wouldn't go, so Steve and Pete Moralee got left behind with a pile of bags amid the clawing little fingers. Off we went, rumbling in this poor beaten runt of a vehicle to the Krishna Oberoi in the Banjara Hills – where we stepped from importunate poverty into a wide white marble atrium, air conditioned, with a cool plashing fountain running off a black marble slab, and a fellow in a tux playing a baby grand.

I wandered up to a spread of vast windows, looked out across spacious gardens, and sighed a doleful sigh – because I wasn't allowed to stay here. It hadn't mattered at the Mela Plaza – but now the cricket was in sight, the agreement I had with Megan was that I could travel with the team, but I couldn't stay with them. She wanted to create a Fortress England, a sealed and focused zone in which her players could dwell undisturbed – and while I was beginning to suspect that in India this might prove something of a pipedream, I'd been happy enough to agree to it. Besides, our agreement was irrelevant – the Krishna Oberoi didn't have enough rooms for England anyway.

I don't know whether the organisers hadn't booked enough places, or whether they had but the hotel had ignored it; either way, the players had to go three to a room with mattresses on the floor. While they stood about disgruntled and confused, I sloped off to have a laugh at the outlandish rates being proposed by the Holiday Inn across the road, and was then advised by Shirley to try the Hotel Golkonda a mile or so away; England had stayed there two years ago, and she said it was fine.

I called and booked a room. By this time, we had in attendance assorted local worthies of the most immensely attentive courtesy. Jyoti Joshi, a short, rotund, and twinkle-eyed lecturer in physical education, was the treasurer of the Women's Cricket Association of India; she was, apparently, going to smuggle in mineral water for England and smuggle out laundry, because the Oberoi's rates for such services were steep. The actual room rates she'd negotiated were spectacularly low – but then her brother was the hotel's credit controller, so that might have helped.

Jyoti's brother was loitering with a shambly old charmer called Mr Pillay of the *Deccan Chronicle*; with much smiling and bobbing of heads these two drove me to the Golkonda, checked me in there, and then stood watching me awhile as if I might do something really interesting, like grow a second head. So I asked Mr Pillay if he thought Hyderabad would put out a crowd to watch England play South Africa. He said sadly, 'People do not watch women's cricket here. But,' he continued with the greatest seriousness, 'as a host and an organiser it is very important to me.'

And there it was again. The bus was too small, there weren't enough rooms – so what? You found yourself so captivated by the deeply decent sincerity of the people supposedly in charge of this mess that somehow the mess didn't matter.

I went to the bar for a Kingfisher ('Most Thrilling Chilled!'), and it came with a plate of peanuts and a teaspoon. Who eats nuts with a spoon? I made a note that India was a wonderful country, and I didn't make any more notes because the next minute there was a power cut.

On Saturday 6 December, England were due to play the Andhra Pradesh state women's team, rated third nationally behind Indian Railways and Indian Airlines. To celebrate the fact that we were going to have a game, for breakfast I ate a chickpea curry of brain-curdling ferocity, then rickshawed off to find the players in the doorway of the Oberoi dubiously eyeing a ten-seat Matador – an elongated VW camper in a fetching shade of snot-green, bearing a sign on the back that said, 'Rash Will Crash'. Connie grinned: 'I'm not getting in that.' By some miracle of compression they did, leaving me, Steve, Shirley, Joce and Pete Moralee to wedge into a cab and come following behind.

Half an hour of deranged traffic later, we pulled into the South Central Railways sports complex. In the shadow of an office building large enough to run several small countries, there were courts for volleyball, badminton, and basketball, and pitches for football and cricket. It was all very interesting but, it transpired, it wasn't where we were meant to be.

Someone tried to find out where this practice game might actually be located, then we shoehorned back into our tatter-demalion transport and set off again. We passed along the Tankbund, a pleasant boulevard by the shore of the lake separating Hyderabad from Secunderabad, and after twenty minutes came to another stadium complex. It was rather grand, with a three-storey exterior painted an appealing lime-green, shuttered shops all round the bottom, and a troop of women bending over to sweep the pavements free of leaves and trash. Inside, there was a substantial roofed oval with gigantic flood-light towers, there was a barking dog on the boundary, and there was no Andhra Pradesh. Megan was saying she wanted to bat first, knock up some runs, bowl them out, then go home for an early tea. Trouble is, you need another team to help you do that.

BB asked how many notebooks I'd filled already; the Lengster said they were running a sweepstake on it. 'I take it,' said someone else, 'it's a comedy, this book.' Out on the pitch Connie was giving herself a black eye, crashing the catching mitt back into her face as she went to take a ball. About this point, the coach of the local boys' side appeared to tell us that this wasn't the right ground either.

Fair enough. If at first you don't succeed . . . with Joce joining them, there were now seventeen people on the ten-seat bus. The rest of us had paid off our cab some while back, so now we had to get another one. The one we found had interesting purple windows, and took us past a political meeting in the middle of a roundabout (where else?) before heading back down the Tankbund the way we'd just come. I passed the time pondering the plight of the cycle rickshaw man in a town that has hills, and suppressing a yearning to visit the Bed Works & Fancy Ladies Emporium. All about us, every time a traffic light changed, it was the scooter equivalent of the start of the London Marathon. It was weird enough, without having to look at it coloured purple.

After three journeys totalling seventy minutes, we finally found our game. It was at the Hyderabad Cricket Association's Gymkhana Ground, which had a foundation stone laid by none other than Indira Gandhi in 1984, but it was distinctly modest for all that. A rusted fence topped with barbed wire ran round the boundary; beyond this lay a patch of waste ground to the left of the pavilion, a dormant fairground on the far side, and to the right a flag-bedecked field of hockey pitches and basketball courts. Some kind of parade was in progress on these, with hordes of people engaged in much drumming and brassy tooting. Beyond all this ran main roads, permanently honking and traffic-clogged.

It was long past ten o'clock, but the umpires still wanted fifty overs a side, and they were fretting to start. England tried politely to evade them, and get a proper warm-up done after their morning's excursions. Mr Pillay appeared. 'I'm very sorry,' he said amiably, 'there has been a communication gap.'

Bev Nicholson and Laura MacLeod were left out; no surprise there, as these two young players both knew they were coming to the tournament more than likely to be back-up bowlers. The third player omitted, as she'd feared, was Helen Plimmer; we had three opening bats and of the three of them, Lottie and JB tended to get going quicker.

Today, however, apart from Sue Metcalfe batting at four and hitting 57 not out, no one got going at all. Rusty after months without a competitive game, out of kilter on a dog of a wicket – low and slow, the ball not getting up at all – England were made to look ordinary. The Indians were nearly all young and tiny, but they were handy enough players and Pete Moralee was pleased about that; as he said, playing a joke side doesn't help you much.

At first I wasn't bothered – it was warm and sunny and I was watching cricket. OK, Lottie lost her off stump to a nasty little grubber. OK, BB was unlucky, run out when JB's straight drive hit the bowler's foot and ricocheted back into the stumps. But when it was 43 for 3 in the 13th over, well – this wasn't going quite the way it ought to. Moralee wandered by muttering, 'Twelve extras. If it weren't for the wides, we'd be struggling.'

JB'd been caught at extra cover for 19; she came off and said she'd been impatient. 'I stood up on it, played too early. But you're always nervous the first time you get on a wicket out here. It must be frightening for the men; you go up against a quick and you don't know if it's going to be round your ears or your ankles. Still,' she shrugged, 'it's good to have a little battle. The beauty out here is that a lot of these sides can really play, and it wakes you up – and we need that.'

It'd be a bit hard waking up, of course, if they were stuck three to a room and couldn't sleep properly in the first place. Selena Colmer, from Vodafone's PR agency Craigie Taylor, now pitched up to say that the Oberoi still hadn't freed enough rooms; the support staff might have to move to the Holiday Inn. South Africa, meanwhile, had got up in Delhi at three in the morning for a six o'clock flight, and arrived at the Oberoi to be told there weren't any rooms for them at all; they were staying somewhere else altogether. Inconvenience, no doubt, was regretted.

Another grubber put paid to Jane Cassar; it was 77 for 4 off 27 overs. The scorer told me not to worry, women's sides didn't often get much past 150 on this track. Over by the scoreboard, Romper considered the business of the hotel rooms and said, 'Winning this World Cup, it's not just about what you do on the pitch, is it? It's about chilling when you're off it. 'Cause once you start stamping your foot about things, it does your head in.'

Karen Smithies came off, lbw for 5, and packed ice round a strapped-up knee. I asked what was up with it, and she shrugged. 'A long word.'

BB grinned. 'She's an old crock.'

It was, according to Karen 'Fizz' Giles, chondramalacia patellar – wear and tear at the back of the kneecap. It sounded horrid, but it wasn't; at this point, the only thing Fizz was worried about was fatigue.

Megan said, 'It's our first game out of season, and people are tired. At least,' she said wryly, 'it's good to get a lot of people out to the wicket.'

England finished 170 all out on the final ball. The Indian fielding was sharp, but their bowlers were nothing special; without an embarrassing tally of 35 wides and 8 no balls,

England's total would have been dismal. Watched by a growing crowd of hundreds of men hanging like sparrows off the wire fence round the boundary, they disposed of Andhra Pradesh for 103 with 8 overs to spare – but again, absurdly, there were 31 wides.

Megan wasn't greatly perturbed. 'I've been on many, many tours out of season,' she said, 'where you're crap first game. But now we've seen what the pitches can be like, we've seen how strict the umpires are on wides – and at least we won, at least we were up for it. After the kind of start we had this morning, at least that proves the spirit's there.'

All the same, it was pretty sorry stuff; the Indians looked as if their bats were too big for them, the English looked half asleep, and the best entertainment was to be got from walking round the fence, greeted all the way by a murmuring ring of big yellow-toothed smiles.

'Hello, hello! What is your name?'

'Pete. Hi.'

'Pea tie? Which country you are from?'

'England.'

'Kind welcomes.'

Back at the Golkonda, I discovered that I couldn't make a phone call without paying for it immediately thereafter. Why on earth not? Why can't you run me up a bill with everything on it like a normal hotel?

'You have very scanty baggage, sir.'

I stared wide-eyed at the implications of this statement, and was met with a charming smile. The receptionist said, 'Forgive me for being blunt.'

I gave them a deposit to reassure them that I didn't mean to do a runner; in their embarrassment, they rang my room minutes later to say that they'd done me the signal honour of unlocking my phone so I could call home direct, rather than going through the operator. I called home, and it didn't work.

Presumably the operator, outraged at being cut out of the loop, had fubared this particular move. I ground a few teeth and called him, gave him the number I wanted, put the phone back down, then stared at it for a while until I got bored of nothing happening and went off and had a bath.

When I took the plug out, half the bathwater immediately reappeared through a drainhole and spread out across the floor. I was standing naked in the middle of this when the phone rang. I lurched out to get my call, at which point there was a knock on the door. Room service wanted to know whether I had enough notepads by the phone. It was like being in a stage farce. Inconvenience, of course, was enormously regretted.

Absurdity piled on absurdity. We were invited to a dinner hosted, as far as I could gather, by a tobacco salesman; the English management and support staff went, leaving the play-ers to rest at the Oberoi. It was a stand-up buffet in a green and roomy walled garden (knockout rogan josh) and during this event, I was informed by Jyoti Joshi that she'd booked me into the miraculously lavish Grand Kakatiya Towers, at the ludi-crous rate of a tenner a night. This meant that, since I wasn't allowed to stay with England, I was now staying with South Africa instead.

To be honest, that was fine; the South African women's cricket team were about the most fun bunch of people I've ever met in my life. Never mind that they'd been up since three in the morning, after twenty-nine hours flying to get to India in the first place; here they all were, mugging up for group photos, singing loud and happy songs. It made England look a bit feeble, tucked away in their rooms.

Megan looked at the South Africans darkly and said, 'You can see their team spirit, how strong it is. But how long will it last?'

Bombs on three trains in southern India killed nine people, and injured around seventy more. It was the fifth anniversary of the demolition of a mosque by Hindu nationalists; in Hyderabad, three died in commemorative protest marches, one stabbed, and two others shot by police 'firing in the air'. Other protestors were subjected to what the *Indian Express* termed 'a mild lathi charge'. A lathi is a very big stick; judging by the paper's photograph, if that was a mild lathi charge, you'd not want to be around for a fierce one.

In the Bombay Test match, meanwhile, Sri Lankan paceman Pramadoya Wickeramasinghe dismissed Saurav Ganguly, gave him the finger and advised him to, 'Fuck off, man.' India's quickie Javagal Srinath then got the Sri Lankan wicketkeeper in the face, splitting his lip in a gash one and a half inches long. Apart from that, Geoffrey Boycott – who, bizarrely, is something of a cult hero in India – moderately opined that India's bowling was, 'A load of rubbish.'

The bowling of South Africa's women plainly wasn't; on Sunday, while England had a rest day, they ran up 191 for 6 against Andhra Pradesh, then got rid of them for 52. But Megan always knew the first World Cup game against these people would be hard; she'd spent a lot of time in South Africa, she loved the people and the place, and she admired everything about the way they approached their sports. With stern approval she snorted, 'Friendlies? In the southern hemisphere they don't know what a friendly is.'

By contrast, neither she nor Peter Moralee had much time for the traditionalists of the WCA in England. The national side might have been hauled into a more professional mindset, but the domestic game remained mired in a lackadaisical amateurism. 'You can put this in your book,' said Moralee. 'You'll go and see people playing these friendly games, they're putting on bowlers that are absolute crap, they're letting the tail bat first – and how is that good for women's cricket? How is that serious? But if you say anything about it, they get all huffy.'

On Monday 8 December, England were due a second practice game against Andhra Pradesh. Now, when they heard what the South Africans had done to the local side, Megan said firmly, 'Never mind that. When we play them again tomorrow, we'll step up another gear.'

I moved into the Kakatiya Towers; when I went to bed, a message was running along the bottom of the screen on the local TV channel. It said, 'Don't Believe Rumours. Situation In The City Is Quite Normal And Peaceful. Commissioner Of Police.'

Not quite true, this. One of those shot by the police had been a woman feeding her infant son in her apartment; the bullet came through the window and hit her in the temple. The *Deccan Chronicle* reported a funeral procession 500-strong turning ugly; police responded to stone-throwing with tear gas, water cannon, lathi charges, and more shots in the air. Someone else was stabbed, someone got thrown off a bridge, and senior police officials rushed to the scene.

Happily, these quite normal and peaceful conditions didn't prevent the local organisers getting England a proper bus this time, or directing the driver to the right ground – and true to Megan's forecast, England did step up a gear. Winning the toss and batting first again, they ran up 222 for 6, then tied down Andhra Pradesh to 92 for 7 for a more convincing win altogether. Helen Plimmer had a bat, and got 47; JB got 36, BB 41, and Jane Cassar knocked 33 off 37 balls. Laura MacLeod and Bev Nicholson both played too, and bowled economically – though no one was as stingy as Clare Taylor, who sent down seven overs, and gave away just three runs.

Overall, the aim in these games was to give all fourteen a chance to play. This was an objective made easier today by the fact that Fresh and Connie had both spent the night throwing up; as to the three who'd eventually not make it, Megan said, 'I think we've built enough of a squad mentality that the three not playing will know they're as important as the eleven who are. But whichever way it goes, it'll be a tough decision.'

One of the more interesting features of these games was

that Charlotte Edwards had a bowl in both of them. Everyone knew about her batting – Jan Brittin said simply, 'She has the potential to be the best we've ever seen' – but to date her leg spin had been thought no more than part-time county stuff. Now, however, she'd bowled just two balls at the tail in the first game, and taken a return catch off the second to finish the innings; then today she bowled five overs, gave away only seven runs, and teased out a stumping into the bargain. As a result, a theory was beginning to germinate that on the spinners' pitches here, Edwards' bowling might allow England to shed a seamer, and let in H as an extra bat at the top of the order.

The pros and cons mulled back and forth; people forgot too easily that Lottie was only seventeen, and what a big task the batting was here, never mind bowling too. Unnerved on an unfamiliar wicket, she only got 4 and 17 in these games; she hated curry too, and was living on chocolate, crisps, toast, and nan bread chip butties. Yet she never looked fazed; she was off in the rickshaws to the Adidas shop with the best of them.

One of these trips became known as 'the fifty-stone rickshaw ride'; four of the party's larger women, Lottie among them, proved too much for a tuk-tuk which, struggling up the hill to the Oberoi, sputtered and died. Now Lottie may have been from Cambridgeshire, but she bore more than a passing resemblance to Graham Gooch, and her accent was purest Essex. So they paid off the unfortunate rickshaw driver and, as they set off in another vehicle, she called out behind her, 'Unlucky, mate, unlucky.' It would, you got the feeling, take something pretty strong to upset Charlotte Edwards.

Romper, Smigs, and Bev ran the scoreboard; shooed off from the pavilion, a big gang of kids went to sit all about them, and were led in applause of good shots and stops. Before long, the three Englishwomen were surrounded by a veritable rainbow of smiles. Watching me scribble BB asked, 'Have you got

Romper on Voluntary Service Overseas?' A pavilion consensus emerged that it was a good job the kids were there, 'cause they could probably all count better than Romper anyway – who, by now, was beginning to disappear among them entirely.

'It's so fascinating,' said Joce Brooks, 'that you just get pulled along with it all.' The sports scientist was a short, athletic blonde, a lacrosse player with a round, appealingly mischievous face. She was twenty-six, she'd been on the previous tour, and she pretty much admitted that she'd been too young for it, that it had been a massive shock to the system; in seven weeks, she'd lost a stone and a half. Now we sat on the pavilion steps as she explained what she did – looking after the food, making sure the players drank enough water, running the warm-ups, trying with Fizz to advise Megan when the squad should train and when they shouldn't, trying to set plans in stone for every next day – and in doing these things, she talked about how much they'd learnt from being here before, above all about being patient.

'It's understanding,' she said, 'that when you ask for something, it may very well not happen. We as a nation aren't necessarily too patient – and then, you don't realise how much you get involved emotionally. When we won at Lord's in '93, I just broke down. But in India, that involvement's multiplied ten times over; things start blowing out of all proportion. You start worrying when people get sick, and it's hard for people not to start getting obsessive about that. You have the problem that, sure, you want people to eat sensibly – but you do still want them to eat. It's more or less a daily question with all of them, to ask what they've eaten. And then claustrophobia's a problem; you're jammed together, and some people need their space.'

Between them, she, Steve, and Fizz had drawn a bead on every single player as a character – what they needed, and how best to keep each of them going. Some you didn't worry about; Melissa Reynard, there was no problem there. 'One of the fittest,' said Joce, 'really motivated, loves curry, eats like a dust-bin.' Then on others, you kept more of an eye.

England finished their innings, and the packed lunches came; tandoori chicken, vegetable pakoora. Skip took one look at it and grimaced, 'Nice lunch, eh?' She reached for a Nutri-Grain bar and said, 'Can't be doing with any of that.'

When I mentioned to Skip's mate Linda Olivier, South Africa's opening bat, that Skip didn't like curry, Olivier gave a dirty great laugh. 'I'll ring her and I'll tell her, Tough luck, sister.'

The England party was growing. Vodafone were paying for an Allsport photographer to join us; Cath Harris arrived, the WCA's press officer, as did a young journalist called Thrasy Petropoulos, covering the tournament for Five Live and *The Times*. Thrasy wasn't greatly taken with the discovery that to keep Megan happy (because he was a rodent of the press) he had to move out of the Oberoi when he'd only just checked in – and when we got into the travel/play/travel/play routine, I could see this giving us problems, especially as none of the other management or support staff agreed with it.

With the possible exceptions of Smithies and Metcalfe, I don't think any of the players agreed with it either. It wasn't pleasant being made to feel unwelcome, when you'd come a long way to pay attention to people whose achievements nor-mally go pretty much ignored; on the other hand, I could see what Megan was trying to achieve, I'd agreed to it myself, and – at least for the moment in Hyderabad – in practical terms it really didn't matter.

So, back in the Banjara Hills, Pete Moralee in the Holiday Inn swapped his room with Thrasy's in the Oberoi. Moralee arrived to find Thrasy somewhat embarrassed, saying there was a problem with the toilet. What problem? It wouldn't flush. In fact, rather the opposite. In fact, it was fountaining. Moralee had a look, and found sewage gushing into his five-star bathroom. He ended up sitting cross-legged on his desk surrounded by his bags while a malodorous flood spread across the floor and out into the hall – a fate which had something ruefully ironical about it. Shit on a journalist, basically, and in this case he'd rather literally shat back.

Overall, I don't really know how I feel about this one. For a start, it was only a few people who wanted us staying elsewhere – and while it's a sorry indictment of the English press that those people should feel such a leery paranoia of anyone with a notebook, it's hardly a surprising one. Even so, from a PR point of view, Selena Colmer thought it sucked – and England are going to have to learn to cope with rodents far more verminous than Thrasy and I will ever be. They'll not be told what hotel to stay in; if they don't get an answer to a question, they'll ask it again and again until they do – and if you're hostile to them in any way, they'll write stuff about you that'll make Thrasy's exploding toilet look like a bowl of roses.

South Africa, by contrast, were massively welcoming; their captain Kim Price was quite one of the most charming people I've ever met. As a group, if the Indians invited them out, they didn't sit muttering in their rooms that they were there to play cricket – they went for it, and they sang at the top of their voices all the way. Their Abba catalogue was impressive; their rendition of 'California Dreaming' (complete with harmonies) was epic. So, on the evening after England's second practice game, they spilt out of the Kakatiya Towers – and were they tired? Nonsense. They'd been shopping. Denise Reid announced fiercely, 'We are a *strong* nation.'

It was throwing down with rain; the evening's dinner was another stand-up affair under a holed and heavily leaking marquee. A banner announced, 'Welcome To The Women Cricket Teams Of England & South Africa Sponsored by Golden Eagle Deluxe Premium Beer & Bhavani Marketing Agencis' (sic). So we wolfed the Golden Eagle and some topping mutton paneer, and Alicia Bezuidenhout from

Klerksdorp in the Transvaal told me about the kid she'd met in the nets the other day.

'He's got a Slazenger,' she said, 'he's eleven or twelve, and he sees I've got a Kookaburra, and he says you can't get one in India. He just wants to touch it, just to touch it, and he was so *wired* when he did, man. And you see that, I tell you – you get so much joy out of so many small things in this country.'

The power cut out; we were standing in a mudbath under a canvas colander in the dark. South Africa sang:

Turn your back on sorrow
And reach up to the sky
We're going up sunshine mountain
You and I

Aluis Kuylaars was a medium pacer from the Cape. She said, 'To me, this is just typical South Africa. We're used to sitting round a camp fire, and this is just the same. So it's raining, so the bus was delayed – there's no use getting a sad face on, is there? And look – Denise is a Cape Coloured, Kim and a few others are English, can't speak a word of Afrikaans – but we've come together over the past few years, and it's a bonding. We have a common background, and we're South Africans.'

Before the evening was out, they'd sung their new national anthem in Xhosa, in Afrikaans, and in English. One of our Indian hosts said, 'The lights have gone out this evening, but you have brought light here by being our guests' – and I was embarrassed to be the only English person there.

Who was preparing better for a game of World Cup cricket, of course, might prove to be another thing entirely – but having watched both sides, Mr Pillay knew what he thought. 'South Africa's bowling is quicker,' he said, 'and their fielding is sharper. They have the edge.'

6

Game On

Karen Smithies said, 'It's not being rude not to go to all the dinners. It's just vital that players get rest.' With sponsors, lottery grants, and the ECB behind them – not to mention their own ambition – England's attitude was that they were now professional in every regard except for payment, and had to behave as such.

Besides, in their own reserved way, they were not less friendly than South Africa; just as Bezuidenhout spoke of the boy who wanted to touch her Kookaburra, so Steve Bull talked about the kids who helped him when he was running a net. He was working the bowling machine – apparently, the only bowling machine in the entire state of Andhra Pradesh – and he had four lads chasing every ball for him. They were in an Under 12 side, they were all in their whites, 'And they were just so made up to have you there. They were totally helpful. Afterwards, the guy running the centre gave me his cap. I felt quite emotional about it.'

The scorer at the first practice game had umpired a match that Megan played in in 1978. He had a photograph – a photograph twenty years old – and he brought it to the Gymkhana for the second game to show everyone. Shirley loved that – but she loved India, period. Forty-one years old, an unruffled, thoughtful woman with a quiet, ironical smile, a few years earlier she'd taken a year out from teaching and travelled round Asia; in India she'd eaten street food, and slept in hotels costing as little as sixty pence a night. Now she said, and she was a little upset with herself, 'We should have thought. We should have brought stuff to give them, caps, badges, pictures, anything. Because we're so rich, and they'd be so made up.'

No one had more time for people than Clare Taylor. Megan didn't always approve ('How can she be focused on the game if she's signing autographs on the boundary?') but she wasn't someone who could turn people away. During one of the practice games, one of the men hanging off the fence asked her, 'Madam. Are you married?'

She fibbed, and said she was. He told her, 'Madam, I am heartbroken.' Next time she was back there, someone else asked the same question and this time she forgot, she said she wasn't – and the first bloke was still there. Appalled, he upbraided her: 'Madam! You lie!'

Now she was wandering about with a jar of Marmite, explaining how she drank cod liver oil neat for her joints. It was the morning of Tuesday 9 December, the day before England played South Africa; they were loitering in the foyer of the Oberoi wanting to go to the match ground for practice, but (of course) there was no sign of a bus.

The World Cup was getting off to a miserable start. The monsoon was meant to be over by the end of November, but global warming and/or El Niño had put paid to that. Downpours in Delhi washed out games between India and Sri Lanka, the West Indies and Holland; heavy rain in

Madras looked likely to see off the Australia–Ireland match as well.

The press coverage wasn't happy reading either. *Newstime* reported, 'Women's cricket in India is still the country cousin of men's cricket and, sadly, the WCAI have failed to properly market the World Cup.' It was 'ham-handed'; after the unattended opening ceremony, Hero Honda was grumbling. One of their people was quoted saying, 'When a sponsor shells out a huge sum to sponsor a sports event, he expects decent publicity in return . . . but the WCAI seems to be putting not much effort to sell the World Cup.'

The forecast for Hyderabad, meanwhile, gave cloudy skies and intermittent showers; Jyoti said the pitch at the stadium was slushy. 'Good,' said BB. 'It'll be just like Hinckley.'

England still didn't have a bus to go to practice there; it was supposed to have shown up an hour ago. Megan said if we couldn't get there, Joce should lead a work-out in the Oberoi gardens instead; Shirley sighed and said, 'If we were playing India tomorrow, we'd assume this was all a conspiracy. But we're not, and it isn't. It's just the way things are.'

The swimming pool was dug into an artificial crater; Joce set the squad to a series of exercises with a sprint up the steps, round the top and back down between each one. Press-ups, sit-ups, squats, triceps; she moved among them barking orders and encouragement as they sweated in the muggy heat. 'C'mon, Jibbsy, great pace, keep it going. C'mon, Lottie, nice and easy, all the way, step up. Keep going, Metcalfe, good job. Well in, Beeby.'

Indians in business suits strolled by, intrigued and admiring. The players worked hard, stern-faced, racing each other round the track with their captain among them clapping them on, calling out their names. Fresh was on her last set of sit-ups; H went to hold her feet as Steve stood over her, pushing her through to the end. 'C'mon, Fresh. Last over, they need four to win. Keep it going. Two balls to go, stick at it. One dot ball and you're there. Well done.'

Whatever happened, no one could say they didn't work for it – and they were always ready to improvise. The bus hadn't come? Fine, get five taxis then. So we got to the Lal Bahadur stadium that way (past an elephant riding down the road on a flatbed truck) and it was the second place we'd been on our travels before the practice game, the lime-green oval with the giant floodlight towers.

It was a Test match ground – but it didn't look as if you could play anything on it just now. The outfield was rough and squelchy, with the odd hole in it, and pools of standing water; one whole corner was pretty much a bog, and towards the middle there were skiddy patches of mud. On the track, two kids squatted by a roller and a pile of grass clippings. Shirley shrugged. 'Who knows what they'll do with it in the next twenty-four hours?'

Craig Prentis showed up, Allsport's Vodafone-funded photographer, and arranged the squad for a group shot, sitting on a wall twenty foot up over a big sign celebrating India's fiftieth anniversary. Lottie looked nervous, she didn't like heights, and the top of the wall was wet – what you have to do in the name of PR, eh? There was supposed to be a press call too, but only one local journalist came. Megan muttered darkly, 'You can see what'll happen, can't you? We'll go back, and they'll all turn up there and ask if they can have it then. Well, I'm sorry. They can't.'

Romps and H strolled out to the wicket. H was pleased with her 47 the day before, 'But it was a bit hairy to start with, there were a good few shooting through. It's not a place to be flamboyant, this; you've got to graft for it here.'

They talked to the local scribe; I walked away to the terraces. There was a guy sat silently by a burning plastic tub in a reechy cloud of black fumes, and three blokes painting the girders high above him. They had no safety harnesses, nothing like that; they'd just monkeyed up a forty-foot strut (three pairs of flip-flops lay at the base of it) then clambered out through the roof, hauling up paint and brushes on a rope. Shirley looked at this precarious undertaking and said, 'Labour's cheap, and so's life. They mow the outfield with push mowers, whole teams of them. And if all these things didn't get done by hand,' she shrugged, 'India'd starve.'

'We've been here a week,' said Skip, 'and we just want to start playing. Because we've been here before, we know what we're going to see, we know ten minutes means an hour, and none of it's a shock. We're rested, and we're ready.'

What about yourself? What about the knee?

'It's been hurting for two seasons, but I've learnt to play with it. I did start with the trots this morning, that's a bit achy – but it's the norm, isn't it? They can dose me up tonight. Then I'll talk with Sue about fielding positions, I'll see Fizz, I'll pack, and I'll do Radio Leicester. I don't mind that – it's my county, isn't it? As for talking to them that aren't in – I want that to be my job. I'm the skipper, and it's my duty to look after them. It's not easy, especially if it's the same people again and again, but it's got to be done. You wish all fourteen could play, but they can't.'

The three not playing would be Plimmer, Nicholson, MacLeod. Taylor got in over MacLeod because, while she'd had a lean summer, her experience was vital. MacLeod did well against Andhra Pradesh – 10 overs, 3 maidens, 16 runs – and it was just hard luck. As for Edwards, Smithies said, 'She's exceptionally talented, and she should play because of that. It's very, very tough on Helen – she looked more at ease than anybody yesterday. But Lottie's got the leg spin too, and we might call on that. I'd say not – but you never know.'

She said, 'We've trained so hard for this. It feels like it's taken a lifetime to get to it, and I can't wait to lead them out.

And we'll win. We don't write South Africa off, but we've seen them, we know them, we've beat them – and with hindsight, the loss at Taunton doesn't do any harm. We know what they can do, we know how good we've got to be – and we will be.'

I got a rickshaw back to the Kakatiya Towers. A sign on the back of the driver's seat said, 'Please check your up beloinging before leaving the auto'. Another on the roadside said, 'If you drink like a fish then SWIM, don't DRIVE.'

In what little time I'd had free in Hyderabad, I'd seen the giant ruins of the Golconda Fort, the mighty bulb-domed tombs of the Qutb Shah kings, the Charminar arch celebrating the end of a plague in the sixteenth century, and a spectacular new temple built entirely of white marble on a hill overlooking the lake. Now we passed a brown and crumbling bus from the Directorate of Oilseeds Research. There was Sangfroid Remedies Ltd., and over here was the Decent Servicing Centre. In India, everything is interesting; you never know what you're going to see next. Yet CNN had a slogan: 'Helping the world become a smaller place.' Now who could want that?

The next morning I got up at six-fifteen, and found big shallow puddles on the hotel forecourt; it had rained in the night. The front desk said it was only drizzle, so the start might be delayed but we'd surely get a game – well, maybe.

At seven-thirty in the Oberoi foyer, the players loitered in that quiet, not-displaying-tension mode. Steve Bull said, 'To be honest, the past week's been a holiday. A switch'll flick today, with the intensity of the game, and this punishing schedule kicking in. And with every passing day, it becomes more obvious how important it's been that they came here two years ago; they're all saying it. Dinner was an hour late last night, and there was barely a murmur.'

There was barely a murmur on the bus ride either. They listened to the Spice Girls, the Backstreet Boys, Eternal, Janet

Jackson. We backed in past a dead animal lying in the middle of the road, and found a dozen starched cops round the dressing room door, the guy with the stripes muttering basso in a walkie-talkie. Out on the wicket, half a dozen skinny men were trying to dry it out with metal trays laden with smouldering coals. Liss grinned: 'That's worth a photey. You can't fault them for ingenuity, can you?'

Romps asked, 'What d'you want from the barbecue then? I'd like it on a length, me.'

There were shallow pools of standing water ten yards square of either crease. The minimum for a game was twenty overs apiece; the umpires said if we were to get that we'd have to start by one-twenty, but if the sun came out we'd manage sooner than that. I can't say I felt confident; the best guess was an inspection at noon.

Still, Indian ingenuity: Shirley once saw a doctor being interviewed on the box. The subject under discussion was male impotence, and the issue was how to determine whether it was physical or psychological. To find that out in the West we'd have tests, we'd have machines – and the Indian solution? You stick a postage stamp on your organ before you go to sleep. If you wake up and it's come off, then in the night you've had an erection, ergo, the problem's in your mind. And if they can figure a little trick like that, maybe they can sort this wicket out as well . . .

A dozen schoolgirls came in wearing ravishing clothes of the brightest jade and turquoise, emerald and cerise, purple and ochre and ivory. They had on lipstick and pearls, gold-spangled embroidery, flashing beads of mirror glass. I took a picture and their teacher said, 'A nice smile for uncle, please.' They went to sit on carpeted platforms under bright canopies of green and red and blue, propped up on wooden sticks swathed in material yellow and maroon, gold and vermilion and royal blue. At one end, a separate platform had five padded chairs, a microphone, a little table piled with bouquets. Romper sat quiet among the empty chairs, writing a letter home. We had a slow morning ahead.

Conrad Hunte was sixty-five. He'd toured India twice with the West Indies, and two other times as well; he'd been Kapil Dev's first wicket in a first-class match, in Calcutta he'd helped save a tour from cancellation amid riot and flames, and he knew very well how to prepare his players. 'India,' he said, 'is the most hospitable of countries – and you have to respond always on the basis of appreciation, not of comparison.'

As for Calcutta, well, that was a story. They'd come into West Bengal for the second Test, started on New Year's Eve, the last day of '66 – and everything was on strike, totally seized up. Sensitive to a touchy situation they didn't know anything about, the West Indians went into the game thinking they shouldn't do anything to make it worse – no disputing any decisions, nothing. The first day, there were minor skirmishes round the ground. The second day, New Year's Day, a huge crowd packed in.

'We were batting overnight,' said Hunte, 'two of our fellows were out there – and I noticed people jumping the fence, there was no place for them. They're ten metres deep into the field, the game can't continue, the police start pushing them back, and people in the stands start throwing sharpened bamboo sticks at them like spears. The riot squad came with tear gas – so now there's people all over the field trying to escape the gas, and the spearthrowers are pouring petrol on the stands to set them on fire. We had gas in our eyes, and fire all around us. All the players scattered – except myself. I had an inner direction that I should stay in the pavilion, that it would be the safest place. As Gandhi said, the inner voice is the only tyrant I'll bow to – and my voice said, Stay. So by staying, myself and two Indians – a physio and a policeman – we were able to save all the kitbags from the fire, and the flags of the two countries.'

Hunte is revered in India for this; the riot had been part of an attempt to bring down the Bengali government of the time, and the decision to play on was taken in the face of that. On 3 January, said Hunte, 'We had police on our coach, in front of it, behind it, and all around the ground with guns. We took the field, and the atmosphere was electric. Then we won in three days and,' he smiled, 'we didn't get shot. 'Cause I'm here, right?'

When Hunte spoke at the end-of-tour dinner in England in the summer, a number of the English players readily confessed that he'd been so passionate for the future of the women's game that he'd moved them to tears. He was, said physio Karen Giles, 'The most inspiring man I've ever met.'

At ten past nine the sun was struggling to emerge, but there was enough blue sky about to make several pairs of police-men's trousers. A team of men were sponging away the puddles by the track with buckets and a wheelbarrow; Romper squatted on the wicket, palm down amid the singed barbecue patches, and a rotund fellow in a blazer told her confidently that we'd be OK, that the coals would be going up and down the track thrice. She smiled and said, 'Thrice, eh?'

An old boy in a cream lungi, sandals, and a waistcoat, with squares of red and yellow on his forehead, wandered about getting autographs. He had cards made up, marked 'Eves World Cup' – sportswomen in India are known, fetchingly, as eves – and he was handing out copies of a newsletter called *Flash & Fellowmen Timely*. It was a mix of politics and cricket, and the mortar in the mix was certifiable loopiness. The main story was headlined:

- GOLDEN JUBILEE YEAR OF UNCERTAINTY
- OF LOOT & SQUANDER, BRIBERY & CORRUPTION
- OF MURDER OF SECULARISM & HUMAN VALUES

'Is it not a daylight and downright murder of secularism

when in the fiftieth Year of Indian In-Dependence the PM dares to hurt the sentiments of Muslim and Sikh minority by allowing the axing of Azhar and Sidhu who were among the best in the team. This is not a laughing question.'

Nor was being dropped. H had learnt late afternoon the day before that she was out; now she sat in a plastic chair in the out-field, and watched the groundsmen in their efforts to prepare a pitch she wouldn't play on. She said, 'I'm disappointed, obviously, but I'm not really surprised. I think their intentions were fairly clear, and I was getting a bit resigned to it. So,' she smiled, 'I'll just hang about and wait for someone to get Delhi belly. Well, I'll hang about, anyway. Maybe I'll get a game against Denmark or someone – but unless I get a really monster score, it'll be hard to break back in.

'Still, look – there are fourteen people needed, fourteen people who need to be united, and it's no good going about with a long face on, because that's not what we need. So I'll enjoy the holiday – and at least it's better happening here than in Australia or New Zealand. It could get boring, sitting about there – but here, everything's so electric that in a way, it's easier to put not playing to the back of your mind. It's very much still there, but it's more foggy, because there's so much to look at. It's a challenge just existing and surviving here – and I do like a challenge. I consider it a real treat to experience this.'

She said, 'I just can't understand people coming here, and not wanting to be here.' To which I say, whingeing blokes who get paid, take note.

We'd not get play before one, if at all. In the dressing room, Jyoti was in tears; she'd put hundreds of pounds of her own money into this, a huge sum, and she desperately, desperately wanted some cricket. Megan embraced her, told her it wasn't her fault – and the saddest thing was, across the lake in Secunderabad it hadn't rained. It had only rained here.

England and South Africa lined up in their playing strips,

waiting to go into Bigwig Mode. The Chief Minister of Andhra Pradesh was coming, a mover and shaker in the United Front whose government had just fallen; Geetha Reddy, the President of the AP Women's Cricket Association, had been a minister in a previous Congress (I) state government too, so there was now a bout of handshaking, bouquet distribution, and speeches. Smoke drifted through the heat haze on the wicket; addressing the Chief Minister Reddy said, 'We've been worried about the weather, sir, but the sun gods have smiled upon us, and we will have a game.'

The APWCA had been founded in 1973 and, she said, it had been an uphill struggle ever since. So now she made a direct and personal appeal for money – and the Chief Minister responded by declaring a grant of 250,000 rupees. That's about £4,000 – and similar disbursements would be made in different venues in the next few weeks, prompting criticism that this was naked electioneering on the back of the tournament. But if India's women got some dosh out of it, who cares?

The Minister was brief and to the point: 'I feel strongly that women are equally competent as men in any field, any venture. Only when women come to the fore will there be balanced development – and I am very optimistic that this World Cup will promote women in India in a positive way.' Then he bundled into a scrum of snappers and TV cameras to shake the players' hands.

Reddy told me, 'Any amount of money is welcome. We have no crowds, no TV, no sponsorship. I see all the staff and material the English have and I'm amazed, I'm really impressed. In the women's game we are way, way behind. We have very good players but they have no fame, no glory, no money. So this event can help and I'm thankful he came, because he's set the ball rolling.'

He would have done, if we could just get a game on; it was an agonising wait. Midday passed; sand and sawdust were strewn about the outfield. But a large patch to the left of the pavilion was still a swamp; where it was dry, it was bumpy and uneven. Megan stood by a slick patch of mud, and said the umpires were talking about a start at one-thirty. 'Well, the rules say they're in control – but this is dangerous. What if someone breaks a leg? I want to play and get six points – but you can't field on this.'

She got the two captains to look at a wide, greasy patch of bog reaching fifteen yards in from the boundary; there were pools of inch-deep mud in it. The umpires' view? 'We are here to conduct the game, not to stop it. It's a very difficult decision – but it's very hard to stop the game for one small area, when the rest of the ground is OK.'

Evidently, different standards applied here – as in, one man's lumpy bog is another man's 'small area'. Karen Smithies said, 'It's nowhere near fit to play. I want to play – but I don't want to play twenty overs, and I don't want to lose any players injured.'

Kim Price agreed – 'It is a little bit foolish' – but other factors were in play. Three games had been lost already, the Doordarshan TV cameras were here, and the organisers needed some cricket. Megan told the players, 'As soon as it's called you get out there with Joce for a warm-up. Let's get that professionalism going.'

South Africa won the toss, and put England in to bat. The Lengster put her left foot down a hole in the outfield in the warm-up, and twisted her ankle. We had an injury before we'd even started – and the first game of the 6th Women's Cricket World Cup was a twenty-over thrash on a mudbath.

Lottie got a single off the first over, another off the second, a four in the third – but the South African fielding was razor-sharp, they'd started with a spinner straight off, and after five overs all we had was 11. What use was that in a slogfest? Trying to step it up, in the sixth over JB was run out – start-stop-start, race back, too late and gone. Lottie tried to thrash the next ball through midwicket, but a flying stop held her to a single. 'Oh,' said an Indian voice behind me, 'what a lovely fielding.'

Alta Kotze was bowling quick and straight; BB went in, got 2, then came back again lbw. Sue Metcalfe faced up to spinner Kerri Laing, prodded forward and missed. The second ball she pulled four through square leg, then she tried to drive the third through the covers and got two from a streaky edge over slip. But in twenty overs, who cares how you get them? Among the applauding English Jane Cassar said quietly, 'Good placement, Sue.'

Every dot ball was a groan, a nervy shudder. There were four of them in the ninth; in the tenth Kim Price put herself on, bowling canny off spin round the wicket. Dot, dot – so the third ball Metcalfe tried to thump it, she didn't connect, and she fell to a fine catch taken low at mid-off. Cassar went in, three more dots, a wicket maiden – and halfway there, all England had was 32 for 3.

Then Edwards and Cassar got motoring. The next overs went for 6, 6, 7, 6, 6 – cuts, nudges, pulls, drives, the business. Cassar was one of the best players we had; her keeping was sharp, her batting direct, intelligent, unfussy. Between them they doubled the run rate, Lottie got to 38 – then Price drew her out with a ball that cut away sharp and had her stumped. Karen Smithies got a single, and that was all she got; Kathryn Leng went out to cries of 'Go for it'. Sue Metcalfe muttered quietly, 'Get to 80 first.'

It became, perforce, a crass and inelegant slog. The 18th went for 6, the 19th for 8, the 20th for 7; Leng was dropped and then stumped, and Jane Cassar was run out racing for an impossible third on the last ball. England had 94 for 7; it might have been more, but in the mud and long grass of the outfield the ball was stopping dead. Given the South African inclination to swing the bat, it looked eminently, unnervingly catchable.

It mattered what happened here – it mattered a lot. These two sides and Australia would surely all beat Denmark, Ireland,

and Pakistan, so how the group finished depended on what they did to each other. If England lost here, and then lost to Australia, they'd come third – and that, almost certainly, meant a quarter-final with India or New Zealand. That was an outcome we really didn't want; we really had to win here.

Sue Redfern opened the bowling; the tension showed straight off in a massive shout for lbw second ball, and two wild overthrows while people were still shouting. Smithies put herself on second over; a single, two dots, a four, a wide. Then the sixth ball she tricked Linda Olivier into swinging, the edge flew behind to Jane Cassar, and with her next ball she had Helen Davies stumped for a duck. South Africa were 10 for 2 – and they didn't look bothered about it one bit.

Where we'd made 22 off 7 overs, they made 42. They were so far ahead – but they were also 42 for 3, because Smithies got another of them. She conned her into lofting a slow one and BB took a fine catch at mid-off, running backwards and sideways to the dropping ball, making no mistake – and maybe here was our hope, that they were inexperienced, and they'd hole out slugging. But how many mistakes could they make, when they only needed 53 more runs and had 13 overs still to get them?

Smithies put the Lengster on – twenty-four years old, a counter clerk with the Yorkshire Bank at Meanwood in Leeds, a quietly spoken woman with a sharp wit, a little bit of a temperament, and a whole lot of talent. She bowled genuine leg spin, classy, bamboozling stuff, whipping it off the top of her wrist – and she stepped up now to stop the South African charge in its tracks. Her first over was a wicket maiden, the next two went for just a single apiece. At the other end, Melissa Reynard came on to bowl line and length seam, and she didn't give away anything either. You could feel the English fielding get tighter, noisier, pulling in the noose; South Africa'd taken 42 off 7 overs, and the next six all they got was 7 more. Shades of panic set in; Denise Reid ran herself out. They were 49 for

5 off 13 overs; the run rate they needed had bounced up to 6.5 an over.

The crowd was only a few hundred; unfortunately, all few hundred of them seemed to be standing round my chair. Padded seats for the nabobs were being carried out to the boundary; a milling throng of worthies and blazers were adding to the confusion. I pushed through to try and see what was happening, and Clare Connor was on; left-arm spin, not much turn but nice flight, and she was putting it on the spot. She reeled in another wicket, bowling their keeper through the gate while she lashed out swiping: 58 for 6, 5 overs remaining, 37 required at 7.4 an over.

Still England squeezed them – and the way Smithies did it was to put on Charlotte Edwards. 'I had a hunch,' she'd say later, 'and sometimes hunches pay off.' So Lottie stepped up with her leg spin. It looked dollydrop stuff, the second ball was a full toss, the South African bat thought she'd have that one – and she went and spooned it to Connie at square leg. Three balls later Aluis Kuylaars had an almighty heave – and found herself bowled behind her legs.

Kuylaars was mortified, she couldn't believe it. 'That ball was fizzing, man. I've gone forward, it was outside leg, I heard a noise behind me, I thought, she can't have stumped me. So I looked and she's *bowled* me. She's hit off stump. How'd she do that?'

Sixty-one for 8, 4 overs remaining, 34 required at 8.5 an over. The South Africans were down to their captain Kim Price, and their opening bowler Alta Kotze; they did the only thing they could do, and threw the bat at everything. The 17th over went for 9 off Connie, the 18th for 7 off Lottie, the 19th for 5 off Smithies, bringing herself back at the death to rein them in with a captain's effort – three dot balls. South Africa needed thirteen off the last over – and Skip threw Lottie the ball. 'Well,' she said placidly afterwards, 'I was a bit surprised.'

Dot, single, two, two – Kotze was facing, and for South Africa to win she had to get two fours. She swung the bat, missed, Cassar stumped her, and England had won. By the boundary Peter Moralee muttered sternly, 'Well bowled, Lottie Edwards, well bowled.'

For her 38 runs and three wickets, just seventeen years old, she was picked by Geetha Reddy as the Eve of the Match. When the announcement was made she was drinking from a Hi-Five bottle, entirely impassive, and Sue Metcalfe had to give her a nudge. 'That's you, Lotts.' She stepped up to make the happy discovery that she was 5,000 rupees better off.

'We lost in the middle of both innings,' said Hunte. 'We let them get away when they were batting – then we made a flying start, but no one stayed there. And Charlotte played very well.' I asked him if it wasn't a bit of a lottery, and he shrugged and smiled. 'That's the game.'

Megan said, 'Twenty overs can go any way; we held up well to a lot of pressure there, and it's a good test for them, because South Africa are a very good side. I know how they'll feel, too – but I won't say I feel for them, 'cause if it was the other way round, would they feel for us? This is the World Cup. If you've got to play, you've got to win. Still, they're a lovely bunch of people, and we've invited them back for a beer, 'cause that's what sport's all about.'

'That's what life's all about,' said Moralee. 'Work hard, play hard. In that order.'

Lottie went off to do Five Live; someone was on the phone from Radio Four wanting the captain. They thought the captain was Clare Taylor. Skip grinned, 'Bloody typical, eh?'

At the dressing room door BB asked, 'Want to see my lbw bruise?' She had to pull her shorts right up to show it; it was slap central way up the top of the thigh, big as your palm, bright red and yellow. '*And* I was jumping,' she said, springing off the ground, '*right* up here. Now how can that be out?'

I asked JB how she'd felt in the last overs, as the tension

ratcheted up. She smiled and said, 'I just stood and watched the nippers do the job.'

The gate outside was blocked by a pack of women pressing forward to see the players. When the bus came and we started loading up, they gathered close all round the door and along the kerbside under the windows, reaching out to touch arms and say, 'Bye bye, bye bye.' As I got on board a hand fell on my forearm, and I turned to be blinded by a radiant smile. She said to me, 'Nice travels.'

Our travels started now. Whether they'd be nice or not, we'd have to wait and see.

7

It Had to Happen

The alarm went off at three-thirty in the morning; we avoided an overnight train by getting up in the middle of the night instead. An hour later, we were picking our way through a carpet of bodies in the ticket hall of Hyderabad railway station. On the cold hard floor, some had blankets, some didn't. A sign over the door said, Cleanliness Is Godliness; a message of Canute-like optimism. At five o'clock a bloke came through with a stick, hit a few people, opened the ticket office, and a minor riot began. Welcome to another day in India.

More bodies lay strewn in dim light along the platform. One of the players spilt their packed breakfast, and a scrawny man swooped from the darkness to gather it up. By our carriage door, Shirley called out seat numbers: 'Miss Charlotte, Miss Beverley, Miss Kathryn – you're all listed.' An old guy with bone-thin legs and a withered woman in a ragged blanket held out their hands as we boarded; behind them, a young man with a bat stood dreamily practising his shots.

We set off on time at five-thirty. I read yesterday's match reports; at Gangotri Glades in Mysore, Denmark had beaten Pakistan by eight wickets before a crowd of 3,000. Pakistan got 31 for their first wicket; 15 of them were wides. They had seven ducks, including the last six wickets in a row; they were 65 all out in 30.4 overs, and Denmark took 29.3 overs to beat them. It sounded awful.

I put the paper down and stared about the carriage. Shirley slept under a blanket; a few players wrote aerogrammes, Laura MacLeod read Michael Crichton, and the Lengster Jeffrey Archer. A bloke came round with sweet coffee in plastic cups bearing the legend, 'Please Deform After Use'. The train trundled over the Deccan plateau past palm trees and paddy fields. We were going 160 miles, and it would take seven and a half hours. Behind me, someone asked wistfully what you'd eat if you were at home right now.

'Yorkshire pudding,' said Romper, 'mashed potato, sausages, lots of onion gravy. And a pint of Pedigree.'

Sue Metcalfe wanted a pork pie and mushy peas; Skip plumped for roast chicken, or an egg and bacon fry-up. Fresh fancied a jacket spud with cheese and baked beans; I'd have had a pizza, heavy on the anchovies. Fizz said she'd drink a bottle of good Chardonnay, and sighed. The day before, she'd had sixty quid nicked from her room. 'Ah well. Have another banana.'

The Lengster said she'd have chicken pieces in batter with chips, 'cause it was all her boyfriend could cook. She'd just recently moved in with him, they were engaged, and she was missing him. During the weeks before the tournament she'd talk to other players on the phone and it'd be all India, India, really looking forward to it, and she'd feel guilty about that; still, he understood. She said, 'We'd not have come this far if he didn't, would we?'

Like most of them, she started playing because her dad

played, her brother played, and her mum made the teas. From when she was nine, she played on the Pudsey St Lawrence boys' team – Sir Len Hutton's club – and that gave her a start, getting accepted when she was the only girl in the Bradford Junior League.

She said, 'You're always different, you always stand out. It's changed a lot now, but fifteen years ago it was a real novelty. It was quite hard, but I had my parents' support; they didn't push me, but I wanted to do it, so they backed me. But the boys, they'd always want to get you out. My first game against Undercliff, there were two boys that we knew 'cause their dads played with my dad, and I distinctly remember when I walked out to bat, they sort of giggled at me. They weren't too happy about it. I thought, you'll get your come-uppance. So I ended bowling one out, catching the other one; they went home with their tails between their legs that day.'

She moved up to the Under 15s; the boys got bigger and quicker, and she wasn't sure she could cope. But she was one of the first intake of girls at Woodhouse Grove, a long-established boys' school – 'You can imagine the surprise, a girl putting her name down for nets' – and she found she could hold her own. She got on the school's first team; now she played for a men's second team in the Bradford League. She said, 'If you're good enough, you'll play. It's up to me. If a six foot quick comes in and bashes your skull, well – it could happen to a bloke.'

She went to Yorkshire's coaching sessions from the age of fifteen, and got into women's cricket from there; now she played for Wakefield with Clare Taylor and Bev Nicholson, and last summer they beat North Riding in the final of the national knock-out cup. She said, 'I enjoy men's cricket, but I'm not going to get anywhere further in it than a second team. For the glory, you play the women's game – and the moment I'm not enjoying it, OK, I'll pack it in and have babies and be a housewife. But at the minute, all that takes a back seat to cricket, 'cause I've worked really hard to get to this. And then, my mum died eighteen months ago. So I like to think now, when I'm doing well, it's for her.'

Her debut for England came at the European Cup in Ireland in 1995; she'd played six Tests and, counting yesterday's thrash with South Africa, seventeen one-days. Her highest score was 144 in the Test against New Zealand at Scarborough; with Barbara Daniels knocking 160 at the other end, they ran up a record sixth-wicket partnership of 132. 'When I went in,' she said, 'all I had to do was support BB. She was in her stride, and she's a beautiful bat to watch when she's going. So I pushed it in the gaps, looked for the singles – then it got to the end of the day and I was eighty-odd. That night I was nervous, I didn't sleep, and in the morning it seemed to take an age to get the ton. But I remember passing the fifty more, 'cause I'd not had one of them, never mind a century. By the time I got the century, I was just thinking how far I could take it.'

I asked if she wasn't irked that they didn't get more attention, as a national side with a world title to their name. She said, 'It's a bit of a get-out, but I haven't really thought about it. It doesn't smack me in the face; it's something you're used to, playing in front of nobody. When you do get a crowd like we did at Taunton, people see you can play, and that's good – but do I get annoyed if people don't come?' She shrugged, and said she didn't. 'It's them that are missing out.'

The Yorkshire Bank had been good to her. She'd been there four years, and when she'd applied for the job she'd put the cricket down on her CV – Yorkshire, Junior England. Later, she found out the managers had looked at that and said, 'Right, we've got to have this lad.' Then they looked again, saw she was a woman – but it went in her favour. Now, when she was away with England they gave her paid leave, and she knew how lucky she was; very few of the others had employers like that.

She looked out of the train window; wherever we stopped, at

a station, or in the middle of nowhere in the green, boulder-specked countryside, people gathered to stare at these women in their powder-blue tracksuits. She said, 'It's an eye-opener, isn't it? To see a leper – you think it's something you'd only hear of in a Bible story – and if we hadn't been before, it'd be a bit scary. You need tunnel vision sometimes – but we've learnt to sit back and laugh about things. If we'd had that runaround before that practice game on the first trip, we'd have been climbing the walls, but not now. Or the toilet on this train – it's got that thing on the door that says "Western Style", and you go in and think, Ooh, this is quite nice. It's not, it's *awful*. But you're used to it, aren't you?'

Being on the fines committee was a laugh too; it was her, H, and Connie, and to date Selena the PR woman had the biggest fine rate. The Lengster grinned, sly: 'There's one born every minute.' People got fined 20 roops a time for impersonating a fish while asleep on a plane, for attempting to get mown down by a rickshaw, for making provocative gestures with a chocolate-covered banana at lunch at the Meridien, for false pretences of friendship – being all nice to the Indians at that dinner in Delhi, then walking off muttering, 'We're going to *thrash* you, you bastards' – and now she had a quick stroll down the carriage to keep things updated.

'Romper's duck impression on the bus was good, and I believe Beebs is doing her fish again. They should learn by their mistakes,' she grinned, 'but they don't, do they? So they can carry on getting fined.'

She expected to be fined herself, for falling over in the warm-up; the ankle hadn't bothered her much in the game, but she was annoyed about a misfield. 'There were potholes everywhere, and I couldn't pick it up; I hope the camera wasn't on me, 'cause I let out a few expletives there.'

As to the success of her bowling, she nodded thoughtfully and said, 'Hmm. Me and Melissa. We pinned them down, and that was the job. But the wicket did the work for me, it was a real ripper, and the batters made the mistakes. A lot of bats in ladies' cricket, if they see it turning a lot, they'll panic. There was some pretty agricultural batting going on anyway, 'cause that was what was called for – but believe it or not, I felt very calm. We'd been in that situation at Taunton, and this time I thought we'd do it.' But when I asked if she was pleased, she'd only say, 'Let's see if I can keep it up – that's the main thing.'

The ankle was bruised and swelling. She didn't know it, but it would keep her out for the next two games – and that, in turn, would have some bearing on what happened to her later.

We arrived in Vijayawada at one o'clock; we were met on the platform by four thoroughly pleasant men from the local cricket association, a small army of porters, a policeman with a megaphone, several photographers and journalists, and a bloke wandering about on his knees because he didn't have any feet.

Outside the station, the sun was burning hot. It was a mercifully short bus ride to the Ilapuram Hotel, where the driver did a 647-point turn before deciding he couldn't get in the gate. In the foyer, Shirley handed out room allocations; England milled around wondering what to do about lunch. Megan wanted them doing a work-out in the afternoon, but where? Joce and Fizz went to investigate the gym, declared it a meathead weightlifter's place, and wandered out into the forecourt parking lot. It seemed to be the only open space; it looked as if England would be doing their squats and press-ups between ranks of scooters and cabs.

The players went up to their rooms to eat on room service; Skip and the Lengster came straight back down again. Skip said, 'It's a bit dim and dismal,' and went to have a look at the restaurant instead. She came back from that pretty quick too, said it was that dark you'd not see the food in front of your face; half a dozen players then trooped forlornly to a shop ('Magazene Paper Food') and stared dolefully at some packets of biscuits.

Being a rodent of the press, I decamped to the Manorama a short drive across town; again, this meant I'd be staying with our opponents, as Pakistan were due to arrive (from Mysore via Hyderabad) at seven in the evening. The hotel looked fine – a tenner a night with air-con – but of course the toilet had no loo paper and (silly me) nor did I. OK then, when in India . . . by the loo there was a bucket, and a tap low down on the wall; I wiped myself clean in the local manner, using the bucket to wash my hand. Along the way, I decided the bucket didn't have enough water in it, so I turned on the tap; it jetted out with such force that the contents of the bucket, faecal particles and all, sprayed all around the bathroom. This is the kind of moment where you wonder what you're in for next.

I investigated the room's wiring system; it seemed to be impossible to turn off the ceiling fan without losing all the lights as well. The smiling but venal child who operated the lift turned some switches on and off to no good effect, then demanded money. Two porters later we'd worked it out, and I went to The King's Table in the basement. The menu announced 'A Tradition That Spells Class'. It was a little hard to read it – murky lighting was evidently the vogue in Vijayawada – but the egg biryani was absolutely top.

It came with a gravy that blew the roof of my mouth through the ceiling. Unfortunately, I can't tell you what this gravy was because when I asked the waiter, 'What's the gravy?', he looked at me like I was a complete nincompoop and said, 'It's a sauce.' That cleared that up then. If not strong on culinary explanation, however, the service was otherwise so remorselessly attentive that one of them even wanted to put my sugar in my coffee for me. Mysteriously, the bill said, 'Do Not Accept Any Manual Writing.' It came to a quid and a bit; I'd definitely be eating there again.

Vijayawada's an industrial town of no particular distinction on the banks of the Krishna River. This is a polite way of saying it's a toilet. I walked a mile or two from the centre of town to the Kanaka Durga Temple; this involved crossing a canal, past a dead rat in the middle of the pavement. The canal was a reechy, toxic green sump bridged here and there by rusted and leaking pipes. People lived on dirt banks along the water in tumbledown huts; they fished in it, and washed themselves and their clothes in it too.

Once through a fume-choked underpass, the main road along the canal was a stenchy mayhem of trucks, rickshaws, buses and bullock carts. The entire length of the canalside pavement was freely in use as a public urinal; streams of piss spread across the broken, calcified stone. It was monstrously minging. At one point, something caught in my throat; an insect, floating ash, I don't know what, but I coughed, and the next minute I was hacking and retching on the verge. There went the biryani, but no one seemed bothered. I guess if they can piss all over it, me puking on it can't make any difference.

Opposite the alleyway leading to the temple, something vast loomed against the skyline. It was the Prakasam Barrage – a massive dam across the Krishna, which lay banked up behind it into an enormous lake. The water was silver-blue, stretching away to a hazy horizon of powder-grey hills; a sharp-prowed boat puttered along the near shore in silhouette against the sun. In the lee of the dam, at the near end of it, water flowed into the canal; beyond that, it sluiced in shallow sheets across concrete slabs and gravel pans. Down by the banks, and out into the water on huge flat boulders and grassy patches of earth, hundreds of people were swimming, washing, doing their laundry; many of them must have been temple monks and acolytes, as they wore robes of brilliant red, and spreads of red cloth lay drying all about. It was typical India – you walk through emetic filth, only to stumble on a scene of mysterious and elevating beauty.

Back across the road, I found the long, winding stairway to the temple. It twisted up the hillside, a narrow, darkening tunnel through a jumble of houses; the steps were powdered the colour of turmeric and cayenne pepper, and the roof of the temple itself was like ornate pink icing on a wedding cake. From up here the town looked better, laid out in pastel shades round a pair of wooded hills. It was just walking through it that wasn't so great.

You get used to people pissing in the street; not infrequently, squatting down to have a dump in them too. Sometimes you wonder what they're thinking – but if they're thinking anything at all, I reckon what they're probably thinking is, I wish I had a toilet.

Late afternoon, England went to check out the stadium; they reported it beautifully prepared, with soap and talc in the dressing room, cases of water already delivered, and an attentive catering manager wanting to know what he should do for their lunch. There was big local interest – a dozen scribes and snappers, a TV crew – and a feeling that we might get a decent crowd.

The hotel, on the other hand, wasn't the greatest. Roaches were sighted in the restaurant; the corridors reeked of rancid fat, and every now and then the air-con belched little puffs of icky dust. There was a lot of noise in some of the rooms, too. They thought maybe it was the air-con fan; Joce and Fizz had to move, it was so bad in their room that the floor was vibrating. Fresh said it was loud enough to drown out the TV – then she shrugged. 'There's glass in the windows, and it's not flea-ridden. It could be a lot worse.' Later, different players would report people following them to their rooms, and people rattling at their bolted doors in the night.

Everyone was tired; Bev lay half asleep on a couch in the foyer. Megan geed her on, 'All right, Bev? You going to last the team meeting?' They would not, however, be as tired as Pakistan – whose 500-kilometre flight from Mysore to Hyderabad had been many hours delayed. They were now expected to land about six in the evening, with a six-hour bus journey yet to come. It was notable that none of the English gloated over that; one representative reaction was, 'Poor buggers. They'll be shot. Bless 'em.'

Thrasy Petropoulos and Cath Harris knew what Pakistan were about to go through on that road. There'd been no train tickets for them, so they arrived from Hyderabad by cab, a journey they described as seriously hair-raising – and they, at least, had done it in daylight.

Thrasy didn't like it any better that he had to go to a different hotel again, either. 'What she doesn't understand,' he said, 'is that she has no right whatsoever to tell people what hotel they stay in. It's purely goodwill that I'm acceding to it, because we've got weeks ahead of us here – but it's the easiest way in the world to make an enemy, and it's just not the way you want it to be. Of course I want England to win the World Cup – but if it's like this, and then you see the South Africans, there's a part of you that wishes you could follow them around instead.'

It didn't help that we couldn't call London from the Manorama – not good, when we both had match reports to file the next day, and Thrasy had to get a preview over right now. We had to use one of the little STD booths in the street, which meant shouting over the noise of the traffic, trying to get them to call you back; it could take an age to get through. We whiled away the time between broken connections over tandoori chicken and some more of that egg biryani at The King's Table; at least the food was good, right?

Pakistan arrived at two in the morning; at five o'clock, a mosque gave the first call to prayer. I stirred, and realised instantly that if I didn't make it to the toilet in short order, my bed was very suddenly going to become a most unpleasant place. I made it with nanoseconds to spare, voided a bucketload of brown water, took an anti-diarrhoea tab, and went back to bed thinking no more about it. It had to happen, didn't it?

By the time the alarm went off at six-thirty I'd had to sprint for the bathroom three more times, and I was thinking about it a lot; I was feeling weaker with each liquid and groaning evacuation. In theory, I was leaving with Thrasy at seven-fifteen; when I now attempted to dress myself, however, I found I was too physically enfeebled to do it. Each effort to stand, never mind to get dressed, produced feverish outbreaks of sweat-sodden trembling. Trying to maintain some sense of order to the day, I fumbled by my bedside for my malaria tabs, and another anti-trot capsule. I downed these with some mineral water, and the stomach cramps started kicking in.

Within minutes, the water was coming back up again. Once more I tried to make it to the bathroom, but this time I couldn't do it; I was on my knees crawling towards it when I projectile-vomited an arc of chalky fluid across the room, a milky spout of dissolved Paludrine several yards long. It was like something out of a horror film; when Thrasy knocked on the door, in the circumstances, I had to tell him I didn't think I'd be making the game.

The next few hours were the sickest I've ever been anywhere in my life. I lost track of the number of times I shat, puked, or both. The cramps came every few minutes, and were so painful that they curled me up double on the bed, moaning involuntarily. At one point, I started wondering if the bug had got into my central nervous system, because I lost all motor control of my right arm; with each cramp, my right hand was fluttering across my torso like a butterfly, not like any part of me at all.

I kept telling myself that in another hour I'd be better. I kept telling myself, it'll be funny when you write it in the book – and I kept telling myself, never mind the bleedin' book, you've got to get up and go and do a match report. You cling to stuff like this – it's stupid, but what else is there to cling to?

By midday, the cramps had receded to every twenty minutes or so, and (trying to take a stoic, Zen-type view of matters here)

I figured my guts must have been so comprehensively dredged that whatever bug I'd ingested would be long, long gone. So I started getting up. My limbs had a fevered jelliness about them; shaving was a slow, nerve-racking business. It took a while to get dressed, taking it one item at a time with a collapsed and panting pause in between; then I wavered my way downstairs, and into the arms of India.

I tried to check out, but they wouldn't take a credit card. I stared. The guy picked up the phone and started writing down unfathomably long numbers, saying he had to get international banking confirmation that my plastic was good. I thought, how can you do that if I can't call home? I paid cash, then waited for the receipt, and waited, and waited. Then I asked for a bottle of mineral water, and waited a while for that too. How long can it take to do these things? In India, for ever – which doesn't incline you to happiness when a) if Pakistan had batted first, the match might already be over, and b) you feel like passing out.

The rickshaw ride brought the cramps back with a vengeance. At the stadium, I waddled with clenched buttocks to the England encampment, and silently decided to levy a fine on the lot of them (bar Metcalfe and BB, who were batting) for laughing at me. Ah well – we like to entertain, don't we?

The Indira Gandhi Memorial Stadium was a basic but pleasant oval, partially two-tiered, cream and ochre in colour, and there were some 4,000 people in it whom England entertained in the most positive fashion. The previous World Cup record total was 297 for 5, scored in 57 overs by New Zealand against Holland at Sydney in 1988. In 50 overs, England smashed it; they finished 376 for 2, with every stroke cheered to the echo.

The previous second-wicket partnership record had been 167, set by Australia's Emerson and Kennare against India in Auckland in 1982. Jan Brittin and Barbara Daniels smashed that too, putting on 203 before Brittin was stumped. She'd scored 138, her fourth World Cup century, and equal to her previous best; it came off 150 balls, included 17 fours, and was described by those watching as a model of patience and classic strokeplay. It was typical of Brittin – a modest, charming, quietly spoken woman – that she herself wasn't entirely satisfied with it, feeling that it had been more grafting than fluid, and that she could actually bat better than that.

As for Daniels' 142 not out – a score one run short of the World Cup record set by Australia's Lindsay Reeler against Holland in 1988 – the other players variously described it as dashing, ruthless, cavalier. It took her only 103 balls, she hit 17 fours and one six – and of Pakistan's unfortunate bowlers, the best of them went for 64 off 10 overs.

In truth, however, England really ought to have clobbered these people. I'm not belittling our batting – if you get bad balls, you've still got to put them away – but Pakistan were woefully inexperienced. I don't wish to criticise them, because the fact that they'd put a team together at all was a brave and worthy achievement – but eight of their squad were teenagers, and they'd only played their first international ten months earlier. They'd gone to New Zealand – who scored 455 against them, then bowled them out for 47.

Pakistan were the creation of Shaiza Said Khan and her sister Sharmeen, twenty-eight and twenty-four years old respectively, whose father had a carpet business in Karachi and Lahore which sponsored the team. The sisters studied textile management and engineering at Leeds University, and played cricket there; they'd been at Lord's watching England win in 1993, and had been inspired to build a team from their own country that could take part next time round. They got IWCC membership in September 1996, and went to New Zealand the next January; Shaiza Khan said, 'Our motive wasn't to beat them; we knew we didn't have the ability for that. Our motive was to get experience, and to qualify for this.'

She was a stout and impressive young woman; when I asked how hard it had been to get this team started she said, 'Oh my God, it was *very* difficult. We were used to England, where right is right. In Pakistan, we had to ignore all the barriers that came our way – we had to have tunnel vision.'

They invited an Australian coach, Jodie Davis, to come and train them; Davis was sponsored in that post by the Australian Sports Commission and Women's Cricket Australia, and she made a big difference. Khan said, 'In Pakistan, people think women can't play at all. They ask, do we play with a tennis ball? But when they saw Jodie come, they saw we were serious – and now we've got 3,000 girls wanting to play, from all over the country.'

The army gave them a ground in Lahore to practise on, a few weeks before the tournament; otherwise, they had next to no help from anyone. The head of the men's cricket authority, said Khan, told her point blank that he wouldn't promote women's cricket, or any other women's sport. To complicate matters further, another outfit sprang up claiming that they were the real Pakistan women's cricket team, not Khan's lot – prompting a chaotic flurry of faxes, and leaving Prasoon Tripathi at the Mela Plaza wondering just how many teams from Pakistan were planning to turn up.

In the end, Khan's team made it. She said, 'It's about going out, doing our best, and learning. Coming from an Islamic state, we've won a battle just by being here – and my main aim is to let people know that if you want to do it, against all odds, you *can* do it.'

In light of which, it's very hard to begrudge them their place in India; Jan Brittin spoke for many of the English players when she said Pakistan had a right to be there, because they deserved to be encouraged, and to have a go so they could learn. That afternoon in Vijayawada, they duly proved they had that right.

Denmark had bowled them out for 65; on the train the

Lengster'd said, 'We've got to go for the kill, and show by our result that we mean business.' Now she wasn't playing; nor was Charlotte Edwards, who was resting a dodgy knee. Fresh was rested too, so Laura MacLeod and Bev Nicholson had a bowl – and neither they nor the rest of England's attack did themselves any favours. Clare Connor had the best figures – 14 runs off 10 overs, two maidens, one wicket – but overall England looked indolent and toothless. In 47 overs (Pakistan were docked three overs for bowling their own fifty too slowly) the debutantes finished with 146 for 3.

From an English point of view, it was tedious and embarrassing. From Shaiza Khan's point of view, it was a triumph – she bashed three sixes on the way to her 41, her sister got 35 not out, and they held their heads up against the world champions with more than a little pride. Given the background to this Pakistan team, when England won by a crushing 230 runs, yet came off the field looking hot in the face and pretty thoroughly disgruntled, who would you say had the better day?

Karen Smithies later held her hands up and said she was guilty of thinking, What the hell. She accepted that, with 376 on the board, they'd pretty much gone through the motions. But it didn't look good.

Outside the dressing room Megan Lear said, 'Six points is six points, but we didn't get them in the style I'd have liked. The batting this morning was brilliant – but we should have crushed them.'

We didn't – and to put this in perspective, two days later Australia played Pakistan in Hyderabad. In the shortest game of World Cup cricket ever, Pakistan batted first, and Australia bowled them all out for 27. They didn't even use their first-string bowlers to do it, either.

England avoided an overnight train back to Hyderabad by leaving immediately after the game on a bus instead. It wasn't a universally popular decision, and Barbara Daniels absolutely hated it. Romper said it was like being in a video arcade game – lots of hostile incoming – and you just had to shut your eyes and pray nothing hit you.

The rodents of the press passed on that experience; we had stories to file, and the Vijayawada people had put together an efficient little press centre at the ground from which we could do it. Given the hoops we'd have to jump through at supposedly superior grounds later, all credit to them; it's such a joy, in India, when things work. I was not, however, in much of a state to feel joy; I wrote something that may or may not have been coherent, then collapsed in a plastic chair outside the office and let the mozzies go to it.

One of the kind gents from the local cricket association appeared, and asked me if I'd had a good time in Vijayawada. The strange thing is, when I mustered the manners to tell him that I had done, I wasn't fibbing. But then, I hadn't been to the railway station yet.

8

Hot and Bothered

Going back on the train suited me fine. I'd sleep, it wouldn't be scary, it wouldn't rock my guts about like the bus would, and it'd have a toilet. Then Mr Pillay appeared, and said the English train tickets had been cancelled. I thought, if I don't get a sleeper berth, I might very well die. The cramps were back; I felt sweat-slicked, filthy, and tremulous. Mr Pillay said we had to hurry up, the train left at nine – so we hurried up as far as the hotel, then he revealed that Pakistan were on the train as well, and he had to hurry up and get them too. Then he sat down and didn't hurry up anywhere. It was seven o'clock. I managed to get him to go and find Pakistan, and said we'd meet him at the station.

At nine-thirty on the concourse, there was still no sign of him – and Vijayawada railway station of an evening isn't a place you want to spend two minutes, never mind two hours. Not unless you like looking at large numbers of poor people sleeping on a grubby floor and being bullied by blokes with sticks, anyway. We still didn't have train tickets, either.

I'd got as far as the counter that said you could buy tickets to Hyderabad at it – and, of course, you couldn't. You had to go somewhere else. I could barely walk, never mind find somewhere else. Mercifully, two Indian journalists showed up who'd been at the game, and went off with Thrasy to engage in the Byzantine process of ticket acquisition. You had to buy one bit here, another bit on Platform Six – but, hey, there were no sleeper berths left. Hadn't our train gone by now anyway?

I'd been trying to stay upright, leaning against a grimy pillar. Now I began sliding. I thought I could very easily just lay down my carcass amid the others on the dirty old floor. I could eat rice off a banana leaf (well, not right now, but generally speaking) and I could piss in the street, I could dress in rags and have limbs like twigs, blokes could come and hit me with sticks, and I really wouldn't care. Among the barefoot, the halt and the lame, this was definitely a low point.

There was still no sign of Mr Pillay; Thrasy had been gone forty minutes. My head was throbbing with the phenomenal, perpetual din of the place – bawling porters, impenetrable announcements, a heaving, honking mess of cabs and rickshaws outside. The only thing that lightened my heart was the little car that played a tune when it reversed. It played 'Twinkle Twinkle Little Star'. I was still considering this surreal innovation in automotive technology when Thrasy reappeared, bearing a tatty scrap of paper with some indecipherable scrawls on it. 'We have berths,' he said, 'on the eleven o'clock sleeper, and apparently it's on time.' He smiled. 'Whatever that means.'

It meant, happily, that we got back to Hyderabad at six the next morning, and I slept like a dead man every minute of the way. England, meanwhile, were jolting down the road in a bus – and BB was finding sleep rather harder to come by. After scoring 142 on a broiling hot day, she was absolutely drained, and going back on the bus really irked her.

The players had been involved in this decision. She hadn't

liked that in the first place; it was management's job to decide what they did, not theirs. In the second place, she certainly hadn't needed it being argued back and forth in the players' area while she was waiting to bat. She didn't think it was the right decision anyway; she'd rather have had a shower at the hotel, then slept on the train. She said, 'It's just rushing all the time, isn't it?'

Romper said, 'I thought she was going to go. Her seat wouldn't recline, 'cause the bags were wedged up behind her. Joce saw that, she tried to recline it for her, so she's settled in, she's got her space – then this Indian lady sat down next to her. Beebs breathed deep, she settled in again – then some mad video came on with loads of shooting, the lights were flashing on and off, and I saw her clutch the armrests and take a deep, *deep* breath. I'd say,' she smiled sympathetically, 'that was very close.'

'Nightmare,' said BB. 'Hooting and horning all the way, six hours of that noise, having to pee on the side of the road – horrible. And a packed meal of cold noodles and chips – just surreal. It was like being in the middle of someone else's bad dream. OK, train or bus, neither way was ideal, and maybe I'm just being a wimp – but I didn't enjoy it. I was irritated with it from the start, basically. But then,' she grinned, 'I'm a cranky old sod.'

England got back to the Oberoi at one in the morning. About eight in the morning, Denmark flew in from Madras; Ireland had thumped them by nine wickets there, and now they had to play us. In Bangalore, meanwhile, Australia walloped South Africa by ten wickets; the South Africans got 163, which at least was a half-decent total, but the Australian openers sauntered past it inside 29 overs. Their captain Belinda Clark, thought to be at least as good a bat as New Zealand's Debbie Hockley, hit 93; it sounded ominous.

I went to the Oberoi about midday, and found England waiting for a bus to take them to practice. *Plus ça change.* Joce gave me some Chinese herbal potions; a mix, apparently, of giant hissop, magnolia bark, perilla leaf, poria, dahurian, fresh ginger, red date, beetlenut and tangerine peel, angelica and balloon flower root. It tasted pretty grim, but Connie assured me it worked; I'd have eaten coal if they'd told me it worked.

Players started heading for the Gymkhana ground in rickshaws. Megan said, 'We only wait so long for a bus these days.' By the time it finally came, there were only eight of us left to go on it; we left the hotel, and were immediately pulled over by the police. Megan said, 'They can't do the practice without us' – but she took this further delay calmly. 'Oh well,' she smiled, 'let's see if they've got any initiative.'

Skip and Sue Metcalfe, meanwhile, were deep in discussion of what went wrong in the field against Pakistan. It couldn't happen again, could it?

A fax from a player back home was passed round the Gymkhana pavilion: 'Ceefax and I have become firm friends & we've decided to spend Xmas together. The words Bish!! Bosh!! Bash!! were mentioned. I have personally declared a national holiday . . . it was v.g. I am h.p. Been out for a curry every night to empathise. Keep going!'

Joce took a warm-up; Fizz worked on the Lengster's ankle. When she went to join the squad Megan asked how it was, and Fizz told her it looked horrible, black and blue all along the outside of the foot, up the ankle and onto the calf – but she didn't think it was too bad. The trouble was, she said, 'It's hard to tell with someone who's desperate to play how one hundred per cent she really is. Still, it's a significant tear, with that degree of bruising. I suspect it'd be prudent to rest her again.'

Megan said, 'She wants it to be better, that's for sure – but I think we err on the side of caution. I'm not saying it's only Denmark – but we don't want to make it worse.'

The players came back from the warm-up, and Liss asked Fizz for bug cream; she'd been bitten by an ant. Fizz asked how big it was, and Liss spread her arms wide. 'I think it were bigger than me, actually. I were very brave.'

Joce went jogging round the boundary; this was to stop herself exploding with tension. It had been sweltering during the game in Vijayawada, it was hot again now, she'd sent the bus off forty-five minutes ago to get water for the players, and there wasn't any sign of it. She did a couple of circuits, then started doing sit-ups; I reminded her of Steve Waugh's three rules about patience and she muttered, 'I've been through them already. I marvel, I tell you, sometimes I really marvel.'

Connie pulled out of the fielding practice to get some ice on a naggy shoulder. When I said her bowling figures had been good she nodded, said she was pleased, and that she just hoped it was enough to get her into the next game, 'Because that's all you think about, really.' She paused and said, 'It must be so difficult, selecting.'

She was reading political cartoonist Nicholas Garland's Indian journal, and enjoying it; she was enjoying being well again too, after her night throwing up a week ago. It was reassuring to be reminded that you did get better.

That evening, while people relaxed watching the men's cricket from Sharjah on Murdoch's Star Sports, Megan got a call to her room from *The Times* in London. There was a bit of chit-chat, then – Are you tired from your bus ride? Is Clare Connor still sick? How are the injuries to Edwards and Leng?

In the foyer at seven-fifteen the next morning she asked me, 'How did he get hold of that?' I shrugged; at *The Times* they'd got Thrasy's stuff, they'd be reading mine in the *Independent*, Cath Harris in the *Guardian*, and whatever else the agencies were sending home on the wires. Megan fretted whether there was some way she could get calls to her room screened, whether that guy was really from *The Times* like he'd said, and how she didn't want anyone knowing any of this stuff anyway.

She got up and paced about on the shining marble floors.

One of the players watched her, then muttered quietly, 'Talk about paranoia.'

I think, to be fair, that what probably bothered her most – apart from being disturbed without warning in her room, which I don't approve of myself – was the looming threat of Australia at the end of the group. On the record, she talked the one-game-at-a-time line; we'd deal with Denmark and Ireland first, and we'd think about the Australians when we got to them. But all the same, she and Moralee were hoping to skip off from the Denmark game to watch Australia bat against Pakistan at the Lal Bahadur – because if they could beat South Africa by ten wickets, then just how good were they?

The bus pulled up at the Gymkhana; the packed meals were last off. 'Now,' said Fizz, 'I really think I ought to eat one of these hot doughnuts. To test them. In the line of duty. In fact, I should probably eat two. In case they come from different batches, yes?'

She was a sparky twenty-nine year old, with freckles and long dark hair. She'd recently been working at Glamorgan; she'd been part-time but she'd always done mornings, so anyone who needed attention could get sorted early doors. That way, she was always finished by lunch, a timetable she'd settled on because Glamorgan did topping lunches. So they'd nicknamed her Scoffanoff.

She tested the doughnuts; England went to warm up and behind us in the pavilion, the phone rang. A bloke came out and waved at me; now who'd be calling me at eight-fifteen in the morning? I picked up the receiver and heard a faint, troubled voice through a storm of crackle and hiss. It sounded like he was calling from Mars but it was, in fact, the Danish coach calling from the Oberoi. 'Hello? Hello? This is the Danish team calling? We have been waiting for a bus for half an hour?' I told him that was nothing new, and he should get some cabs together – so Denmark arrived for this game of World Cup cricket by taxi.

Fizz, meanwhile, was treating more tender shoulders. Besides Connie she had Skip, Metcalfe, Lottie and Bev Nicholson all feeling achy; she reckoned JB was too, but that she wasn't owning up to it. Women, she explained, didn't have the same strength of musculature round their shoulder joints as men did – and they were amateurs, they had jobs to go to. Maybe if they could train every day, it'd not be a problem, but they couldn't – so when you got to the full-on intensity of a World Cup, playing and training every day, little things like this did start to flare up.

Still, England were mightily better prepared than Denmark. Their coach was Allan From Hansen, thirty-three years old, a local government tax officer in Copenhagen, and a thoroughly congenial man. 'My players,' he told me, 'play five games in nine days here. Normally in Denmark, they might play five games in a year.'

There were only about a hundred women playing cricket in Denmark. They had no backing or sponsorship; the Danish Cricket Association (which ran the game for men and women alike) had paid for their plane fares, the Indians were hosting them, and everything else came out of their own pockets. He said the Indians promised them playing kit, but it never turned up; they'd had to go out and buy it themselves, so now they were playing in short-sleeved yellow polo shirts and red tracksuit bottoms.

He said, 'We just hope to learn, and to enjoy ourselves. No matter how strong or weak you are, you have to turn up – because it's an experience to come here, isn't it? It's a bit chaotic – our last two flights, we had to get up at two in the morning – but I think you learn a lot, don't you? I think I'll be a lot more patient man when I get home. When anybody complains about paying taxes, I'll remember all you see here, and I'll be happy I pay taxes.'

Then he smiled and asked me, 'How come Pakistan got 146 against you anyway?'

*

Denmark won the toss (the third time Skip had lost it in three games, prompting a voice in the pavilion to observe, 'You're the worst tosser I know') and they put England in to bat. That was fine by England – more practice, basically. H was opening with Lottie; against Pakistan, she'd got 36 off 45 balls before they stumped her, and now Megan wanted her having another knock. Lottie playing, meanwhile, meant BB could rest after her 142.

Lottie pulled the first two balls for four through square leg, and another massacre began; BB went to sit quietly by the boundary and watch on her own. She wasn't in a huff; she was just something of a loner by nature. She said, 'I'm quite happy not to be throwing myself about today – I'm not one of those who thinks, Oh God, I've got to play every game. I was knackered after Vijayawada; the travelling takes it out of you, and,' she smiled, 'I'm not the youngest in the team.'

She'd turn thirty-three in three days' time. She stood five foot four ('on a good day') and she'd grown up in Atherstone, near Nuneaton in Warwickshire. Her mother was a nurse; her father, now retired, had been a primary school headmaster. He played cricket, her three older brothers played, she grew up watching the game, reading about it, talking about it – but she didn't play competitive cricket herself until she was sixteen, because for women, she didn't know it existed. Then her father rang Edgbaston one day to get a Test score, and by chance the woman who answered the phone was an England player; she told him Edgbaston had a women's club, and his daughter could go and play there.

She played her county cricket for the West Midlands; she read English at Lancaster, and became a teacher in that subject. In 1991, she moved south to take a job near Tunbridge Wells; in 1993, she made her debut for England in the World Cup. Twenty-eight was pretty late for a debut, especially when she'd played for both Junior England and Young England – but, she said, 'I think I genuinely wasn't ready for it before. I'd never been a particularly confident player, and I found the senior squad intimidating. There were a lot of strong-minded people, and I didn't feel I fitted in. I felt vulnerable, I wasn't sure I could do it – so I concentrated on my teaching. Then the World Cup came round, and I thought I'd give it one last go.'

She got picked, she was at backward square when JB took the winning catch, and she remembered everything feeling really, really quiet for a moment. 'Then suddenly all these people were on the pitch, all your family and friends – and you couldn't ask for a better time to make your debut, could you?'

She gave up her job, and worked as a supply teacher so she could go on playing for England. When she got back from the first tour to India, the post of Executive Director at the WCA came up, so she went for it – and when I met her in their office at Edgbaston the week before England left for India, she was clearly just a little stressed out. Commuting from London, she was dealing with the lottery disbursement, the Vodafone sponsorship, and trying to push forward plans for their merger with the England Cricket Board.

It wasn't a foregone conclusion that this merger would happen. Like any amateur sport, women's cricket relied on the work of many volunteers; these people served on a plethora of committees, and naturally wanted their democratic say. Some of them were the kind of traditionalists who still thought women should play in skirts, while others were nervous about losing their identity (and their committees) inside the bowels of the ECB. Daniels wasn't sure, when it came to the vote in the New Year, that they'd accept a merger – and she felt pretty strongly about it. She said, 'The time is right, the people are right, and it has to happen. I don't see any other way forward. If it's a no vote, I resign.'

On top of that, she had to get England ready for India – not easy, when the itinerary changed by the day – and she had also to prepare herself as a player. 'In theory,' she said, 'I give up being Executive Director when I get on the plane. When we get to India, Shirley's there, the Indians run it, and it won't be anything to do with me. I'll just be a squad member.' A week before they got there, however, she said that between playing, the job, and her private life, 'When I get back, something's got to give.' With regret, I took this to mean that after India, she'd give up playing – something England would sorely miss.

While the older player contemplated retirement, a new young one shone brighter every time she went to the wicket; feasting on the wayward bowling of the Danes, Charlotte Edwards hit 11 off the first over, 8 off the second, 7 off the fourth. H said afterwards, 'She was awesome, she was seeing it so well – I just gave her the strike.' When England's 50 came up in the ninth over, Lottie had scored 45 of it.

Thrasy said, 'You can tell, she's just a class above everyone else. That shot she's clipped in front of square where there wasn't a fielder, she's just eased it into the gap for 2 there, and she knew exactly what she was doing. She didn't need to belt the cover off it, and she didn't try to.'

She was caught in the gully in the thirteenth over; she'd scored 72 off 54 balls, including 13 fours. JB went in, and she and H kept it nudging along, two assured team seniors quietly pushing the singles after the fireworks from the tyro. After 25 overs England were 141 for 1, and people were beginning to say it'd be good to top 300 again.

On the boundary, meanwhile, BB mulled over the news of Australia's result against South Africa. She said, 'We've not played them since '93 – but we stuffed them out of sight then, and we should remember that. We shouldn't build up a fear thing about them. Ooh, they beat South Africa – so what? We should look at us, and how well we've done – we've gone up a gear every game. But we're too good at saying things like, Oh, we didn't beat Pakistan as well as we should have done – well, c'mon. We bloody stuffed them. And this batting here now – we're building up to the point where the big performances are definitely going to come out. The self-deprecatory stuff – Australia won't be doing it, will they? And I'll be very happy to beat them, 'cause I hate them.'

I raised an eyebrow. From a markedly intelligent woman, it seemed an extreme remark. She said, 'Well, hate's a strong word. But they are Australia.'

JB was bowled in the thirty-first over; she'd got 51 off 55 balls. Sue Metcalfe went in, got 4, and then got stumped chasing a horrid ball that bounced twice before it reached her. England were 178 for 3, with sixteen overs still to go, and after playing the anchor for Lottie and JB, H was steadily stepping up her strike rate. The players watching, however, were somewhat distracted; there were rats in the dressing room and the toilets. When Connie went to the loo she made the Lengster go with her, and stand guard with a bat.

The Lengster said she wasn't too bothered. 'They don't go for you, do they?'

So, I said, some of these others were southern softies then?

She grinned. 'I think so. Metcalfe, she'd pick it up by the tail, swing it round, then *cccrrrrkkk*. Snap his little neck.'

Out on the field, H took a tired swing and edged a catch to the keeper. It was the forty-fourth over, she'd made 87 off 113 balls, and stayed solid as the heat grew steadily more muggy. England were 243 for 4 with six overs to go, and Hansen professed himself relatively happy: 'I'd been scared of another record score.'

Peter Moralee was happy too. 'Of course we're pleased,' he said, 'we're in the quarter-finals. I know they'd have wanted 300, but cricket's like that, it doesn't always go your way. And it's easy to be critical from the sidelines – but there are little things we need to look at. Lottie was brilliant, but when she's running to the bowler's end she doesn't slide her bat. Now the Australians will be so smart fielding, they'll pick up and throw in one go, and they'll spot that. Another thing – Helen's done an outstanding job, but she's got to get the confidence to start hitting over the top after twenty overs. She's technically immaculate, she's a great sportswoman – but she can go quicker.'

It was typical of Moralee to note these things; in the sixties he'd played for Kent (and been a semi-pro footballer too) and he brought an extra touch of professionalism to England's work, quiet words behind Lear's leadership that sharpened everyone's attention. He had a nice, dry sense of humour too. When he heard about the Australians getting rid of Pakistan for 27 he smiled grimly and said, 'Not much point going to watch them bat then, is there? Only question's whether they do it in three or four overs, isn't it?'

Megan said sternly, 'Might get some visitors this afternoon ourselves, I'd imagine.'

Skip and Smigs were batting; the forty-ninth over began, Smithies clattered the first ball for four, then the scorer started shouting and waving. He was a dapper, dark-skinned little gent called Sam Swaminathan, and he knew his business inside out. It was a blessing when you got a good scorer; the scorer's desks were usually a turmoil of hopelessly differing tallies buried in a pestersome scrum of kids wanting autographs. But now Swaminathan was onto the umpire, because the Danish bowler had had her ten overs already. That umpire wanted his wrist slapping – and he was an ICC panel boy too. Anyway, someone else came on to bowl, so Smithies shrugged and gave her a clout instead.

To be fair to Denmark, they'd stuck at it; several of their players were sick, their keeper had fainted and had to be replaced, and at one point in the last over, the bowler had to stop during her run-up to heave on the pitch. England went into that over on 289 – so the only question was whether they could pass 300 again.

The first ball was a wide; Smithies crashed the second back over the bowler's head for four. She rolled a single off her wrists to square leg; Cassar drove another one back past the bowler. There was a dot ball, Skip lofted two to deep square leg – then the poorly Dane gave us two more wides, and that was 300. With a single driven to cover off the final ball, England finished on 301 for 4, beating the previous World Cup record for the second match running. Cassar had battered 43 off 45 balls, Smithies 29 off 19, and – even if Denmark were pretty weak – it was plain as day that these people could bat.

It was what they did in the field that we had to worry about.

The Danes slumped into their chairs looking deeply weary, and watched England's fielding work-out. The routine was sharp stuff, well drilled and busy. I wondered what the Danish thought; here we were with our logo-decked one-day pyjama suits, names on the backs of the shirts, baseball mitts, coloured pads, enough balls to play a whole tournament on our own – we had backing they could only dream of. So why couldn't we bowl them out?

The afternoon ended up dreary and dispiriting. A spot of bad temper kicked in from the start, when drizzle during lunch had the groundsmen hauling a tarpaulin over the wicket, and then Denmark asked for the roller. Megan wasn't happy, England were ready to go out, she got into a taut discussion with the umpire, then came back muttering, 'He just wants to finish his cigarette.'

After nine overs, Denmark were 15 for 3; Romper was beating the bat again and again, and to begin with it looked pretty good. It needed to, because Australia had turned up; their coach and captain walked round the boundary, doing their homework. Megan met them on a perambulation of her own, and came back fizzing with mistrust; they'd told her their travel had all been fine, the hotels were lovely, the food was great. Now she muttered, 'Doing a number, aren't they? But they're like that. They're hard as nails, and they're bloody good. Every one of them that's here will have been told what to watch, too.'

Out in the field, England were bowling dot ball after dot ball. Romper finished her ten overs with four maidens, twelve runs and two wickets. The Australians left; the Danes stuck in, prodding. I went to the loo, dodging a pair of rats. In a rancid ditch behind the pavilion, half a dozen water buffalo went wandering by. The game drifted along too, going steadily nowhere; it was getting to where the drinks break was an event. Lottie got an lbw, fourteen overs crawled past, then she got someone caught behind. The Danes were 57 for 5 off 35 overs; they were barely playing a shot. By the end, we'd bowled 18 maidens.

I asked Megan if she wasn't fed up that we weren't killing them off and going home for tea, and she said she wasn't. 'We're doing the right thing. It's not a killing-off game. Bowl tight, get the field placing right, put pressure on them – all right, they're not trying to do anything, and that makes it difficult – but if we keep it tight, we win the game. What would be silly would be to start chasing wickets, give away a few fours, then you're not in control any more.'

Well, yes, but . . .

'One-day cricket's not about bowling a side out. Wickets don't matter. It's about the team with the highest score. The fielding and bowling's a lot better than it was against Pakistan, and that's what we wanted.'

The conversation was interrupted by Danish people singing in the toilets, presumably to scare off the rats. The game crept into the final overs, two more wickets fell, the ninth Danish bat went out, and Hansen came over to say he didn't have any more players to bat 'cause everyone else was ill. Skip put Bev Nicholson on, and – no doubt nervous, unsettled, trying too hard – the unfortunate youngster got hit for ten runs off the final over. By Denmark, for goodness' sake – who finished 107 for 7.

Again, England had won by a crushing margin – by 194 runs – and again we left the field looking hot and bothered. Nicholson went to Moralee for advice, and so did Melissa Reynard; Sue Metcalfe left the ground saying bluntly that it had been a long, tiresome afternoon. The batting, obviously, had been potent and classy – but against Denmark, so it should be. As for the bowling – well, strictly speaking, Megan was right. One-day cricket was about tying people down, not letting them score runs – but one of the ways you do that is you get them out. And if you can't get Denmark out, what are you going to do against someone who can bat?

The other top sides were crushing minnows as a matter of routine. Apart from Australia destroying Pakistan, India dismissed the West Indies for 83 in Faridabad, and New Zealand saw off Sri Lanka for 71 in Chandigarh. England, by contrast, seemed to have no edge of ruthlessness about them. It may not be a desirable quality in daily life – but in sport, it's the essence.

I got a rickshaw back to the Kakatiya Towers with Thrasy, and we weren't happy bunnies. It was unprofessional to say it, but we couldn't see England keeping their title. They hadn't shown the hunger and desire in the field that winning would require; it seemed more than likely that we'd lose to Australia in Nagpur, come second in the group, get to a semi-final against New Zealand, and lose that too.

The Australian coach was called John Harmer. Despite Megan's initial, almost ritual suspicion, he was an entirely friendly and forthcoming man (something she herself readily acknowledged, when she'd spent more time talking with him) and that evening in the bar of the Kakatiya, he readily gave me his time.

He was fifty-five, and he lived on the Snowy River two hundred miles east of Melbourne; he'd been a university lecturer in bio-mechanics, and he now worked as a consultant in that field. He'd been running the Australian women's side since they returned from their poor showing in England in '93 – and he'd plainly been targeting this World Cup from the moment he'd taken over.

Women's cricket in Australia was stronger than anywhere

else in the world; over 20,000 women played the game, club and state competition was well established and structured, and in the past few years it had become an accepted part of the cricket scene as a whole. In short, no matter how much progress we'd made ourselves, we were up against something here that ran on a higher level altogether.

Jane Cassar, recently married to Derbyshire's Australian all-rounder Matthew Cassar, had gone out there with him one winter, and played three months for a club side; she spoke of the jump in standards from the English women's game with something approaching awe. It was fiercely competitive, if you didn't go training you didn't get picked, fitness levels that passed for normal in England would have been laughed at – and the sledging was something else. The first time she played and missed, a close fielder leaned towards her and asked idly, 'Would you like us to put bells on it to make it easier for you?'

Now Harmer told me, 'Today's the first time I've seen England. At a cursory glance, our girls are more athletic; whether that makes them better players I don't know. It'll be a tight game, a good hard fight; the talent's probably close, so it's who puts it together in the middle, isn't it?'

For all that, the fact that England hadn't killed off Pakistan and Denmark surprised him. He said, 'Either your batting's a lot better than your bowling – or they've just thought, let's see out fifty overs.'

And would he want an Australian side doing that?

He frowned, then gave a fierce little smile. 'I'd hope not.' With this guy around, I'm not sure I'd want to be in the dressing room if I did do it either.

Oh well – maybe we could put it right against Ireland in Pune. Australia, meanwhile, had Denmark up next. I asked Harmer if they were playing them here in Hyderabad, and he laughed. 'Don't be silly. We're here, they're here – so we've both got to get up early in the morning and fly to Bombay.'

9

The World Record that Wasn't

The alarm went off at four-fifteen the next morning; an hour later we were at the airport. Romper's overladen trolley had a dodgy wheel; she lurched towards the check-in, obliging BB to take evasive action. As she hopped away Romps told her, 'I have got a licence for one of these, you know.' She muttered, 'Like one of bloody Morrison's trolleys, these buggers.'

Metcalfe was shaking her head over the dreadful ball that got her out. It's dribbling down the wicket, she's steamed out to clout it, missed, got stumped. Romps told her, 'I feel for you. All you want to do is get back in the dressing room and throw your bat around. And you can't, 'cause there's people in there screaming about rats.'

Connie was having a panic attack by the security scanner. 'Oh no,' she moaned, 'I don't want them taking my batteries.' They had a tendency to do that, there being every possibility that we were, in fact, the National Liberation Front of

Bodoland. The Lengster had the boom box; she told Connie it was all right, she'd taken the batteries out. Connie asked her what she'd done with them, and Leng puffed her cheeks out like a hamster swallowing billiard balls. Connie rolled her eyes. 'Where *are* they?'

The Lengster told her, 'I'm an international spy, me.'

Bev said we needed new tunes, needed to get down to a music shop; Leng said she was well into Indian pop music. The current No. 1 was 'Bolle Bolle', sung by an immensely cheerful portly bloke with a turban and a tangerine jacket. I asked where the batteries were; she said she'd put some of them in Fresher's bag so she'd get in trouble, and rolled the others up in her shorts. She had X-ray-proof shorts then?

'Must have.'

Shirley marshalled a sheaf of boarding cards at the check-in counter; she remarked encouragingly of our travel arrangements, 'So far it's been a training camp.'

People scanned match reports in the papers; at one point the Australians had had Pakistan on 4 for 4. Twenty-seven all out was the lowest total in Women's World Cup history, pipping Holland's 29 against Australia at Perth in '88; Pakistan had taken 48 minutes to get it, and 8 of their 27 had been extras. Six of their bats got ducks – then Australia sent in their second-string openers, and one of them got run out. 'I should imagine,' said Peter Moralee, 'when Pakistan had Australia one for one they got quite excited.' It took Australia twenty minutes to win the game.

The plane boarded on time; it was, disturbingly, making a noise like a steam train. The passenger in front of me had a walking stick as tall as he was, a long white beard, flowing orange robes, three stripes of white paint on his forehead, and deck shoes. We taxied past a shanty butting right up close to the runway. They must have been breathing pure aviation fuel in there.

BB read *Fever Pitch*; JB read Bernard Cornwell. The flight to

Bombay was an hour and five minutes; on arrival we trans-
ferred to another terminal, and were filmed and photographed
by the local media as we did so. The players submitted to their
attentions with good grace – but when you're starting half your
days in the small hours, every little thing feels an extra effort. It
was 15 December; today, I thought, we are half-way through
this.

At least the Bombay organisers were on top of the game;
they had two buses, one for us, one for the luggage. We clambered on board and BB said dryly, 'Now this bus isn't going to
take five hours, is it?'

We were about to pull off when someone realised Lottie
and the Lengster weren't with us. They'd dived aside for some
sharp-eyed shopping: *Spiceworld*, and a *Best of the Eighties* com-
pilation. 'Got to have something for the oldies,' said Leng.

The tapes were a quid apiece. Romps said, 'You got the
Spice Girls for a quid?'

'Yeah.'

''Bout all they're worth, eh?'

Another terminal, another check-in; to while away the time,
I conducted a survey. If you could have any one song, album, or
piece of music on tour in India, what would it be?

Romps plumped for Everything But The Girl, 'Because it's
chilling-out music. And, incidentally, they got the name from a
bed shop in Hull.' Connie picked the soundtrack from *Stealing
Beauty*, the Bertolucci movie; Skip went for Whitney Houston.
Laura MacLeod said it had to be something relaxing – Texas,
'Black Eyed Boy'.

Bev asked me to leave it with her for five, then came out for
REO Speedwagon. H said it had to be 'Always Look On The
Bright Side Of Life'; Fresh took Erasure, 'Because all their
songs have meanings for me.' Sue Metcalfe's vote went to the
Beautiful South, 'Blue Is The Colour', while Lottie grinned
and gave an ironical yelp: 'Spice Up Your Life!'

With a whisper of a smile JB said, 'It wouldn't be the Spice

Girls, that's for sure. It's got to be "Land Of Hope And Glory", hasn't it? And a flag to go with it.'

I wrote the answers down by numbers, to make sure I got all fourteen of them; when the Lengster saw she was No. 13 she said, 'Can I be 13A? Not that I'm superstitious or anything. Now then, where's me rabbit's foot . . . anyway, Prince's *Greatest Hits*. Best album ever, it's got everything in it, jazz, funk, the lot. Got to be.'

Liss said, 'Not bothered whatsoever. Not interested.' Then she went away and thought about it, and came back with Mansun, 'Wide Open Space'.

Fines were noted for Smigs and BB. The former, asked if she could have any one song, album, or piece of music on tour in India, said, 'What, to listen to?'

BB said, 'I don't know. I'm tired, I'm pissed off, and I don't want to talk about it.'

We stumbled through another security check. Laura said, 'That was a good frisk, girls.'

The Lengster grinned. 'Nothing like a good frisk.'

We were on Jet Airways to Pune, a half-hour hop over a jagged patch of mountains that necessitated a steep descent at the other end. The pilot blew it first time round, circled three-sixty degrees, and tried again; he definitely brought that one in by hand. At the baggage reclaim, Megan looked absolutely wrung out. No time to be nervy, though – another welcoming committee was on hand, another gang of suits, scribes, snappers, and lavishly dressed women handing out garlands of lilies so big they hung down past your waist. Connie ducked away, grinning. 'Lovely,' she said, 'I've had no sleep and I've got half a friggin' flowerbed round my neck.'

Romps had another rickety trolley. 'It's what happens when you've got crossply and radial on the back. You've no chance.'

Outside, the way they loaded the bus made a terrifying spectacle. One of the porters climbed the ladder to the roof rack, then stood with one foot on top of the bus, the other on a first-floor ledge jutting out over the terminal doorway. Splayed out way above our heads, he couldn't use a hand to steady himself; he was heaving up the kitbags with both hands, teetering alarmingly under their weight. Fresh gaped: 'I don't believe I'm seeing this.' Personally, I couldn't look.

One likely outcome of all this dragging and hauling would be half the bags getting ripped again; a tailor had been called on in Hyderabad to patch them up once already. BB sighed, 'It's a pisser, isn't it?'

Joce shook her head. 'You'd think they'd look to put the lighter bags on the roof, wouldn't you? I don't know. They just don't seem to have any sequential thought, do they?' She sighed. 'Ah well. Every day a new experience. Or several, indeed.'

England watched the chaos aghast; Fresh put on some music. The Lengster said, 'You'll notice the significance of the music. People put it on when they're pissed off. Tap your foot and keep smiling, eh?'

Romps did a dance routine: 'Pan's People do Pune. Still, look at it this way. I could be driving a Royal Mail van round Bradford, couldn't I?'

We boarded, Hot Chocolate singing that they believed in miracles. Connie smiled wanly and said, 'You bloody have to, don't you?'

The Hotel Shantai laid on more garlands, more dobs on the forehead, and trays of juice with some marzipan sweets. You had to smile politely and turn down the juice (in case it had tap water in it) and try surreptitiously to salt the sweets away in the nearest bin. It sometimes meant struggling hard not to offend, but zero risk was the only possible approach – not that it had helped in my case. Apart from Joce's weird Chinese pellets I still wasn't eating anything; I had bowels like Niagara.

I sat with Thrasy, and watched porters clear the luggage-cluttered foyer. We decided we weren't mucking about going off to some other hotel any more, and checked in; whether Megan noticed or not I don't know, but nothing was said. I arranged to meet Liss later in the afternoon, then studied the *Lonely Planet*. We had two hours; Pune had a temple, a museum, the Bhagwan's ashram, and a ruined palace with a door with big spikes on it to stop enemy elephants bashing through it. We plumped for the palace, where the spiky door was impressive, and the gardens pleasantly restful.

We sat in the sun, and Thrasy said Karen Smithies had lightened up with him. She'd stopped giving him the clipped sentences, the mistrustful you're-a-rodent-I'm-a-clam act; he was now finding her refreshingly honest. He'd asked if she was happy so far; she said she was, but the bowling was a worry. What we rodents should understand, however, was that England didn't have an out-and-out strike bowler; they had a stock bowling attack that relied on consistency, on line and length, and looked to tie people down. But, sure, they were disappointed after Pakistan; they'd fielded badly against stonewalling bats, they'd not adapted, they'd just carried on humdrum as if they knew they were winning so it didn't matter. Whereas the Aussies, of course, had annihilated Pakistan – and she agreed, that had to be in the back of your mind.

The rodent line at this point was that, unquestionably, England had quality players. Edwards was hugely talented; Thrasy said simply, 'She bats like a man.' Brittin and Daniels were fine bats; JB's record stood for itself, coming into the tournament as she did the only woman with over 1,000 World Cup runs to her name, and an average of 42.11 in 49 one-day innings. Cassar was also a strikingly good cricketer – while among the bowlers, Leng's leg spin was a class act, Reynard was tidy and athletic, and Clare Taylor was plainly an exceptional sportswoman. But otherwise . . .

The nagging worry (this one applies to our women's football

side too) was how many of them were really athletes? OK, we were never going to have that burnt-in-the-sun leanness, that out-of-doors wire and muscle of the southern hemisphere players. And OK, their lottery grants had only just kicked in, they'd only just lately got their gym memberships, whatever. But all the same, you wondered if it wasn't just a bit, like – c'mon, eh? If you're playing for England, shouldn't you be fitter?

There were many ways in which England had improved their approach as the World Cup drew near, and their backing grew more substantial. But it was still a doubt in the mind that maybe the difference between us and the Australians would turn out to be that when we got serious, we got better playing kit with a snazzy logo on it – and when the Australians got serious, they won.

Everything about Australia spoke of a supreme confidence. The night before, Harmer had told me casually that once the tournament and the travelling began, he'd scrapped all practice – as if to say that they didn't need to practise, because they all knew exactly what they were there to do. In Pune, by contrast, Fizz and Joce said they had to stand a bit firm with Megan to let our players have a rest day.

I'd arranged to meet Liss. The palace was only five minutes from the hotel; unfortunately, we got the worst rickshaw driver in India. He was a total psychopath; it took forty minutes to get back, veering all round Pune with three stops for roadside discussions with strangers as to where the hotel was (he knew perfectly well), one stop to call the hotel from an STD booth so they could give him instructions as to how to get there (which he completely ignored), and one petrifying incident where he got into an argument with another rickshaw driver, and careered at full speed across a crowded bridge going fender to fender with his victim, not looking where he was going while he yelled a manic torrent of abuse. He then followed us into the hotel demanding more money than we were ever going to give him, and we had to get the people at reception to see him off. Result? I'd stood Liss up, she'd gone shopping, and my brain was boiled. You don't need it, you really don't need it.

Five local journalists were in for a press call with Skip. We had a quiet word aside while snappers took shots of other players; she said Bev, H, and Connie would be left out against Ireland. The Irish were a markedly better side than Pakistan or Denmark, they knew England well, they'd definitely be up for it (they were trying to get England to give them a Test match, a notion England weren't too impressed with) and the thinking was straightforward.

H was out because they wanted another look at Lottie and JB opening. Bev hadn't performed too well, so they wanted another look at Fresh (who hadn't performed too well either) and playing three seamers meant losing a spinner. With the Lengster back, that meant Connie resting.

Skip went to sit in the restaurant with the Indian scribes, who pressed her several times on what team England would put out against Ireland. Politely, fluently, she lied; they had not, she told them, had a selection meeting yet. I don't mention this to be critical; it's what's known as being a professional sportsperson. On the other hand, if we knew Ireland and they knew us, and if we were going to beat them anyway, what was the point?

Smithies on Reynard: 'Her heart's there, and she's got the talent. I'd let her bowl the last over; I'd always back her.'

Liss worked for Yorkshire Water, in an engineering depot on the outskirts of Harrogate; on the wall of the office where we talked a few weeks before the tournament, one of the lads had a naked totty calendar over his desk from the Teeside Valve & Fitting Co. Liss said, 'Lovely, isn't it? You'll find her everywhere.' She shrugged, 'It's up to them. They introduce them gradually. They start in the corners, then work their way out.'

She was born in Knaresborough; her dad was a retired

insurance claims inspector, and her mum worked in a china shop. She had one brother, seven years older, and the cricket came from messing about with him when she was little. She joined a lads' side when she was eleven or twelve; she said, 'I just enjoyed it. I thought I could do OK, I wouldn't be letting anybody down, and no one ever commented.'

When she was eighteen, a PE teacher at her school found her a women's club, Green Hammerton in the local evening league; she played for Lofthouse now, up in Nidderdale, and for Sue Metcalfe's North Riding at the weekend. It took up nights, weekends, all her holidays; she didn't get paid leave, but the people at work were good about it. When she started there, she didn't tell them about it – then she'd only been there two months when the first India tour came up, and she had to ask for two months off. Before she got round to asking, unfortunately, her boss read that she'd been picked in the local paper – so, seeing she was still there, one did assume he had to be a decent bloke.

Still, she wasn't the kind to make a meal out of being an international. She said, 'I'm not really one for ambitions; I don't set goals or targets. I'll drive myself to do things, I'll play to the best of my ability – and if that's for England, that's a bonus. If it's not, that's the way it goes.'

For all that, she loved that first trip to India; the way the people were so welcoming, the way every place was so different from the last one – and the simple fact that when you played, you got a crowd. She said, 'You're in the middle, you're playing your game – and all of a sudden it hits you. My God – all these people watching me. But they're great, because they appreciate good cricket; it doesn't matter who's playing it.' The only thing she didn't like was all the flying – but then, she shrugged, 'If you don't get on 'em you don't get anywhere, do you?'

The lack of attention in England didn't bother her. She said, 'It's the way it is. It'd be nice to get paid, I'd be lying if I didn't say that – but money's not why I'm playing, is it? I'm playing because I enjoy it, I like the challenge, I like being in a team that's successful – and then, one of the advantages of not being paid is you know you're all there because you want to be. I don't know how the chaps go on – but if you took the money away, would they all still be there?'

On the other hand, she said, 'It's a great story, and you do wonder why people don't follow it a bit more. But when the press do come, you have to be careful, because all they want you to do is slag off the men – aren't they terrible, all that. Well, no, they're not – they're a lot better than we are, and they ought to give them a break. Anyway, you can't make a comparison. I mean, people ask if we could beat the men – well, really.' She shook her head. 'How are you supposed to give an intelligent answer to that one? Do I want to face Courtney Walsh? Mind you,' she laughed, 'I'd probably be OK. It'd be flying that high over my head that I'd be fine.'

So what did she want? She said, 'I'd just like us to be seen in our own right. This is who we are, this is what we do, we work hard at it, and please don't compare us to anyone but the teams we play against. It'd be nice to read a paper and they'd just give a scorecard, they'd talk about someone's bowling, or someone's innings – not, we're so poor that I've had these shoes for ten years 'cause I've spent all my money on cricket. Who wants to read that? It'd be nice just to talk about the cricket.'

Melissa Reynard's figures against South Africa: 4–0–10–0. Against Pakistan: 10–4–36–2. Against Denmark: 6–2–18–1. She thought it was OK, but not great; she'd gone to talk to Peter Moralee after the Denmark game because she felt she'd not been pin-pointing it, and she wanted to know why. He asked what she was looking at; she told him, top of off stump. So he told her to try looking at the base of it, and he had a word about her action – about getting the front arm up, and taking her body through.

It was only fine tuning; she wasn't going to go mad trying to change things. Besides, she'd just been out shopping, she'd had another blast of India on the pavements of Pune – and now she said, 'I don't think about cricket all the time. You could turn into a bit of a bore like that, and I don't want to get bored of it. But that's no problem here, 'cause there's so much to look at; you don't think about cricket or home or anything, you're too busy looking. It's difficult to get your head round some of it, and you do get quite hard. There was a blind man in the middle of the road today – and you find yourself just look-ing, not thinking anything. But the people, the diversity . . .'

She was enjoying it; she was only disappointed they'd not be seeing Bombay. As for what happened with Pakistan and Denmark, she wasn't going to get fussed. 'Look,' she said, 'we've got an immense batting team. I can't envisage Australia being any better at batting. But bowling, we're a containing team; that's good for one-day cricket, and we should concen-trate on that. So if sides are going to shut up shop on us, and not play any shots, there's no point thinking what Australia might do to them. You're aware of it – but people have got to be care-ful not to let themselves get wound up about it.'

All the same, they'd have to start getting a bit more ruthless, wouldn't they? She said, 'Yeah, definitely. And it'll come. When we play Australia, it'll come. 'Cause we've got a game on our hands there – and people bring out the goods then, don't they?'

Ireland's coach was a courteous and exceedingly tall man named John Wills, an Englishman who'd moved to Ireland twenty years back, and now lived in Killarney. His squad, he said, had received a £4,000 government grant towards a total budget for their World Cup of something near £35,000; one of his players had done a sponsored cycle ride from Donegal to Dublin and back to raise money towards getting to India.

They were a young side; he'd recently lost an opening bat and two opening bowlers who'd retired, so now he was building the team towards the next European Cup, and the 7th World Cup in New Zealand after that. He'd blooded three new caps against South Africa in the summer, when Ireland lost a one-day series 3–0 before the South Africans came to England; he had a seamer who was eighteen, and an off spinner who was sixteen. He smiled and said, 'Against England. That's the deep end, isn't it?'

The pool of players from which he'd pick a squad would not, realistically, be much bigger than twenty – but for all that, they weren't a bad team at all. Further down the track, they'd get Pakistan all out for 60, which made England's lackadaisical effort look even worse. Unsurprisingly, therefore, Wills was opposed to the notion, mooted more and more around the tournament, of a two-division World Cup. The ongoing slaughter of cricketing innocents by the top teams in hopelessly one-sided contests was encouraging this idea, but Wills didn't like it, for two reasons.

'The little teams,' he said, 'have to come with at least the chance of winning. In fifty overs, if you've got five good players, they might do it for you – and if England are upset, dead and dying, we can beat them. We could have beaten South Africa in the summer – we had them 135 all out, and we blew it. But there's another factor. Maybe with Australia and England it's getting different now, a bit more professional – but for the rest of us, the friendship thing in the ladies' game is still as important as the playing.'

We were talking over a buffet of vegetable and chicken chow mein laid on for both teams by the Shantai on a pleasant, tree-shaded terrace – a buffet so palatable that I ate some of it myself, with predictable results. Wills was friendly and relaxed, and pretty happy with India – as you would be, if your itinerary involved little more than eight days in Madras, six days in Pune – and he was pretty certain what would happen, too. He said, 'I think Australia will walk it.'

Then he got up and smiled, with a pained little wince. He

said, 'If you'll excuse me, anyway. I've got to go and break three ladies' hearts now.'

I stayed up 'til midnight watching England's gripping win over Pakistan at Sharjah. This involved two priceless Boycottisms; firstly, 'Cindy Crawford. I'd like her for Christmas.' Then the second came when he described England's opposition as, 'The Pakeeeee . . . stanis.' My, but that was close.

All the same, I didn't actually want to stay up that late. I enjoyed the unusual pleasure of watching England win, obviously, and Star Sports anyway had a kind of horrid fascination – this was cricket commercialised to an all but grotesque extent. It wasn't just the ads screaming noisily through every change of over, every fall of wicket, or the irritating little slogans promoting some brand of bourbon zipping along the bottom of the screen during play. You get that elsewhere, and anyway, Indian ads are a hoot – frantically aspirational paeans to the virtues of men's suits, whisky, beer, and bathroom fittings. One brand of taps was 'Beyond Your Imagination' – which, if you were living on the pavement in Calcutta, was no doubt literally true.

It was, instead, that the entire Sharjah tournament was effectively a promotional video for the United Arab Emirates. You had shots of Dubai Creek, the souks and duty-free shops, the hotels and the yacht club all cut into the cricket, with the commentators burbling on about how triff it all was. As it happens, I've been there, and it is a pretty nifty place – but (seeing I'm stuffy and English) I thought using cricket to flog it to Asia this brazenly was just a teensy bit minging.

Anyway, I stayed up to watch it because I didn't have much choice. Firstly, there was a party going on in the hotel, half of whose guests appeared to be having their fun in the corridor immediately outside my room. Then secondly, right outside my window, an industrial-sized ventilator was roaring and grumbling 'til after midnight like something out of *Eraserhead*.

No surprise, then, that when the alarm went off at six-fifteen, my head felt like a lump of dead wood. I crawled through the shower and into my clothes, went downstairs, and met the Lengster. The evening before, she, Connie, and Smigs had come tearing into the hotel ten minutes late for the team meeting; Connie had panted, 'Bad rickshaw'. Well, I knew all about bad rickshaws in Pune – so now I asked what happened.

Two local girls, England's minders and helpers, had taken them shopping; five minutes down the road there was Adidas, Nike, a jeans store, and a music place called The Jukebox. They bought half the shops out, then the Lengster remembered her boyfriend was an Eagles' fan. She saw a CD, she thought she'd not bother – then by coincidence they started playing it, and she had a pang of guilt. It was only a quid. So she bought it, they got back, she was having a natter with some of the others, she showed someone the CD – and the case was empty.

She said, 'You should check, shouldn't you? But when you've got up at four and you're walking round like a zombie, you don't. So I thought, they've skanked me. I felt really stupid. We went back there – and the bloke had the CD all ready in his hand, waiting for me. I was gobsmacked, he was so nice about it; I was apologising all over the place. Only now it's getting late, we've the team meeting to get to – so we get a rickshaw and the driver's a maniac, he's definitely not all there. It's rush hour, the girl we're with doesn't know where we're going, we're trying not to watch the road – and after ten minutes we're up and down all these backstreets, the girl's jabbering at him – then the rickshaw breaks down. Oh, and I've missed the bit where we got shunted by a bus. It was really, really scary. It must have been, 'cause Smigs doesn't usually swear – but we could've been knocked over easy. Anyway, the girl's yapping at him, we've no idea where we are – what a day. I was so on edge. First I thought I'd lost me traveller's cheques, then I thought I'd lost me washbag, then the CD, the rick-shaw – I can't have another day like that one.'

'She was,' said BB mildly, 'on another planet yesterday.'

She had to rejoin earth today though, didn't she? She'd found out at the team meeting that she was back playing again; now she said, 'If I'm going to play in the quarters, the semis, I needed to play today. Shit or bust, eh?'

The Pandit Jawaharlal Nehru Stadium in Pune was opened in 1969 by Indian captain C. G. Borde and Bill Lowry, captain of the touring Australian team. The Maharashtra State Women's Cricket Association had an office there, beneath the stand facing the street, with a dozen pictures on the walls of local players who'd played for India. One of their officials told me proudly that it was the first place in the country where a female international had a stadium gate named after her – which might not sound like much, but in a nation where form and ceremony mean a lot, I'd guess it's no small thing to get your name on the door.

Crowds of girls were gathering round the main entrance. The organisers had given out free tickets to schools and col-leges, they'd laid on buses to get people to the ground, and by doing that they reckoned they'd got over 7,000 people watch-ing Ireland–South Africa on Sunday (a game the South Africans won by nine wickets, after bowling Ireland out for 155). 'We do everything possible for the promotion of women's cricket,' said my charming and eager host, 'we provide poor girls with bats and playing kit, we take exhibition games to rural areas – we want the creation of a sports atmosphere everywhere.' Happily, that work would be repaid today; they'd be shown just how good a woman can be.

The Nehru was an appealing arena; the pavilion was four storeys in a faded pale green, with open, palm-fringed terraces fanning round on either side. One reached to a two-tier, sky-blue stand on the far side; the other stopped half-way, breaking up into a minor jungle of hanging ivy and flowers. There was a heavy dew, but the dense mist and grey skies of dawn were clearing fast; it was going to be a hot one. Out on the wicket, the groundsman told Liss it was a batsman's paradise; she smiled and told him, 'That's nice to hear if you're a bowler, isn't it?'

The scorer came to get the batting order. We got as far as seven, then he said after that it didn't matter. 'From what I read in the papers, only your opening pair will bat anyway, yes?'

Elsewhere, more minnows were getting squashed. In Ghaziabad, in a match reduced to forty overs a side by rain and bad light, India beat Holland by 93 runs; in Chandigarh, New Zealand ran up 253 for 9 against the West Indies, then skittled them out for 55. New Zealand's total included a century from Debbie Hockley, her second neat round number of the tournament – 100 exactly in this game, to add to 100 not out against Sri Lanka. During that first knock, she joined JB as the second woman to pass 1,000 World Cup runs; she also became the first woman to top 3,000 international one-day runs.

With results like that coming in, England needed to do something good against Ireland, if they wanted to look as if they could stay in the frame – above all, they needed to step it up in the field. For the first time, however, Skip won the toss – so Lottie and JB went out to bat, and in the second over Lottie pulled two successive boundaries through square leg. It was the day before her eighteenth birthday – but already she'd gone beyond being a player you could talk about as 'promising'. Put a bat in her hand, and she was irrepressible.

Megan said Lottie had a plan for the Australian opening bowler, a quickie called Cathryn Fitzpatrick – by all accounts, a serious quickie. 'She says she'll go out with a helmet on. Then after the first ball she'll put her hand up, call for the twelfth man, and get her to take the helmet away. Nah, she'll say. You're not fast.'

I gaped. Megan laughed and said, 'Course she'll not do that. But that's Lottie.'

Romper wandered round the boundary. She said her achilles kept tightening on her, so she'd gone to see Fizz, and Fizz had worked her fingers good and hard into her foot and her ankle. 'Before too long I was hanging from the ceiling. So Fizz says to Joce, "Turn up the TV. We don't want to disturb anyone with the screams."'

We sat on a roller by the wire fence round the base of the terrace, and signed autographs for packs of smiling children. She said she was keeping a diary; she said, 'I can shut myself in my room, and if I've got frustrations I'll put them in there. I don't always want to be Miss Happy, and it is tiring here, it's hard work physically. You grab the rest where you can; you exist on cricket, sleep, and TV. Steve Bull talks about the three C's – Concentration, Commitment, and . . . I dunno, something else. My three C's are Coffee, Chat, and Cricket.'

So we chatted about the cricket – and she wasn't worried about what happened with Pakistan and Denmark. Against Denmark, her figures had been 10–4–12–2, and she was naturally pretty happy with that – but overall, it wasn't the point. She said, 'It's who gets the most runs. Those teams want to do well, and if they shut up shop and don't get all out, that's a feather in their cap – so if they're not even going for your score, wickets are academic. It's nice to get them, but if I've bowled my ten for less than twenty, I can come off and I've done my job. But still,' she shrugged, 'it's hard to keep going for fifty overs against people that aren't trying when you've already won.'

Australia wouldn't think like that.

'They wouldn't admit it. But deep down, if they'd been where we'd been, they'd have been bored too. Besides, who knows what happened when Pakistan got 27? They won the toss, so why didn't they field first? 'Cause they didn't want to get whacked to kingdom come for fifty overs again? Did they go out and think, let's have a go and then go home? Who knows? We weren't there. And what matters where we were is, we won.'

According to one cricket journalist, Taylor shouldn't have been in India at all. 'OK,' she said, 'I didn't do well in the summer against South Africa. So I can give up, or I can do something about it – and I don't like being twelfth man. So I've done something about it – and I needed to, 'cause in this squad you do look over your shoulder. But you're selected by the selectors, nobody else – and if you've been around long enough, you must have broad shoulders. Anyway, all this talk'll stop on Thursday. We'll see what Australia are like then – and they'll be just as worried about us as we are about them.'

Out in the field, England were 170 for 2; JB got 37, BB got 4, Sue Metcalfe was in with Lottie, and in the thirty-second over Lottie reached 100. It was her second century for England on her ninth one-day appearance; by her standards she'd started cautiously, taking 66 balls to reach 50, hitting five fours along the way. Then she cut loose; the second 50 came off 34 balls, with seven more boundaries. There wasn't a corner of the ground she wasn't reaching, and she hadn't offered a single chance.

Connie sat in the sun on the boundary, restless, stamping her feet. She hated not playing; Skip had told her she'd been bowling well, she was just being rested and she was probably in the strongest eleven, so she was sanguine about it, but she was disappointed all the same. She said, 'You just worry about getting back in, from a selfish point of view. I hope everyone does well, obviously – but I want to get back in.'

After she'd been in hospital on the first tour, falling ill had made her paranoid. She thought, oh no, here we go again. Can my stomach not hack this? Getting better was a massive relief –

but it threw her a bit; with the travelling she was tired, and she was homesick too. She hadn't expected to be; when she was sixteen or seventeen in Romania, sure, she'd missed home then, but later on she'd been to Zimbabwe and India, and she'd been fine. Trouble was, it was Christmas coming up, wasn't it? She had a ten-year-old brother, and with him about, Christmas at home was still magical. She'd called, and he was decorating the tree – that got to her a bit.

She said, 'I'm not miserable; I'm just aware of it, it's just the time of year. Still, everything fades into insignificance when cricket's around. I've bowled twenty overs, I've got 2 for 38 in three games – I'm happy about that. And if I'm picked to play Australia, I'll be happier. And if we beat them, I'll be happier still. Because that,' she said, 'is the focus in everyone's mind.'

It wasn't the focus, just then, in Charlotte Edwards' mind. It was now searingly hot, and she'd been batting from the start; she'd put on 108 with Sue Metcalfe for the third wicket. Metcalfe was stumped for 29 in the thirty-fifth over, so now Jane Cassar went in. What followed grew more impressive with every ball.

Edwards' innings was already stunning in its range, in the variety of her shots; it now became admirable in its character. She had to call often for water; she was beginning to feel sick, and to get cramps in her feet and her ankles. There was bound to be a tired shot or two; she was dropped twice at square leg on 110 and 131, and after she'd passed 150 she was put down in the covers. But with Cassar batting quite splendidly beside her, she kept going – kept going all the way to the end.

Cassar hit 50 not out off 55 balls; their undefeated stand of 131 was a new record fourth-wicket partnership for the Women's World Cup. This, remember, was against bowling some way better than anything Pakistan or Denmark could muster – but Edwards had tumbled a bigger record than that.

The previous top score in this tournament had been 143 not

out by Australia's Lindsay Reeler against Holland in Perth in 1988. Edwards passed that mark in the forty-fourth over; that she went on to thrash 30 more runs before the innings finished spoke a heart as big as her cover drives were sweet. She finished on 173 not out; she'd faced 155 balls, and hit 19 fours.

Smigs said later, 'I kept telling her to see it out, that she was batting really well, how she was the one that could get the big score. She said she had cramps so I told her to take her time between overs, to get a drink whenever she wanted one – but she was knackered when I got there, and we had fifteen overs still to go. She got a bit of a second wind, she started running the two's again – but bless her, by the last five overs she could barely run at all. I was only out there an hour and I was really, really feeling it – it's one of the hottest I've ever played in – so how she lasted three hours I don't know.'

She smiled and said, 'Every time we passed, I'd check if she wanted to go for a second. When I got out there she said, I do one's, I do easy two's, and I don't do three's. Oh, but I do enjoy batting with her. She's really psyched up; you see her stroking it about, and it really gets you going.'

It was a world-class performance; England finished 326 for 4. John Wills said, 'That was an exhibition of how to play proper cricket. They respected the good ball, and the bad ball went for four. I think Edwards is tremendous.'

Joce got her in the dressing room; she was too exhausted to take the field in the afternoon. Joce said, 'We've packed her with carbo-drink. She'll have a raised core temperature, she'll have sweated four or five litres – but she'll be fine, she just needs rest.'

She thought about that a minute, then asked grimly, 'What time are we getting up tomorrow morning?'

Now England had to show that they could bowl as well. The Irish, to their credit, didn't try to stick at the wicket doing nothing; they set themselves a target of 180 to 200. Wills said,

'We're here to learn, not to block it all day. We've got a lovely field, a nice big crowd, and some good bowlers to face. Let's enjoy it.'

I don't know if they enjoyed it or not, but they didn't get anywhere near their target; England bowled them all out for 116 in 41.1 overs. After an iffy tournament so far, Sue Redfern's opening spell was blistering; she took a wicket clean bowled second ball, and she got an lbw with her fifth. After that, there were no more wickets for her – but in six overs, she gave away only five runs.

I was going round to the scorebox when she came out to the boundary after her first over, a pair of wickets in her pocket; Connie was coming the other way, laying drinks out round the rope for the fielders. The minute she got to Redfern, she high-fived her. It was conceivable – unlikely, but conceivable – that Fresh had just bowled Connie out of a place in the team against Australia, but she gave her the big hand all the same.

I said to Connie that I'd noticed that, and asked if she was generous, or an actress. She laughed and said, 'Generous of heart.' Behind us, another horde of kids was hissing and screaming for autographs; you had only to stop for a nanosecond, and the entire cast of *Oliver* were waving tattered pads under your nose. Connie sighed and said, 'Oh go away, horrible children.' Then she walked over and signed her name for them all anyway.

High up in the scorebox was a good place to see the tricksy canniness of Smithies' flight; she teased out a stumping, and Ireland were 47 for 4 off 20 overs. I said idly to an Irish bloke that there was a long way to go yet, and he laughed. He said, 'Cricket's a funny game. But it's not that funny.'

Another wicket fell – then two of the Irish stuck in. The game went a bit dreary for a while; the fielding had been the sharpest since we'd played South Africa, we'd looked tight and controlled, only now it was drifting away again. A dozen tooth-less, soggy little overs wandered by; rusty after two games injured, the Lengster got a wicket, but she went for 37 off 9 overs, and I started fearing that we'd let another team stay in again. Where was the ruthlessness?

Smithies put Liss on. She bowled 4.1 overs, got four wickets for six runs, and Ireland were gone. Line, length, and a tidy bit of swing – that's the way to do it.

Then came the news: Lottie's 173 wasn't a world record after all, and our 376 against Pakistan wasn't a record any more either.

In Bombay, Australia played Denmark. They batted first, they scored 412 for 3 – and their captain Belinda Clark got 229 not out. It was the first double century in an international one-day game by anyone, man or woman, and her first hundred along the way was the fastest in the history of women's cricket – she got there off just 64 balls. To rub it in, they then bowled Denmark out for 49; the only name on the Danish scorecard to make double figures was Extras.

There was no point being glum about it; you just had to reckon that the meeting in Nagpur between England and Australia now looked more enticing than ever. But there was, of course, the small matter of getting there first.

10

Proper Cricket

The original itinerary had us staying in Pune after the game, getting up at God knows what hour, flying to Bombay, sitting in Bombay airport for seven hours, then flying to Nagpur. Megan wasn't having it; seven hours in the airport would be deadly, and it meant arriving so late that all the team could do was go to bed, get up, and play – which was no kind of way to prepare for Australia.

The other option wasn't much better, but here it was: get a bus back to Bombay after the game, sleep there, then get a flight in the morning. The problem this presented the rodents, however, was that we had to file match reports – and, obviously, we couldn't expect the bus to wait for us.

Rodent grief was further enhanced by the fact that the stadium in Pune seemed to have only one telephone – which, seeing there were four us (me, Thrasy, Cath Harris, and Craig Prentis wanting to send pictures back) wasn't fabulously helpful. So I span on the spot for a while, then decided to leave the ground the minute the game was done, get a cab with Craig and Selena to Bombay, and file from there.

I grabbed a scorecard and ran. By the pavilion, bigwigs were giving out awards; Lottie, unsurprisingly, was Eve of the Match for her 173. 'That,' said a bigwig, 'is a world record.' I didn't have the heart to tell her it wasn't. To one side, Smithies was doing TV; assorted soldierly women trooped about in khaki saris, and dainty berets with puffy red feathers. Outside, the cab was waiting – another tinfoil 4×4. It didn't have any seat belts.

Selena was going ahead to sort out rooms at the airport hotel. Too many PR people are slapdash slimeballs – I had one tell me once that there were no hotel rooms in an entire country, when she was supposed to be representing that country – so when you get a good one, they're worth their weight in gold. It was Selena who'd got a Union Jack out of the British High Commission in Delhi so we'd not be flagless at the opening ceremony; it was Selena who'd been toting a Christmas tree all round India in her Vodafone coffin. Now she sat in the back with Craig, and confronted the Worst Car Journey In The World with regal aplomb.

We left the stadium at four-forty. Once out of Pune, the road was a deranged two-lane parade of belching trucks, dead dogs, and madmen who overtook on blind corners and over the brows of hills as if nothing ever came the other way. There was, of course, *always* something coming the other way. To add to the fun, our driver was intent on proving himself even madder than everyone else – so you got to check out all the vehicles coming the other way up close and personal.

It was like a stockcar rally, but with trucks instead of cars. If you could tear your eyes away from it, the countryside through which this death race passed had middle-sized mountains lining a pink-tinged sunset over a tree-scattered plateau. But I couldn't look at it much; mostly I was looking at the radiator grille of the next oncoming truck while the driver tapped his cassette on the dash to try and get it to work, and gobbed out the window, and generally paid no attention whatsoever to the teeming mayhem on the road ahead. I sat thinking, I'm spending four hours risking my life with this lunatic so I can file a cricket report?

It got worse. As night fell, we tumbled through countless vertiginous hairpins down the flanks of the mountains to the littoral plain before Bombay. Wrecks lay rolled and dented along the side of the road, including a lorry that had gone through the front of a Jeep. There was no chance anyone had walked away from that one; they sat melded together, rusting in the ditch.

When we pulled up at a truck stop for a toilet break, our go-faster stripes fell off. Out of sheer fright, probably.

It was four hours to Bombay, and then another hour through it. I wrote the match report in the cab (it beat looking at the road) and filed it from the front desk of the Centaur Hotel at the airport. The squad arrived about eleven; there weren't enough rooms, so I shared with Peter Moralee. The room cost us £120, for the privilege of sleeping in it for four hours; the alarm went off at three forty-five, and we were checking out by four-thirty.

Lottie leaned against the front desk looking absolutely shattered. She asked, 'How long's the flight?' I said she could sleep in the afternoon, but she shook her head. 'Got training.' It wasn't so much spoken, as moaned; welcome to your eighteenth birthday. Later, Fizz wrote on Lottie's card, 'Not the most riotous birthday you'll ever have – but certainly the longest.'

At least the Bombay organisers were on the ball again; they'd relieved England of their luggage when they'd arrived, and taken it away to check it in ahead of us. So, said Shirley, 'I haven't seen the bags for six hours. I might live to regret it, but right now it feels great.' Then she went outside, looked at the bus, and – seeing the terminal was only down the road – she asked brightly, 'Can't we walk?'

That got rolled eyes all round. Romps said quietly, 'I knew there was a reason I gave up doing earlies at work.'

It was BB's birthday too; Romps said she'd wished her happy birthday, and BB told her glumly, 'It's not my birthday. It's the middle of the night.'

We got to the check-in – where Shirley, still remarkably on form, talked contentedly about what she liked about India (most of it) and what she didn't. 'I would just like it,' she said, 'if now and then someone would hold open a door for a lady with a bag. But there you go. Can't have everything.'

She gave out name-tags for the hand baggage; Romper took two, gave BB one and told her, 'There's your birthday card.' Then there was a big burst of jarring music. Whhhooooaaahhh BABY! My heart is full of LOVE and DESIRE for you! I turned round, and it was Australia. Brilliant. Here we both were in Bombay – so, obviously, to play our game we both had to fly to Nagpur on the 5.45. It made perfect sense.

The Lengster said quietly, 'Anyone object to loud music?' On went the dance mix – couldn't be outdone, could we?

Moralee said one of his daughters went to Australia to play for Fitzpatrick's club, Buckley Ridge in Melbourne. Now he said, 'Every little thing's a stunt, a head game. Every ball's a Test match. That club, they won a competition – so when they went up to get the trophy, they walked slowly so everyone had to clap them for longer.'

In the departure lounge now, they blanked us – not a flicker. Maybe they were knackered too – but on the other hand, if they were I doubt they'd show it.

The flight was a real sweaty palm job. We went along fine – then the descent brought us down into thick grey cloud, near-snowy looking stuff. We went into it, we levelled off, and we stayed in it. After twenty minutes, I was finding this far more

dread-inducing than the drop into Pune. Were there mountains out there? Did he know where the ground was? Finally
the pilot said he was holding to let the weather clear – and
after half an hour, we started getting the odd glimpse of the
ground.

This was welcome on the one hand, but nerve-racking on
the other, as it wasn't too far away. I started thinking I was glad
it wasn't my eighteenth birthday – 'cause eighteen years isn't
much of a span, is it? Mind you, never mind dying in a plane
crash – what if the wicket was wet? Nagpur, after all, was the
place India's men had just had four days of a Test match with
Sri Lanka rained off.

The pilot was Joe Cool; the landing was one of the
smoothest I've ever had. This confirmed my belief that the
only way to approach flying in the third world is to believe that
if these guys have learnt to fly there, they can surely fly anywhere. You have to believe this, because the alternative is to
believe that they're a bunch of feckless, ill-trained, over-macho
cowboys, and that death is imminent every time you board a
plane.

We staggered through fine drizzle to the baggage reclaim.
Right now – after Australia had dropped three points to Ireland
when their game in Madras was rained off – we were top of the
group. So if the pitch here was unplayable, said Moralee,
'Thanks for turning up, Australia, and we'll see you in the
final.'

Liss came up, and he told her how good her bowling had
been against Ireland. She smiled and told him, 'There you go,
Pete. Quick word with you and I'm right.'

BB stared wearily out of the window at the damp grey skies.
She said, 'I know we won't get it, but I'd like a decision today.
What I don't want is a twenty-over thrash, and what I do want
is two rest days – because no one, *no one* has been made to
travel like us. I don't know where we are, I don't know what
day it is, I don't know what time it is.'

Joce was trying to work through the schedule in her head, if the game was rained off (or, indeed, if we won) and we topped the group. We'd have to leave tomorrow night, get into Delhi about ten in the evening, stay in another airport hotel, leave for Lucknow at five-thirty in the morning . . . England's motto was now, 'We wash and go.'

Fizz said, 'They might as well forget the cricket. They should just stick the teams in an airport lounge, feed 'em all curry, and whoever stays standing longest is the winner.'

Selena From Kensington blithely asked some of the players, 'Have you seen Craig's equipment?' Cue gales of laughter.

Picture technology: during the Ireland game Prentis shot five rolls, thirty-six shots a roll. He had two weighty cases, one for all the developing clobber, one with an Apple Mac and a scanner. To develop and fix the film took a shade over six minutes; then you washed it, squeegee'd it, hung it with gaffer tape on the back of the door, and dried it with a hair-dryer. If you were quick, you were ready to send in ten minutes.

You cut the film into strips of six, slid it in a clear sheet, checked it on a light box, and edited. The Apple had a pro-gramme called Photoshop; you fed the negs into the scanner, acquired your image, cropped it, whacked it down the wire on a modem and all being well, it was in London in three minutes. To Craig's relief and astonishment, the phone lines – once you'd got hold of one – were holding up pretty well.

He said, 'I haven't had to tear any skirting boards out yet. Basically, you strip out a bit of the phone line with a pen knife, then tong the modem on the line.' Result? Pictures in all the papers, including one of Lottie in the *Sun* memorably cap-tioned CHAR ON BOIL. There was another good one of Lottie and the Lengster in *The Times*, celebrating the win over South Africa with BB in the background; with the funky pyja-mas and the rimless wraparound shades, it made England's women look what they were. I know I've quibbled here and there – but for all that, they were proper cricketers.

When I asked BB how she'd like them to be seen, she said simply, 'As a cricket team. As a team that plays to a high standard, works hard, works together, enjoys its cricket, knows about its cricket, and is prepared to learn more. We're not the best team ever, we haven't got it all sorted, we've still got stacks to learn – but we're desperately proud to be playing for our country, and we'd like people to know that.'

Among these fourteen people, Thrasy was growing steadily more impressed with Jane Cassar. Of her partnership that helped Lottie carry her bat against the Irish he said, 'She's a thinking cricketer. That was proper stuff.' So the only question now was, how proper were Australia?

Both teams stayed in the Jagson's Regency, five minutes from the airport across open, scrub-strewn ground that looked sodden, and had muddy pools of standing water lying all about it. The hotel staff said it had been raining since three in the morning; it was only starting to clear up now.

England, meanwhile, had been raining fines on Fizz; at the team meeting in Pune, she got fined seven times. She got fined for walking behind the bowler's arm (twice). She got fined for saying, when someone asked who'd taken a catch and the answer was JB, 'That one in the hat.' She got fined for asking Connie if she was left-handed when Connie was sitting there writing a letter (and which hand was the pen in?) She got fined for being a member of the fifty-stone rickshaw ride. She got fined for running on to treat the wrong player – running on to Bev and asking, 'What's the matter?'

Bev says, 'Fresher's hurt herself.'

'Where is she?'

'She's gone off.'

And she got fined for getting fined so much.

Joce went to change some money; they gave her 3,500

roops – in ten-roop notes. She was muttering something about an order she'd put in for chicken stroganoff; Fizz told her what she'd really like herself was, 'A proper curry. Like they make 'em in Cardiff.'

She was looking through the double doors in the foyer, and looking happy; she said, 'Looks like more rain coming on.' Then she opened the doors, and there was no sign of any rain at all. 'Oh,' she frowned. 'Tinted glass.'

Joce, Fizz, Selena, Craig and I were going into Nagpur to get presents for the birthday girls. We asked for a cab (for a trip of eight kilometres each way) and were quoted a minimum rate of fifty kilometres. Why not? The guy said it'd be there in ten minutes; Fizz asked him, 'How about five?' He laughed at her like that was the funniest thing he'd ever heard – and five minutes later, there it was. It was a kind of Matchbox version of a Bedford Rascal and it proclaimed on the side, 'Tourist Vehicle'. We puttered into town past a sign saying, 'Go Slow And See Our Town. Go Fast And See Our Prison'. Then we got a puncture. We got the puncture just past another sign at some roadworks saying, 'Inconvenience Is Regretted'. It always is.

So we clambered out while the driver changed the tyre, and a cycle-rickshaw driver of wizened and haggard demeanour stopped to peer at us hopefully. How he thought all of us were to be loaded on his rickety conveyance, I'm not sure. How he was to avoid a massive coronary trying to haul us if we could be, I can't imagine.

When the tyre was changed we set off again, past another cycle rickshaw that said on the back, Jesus Leads Me. The driver of this one looked so gnarled and racked with his load that, never mind leading him, it seemed more probable Jesus was coming for him at any moment. We went past him and I forgot him, until I realised I'd just casually contemplated the death of this man in his straining poverty without the merest flicker of emotion. It was two weeks to the day now since

England had arrived, and in just a fortnight it seemed I'd become a completely heartless bastard.

The others went hunting goodies in the Nike shop; I sat outside thinking. On the way through Bombay the night before, a child beggar with a filthy rag to wipe the dirt round on your bonnet had come to my window at a stop light amid six lanes of traffic. His left cheek was swollen out in some deformity, his face was a pleading rictus, and his hand was a begrimed little bird fluttering at my arm, fingers like twigs. I put my hand in my pocket, and I had no coins; I asked Craig and Selena if they had any, and they didn't either. So I forgot it. The kid wasn't eighteen inches from me, the stop light turned green, and I forgot all about him.

Why didn't I give him a ten-roop note? It's sixteen pence. Why didn't I do that? People tell you the beggars are all controlled by brutal Fagins, beggar pimps getting stonking rich out of it – but so what? If that's true, and Fagin takes ninety per cent of what you've given, isn't the kid still one roop better off? Or if Fagin takes every bit of what you've given, and the kid doesn't get clattered 'cause at least he's brought something back, isn't the kid still better off? But then the light turns green, and he's history anyway.

I saw another kid on the roadside in Bombay. We were snarled up in heaving, minging traffic under a gigantic bamboo-frame billboard flogging televisions; underneath it the verge was mud, water, indeterminate piles of rubbish and rotting vegetable matter. A child was squatting in all this crud, a tiny, skinny child not more than three years old. He had on a holed, stained yellow jumper, and nothing else; there was no sign of any adult anywhere around him. He sat motionless in the dark, staring into the road. And then the light turned green.

Megan let the players off training; Lottie, Liss, Romps and BB went along to the stadium with her to have a look at it anyway. They waited for the bus by a little drinks stall outside the hotel

England in India, top row, l to r: Helen Plimmer, Charlotte Edwards, Jane Cassar, Clare Connor, Laura MacLeod, Clare Taylor, Sue Metcalfe, Megan Lear, Suzanne Redfern. Front row, l to r: Barbara Daniels, Bev Nicholson, Karen Smithies, Kathryn Leng, Melissa Reynard, Jan Brittin.

Lottie and the Lengster celebrate beating South Africa, while BB demonstrates how long your arms have to be to play cricket these days.

She bats, she bowls… Lottie, a star in the making.

Romps and Lottie help out at the Hyderabad barbecue.

Have rickshaw, will travel.

Connie suggests the third umpire won't be necessary. Good job, seeing there wasn't one.

No doubt about it this time; Liss nails one of the Sri Lankans.

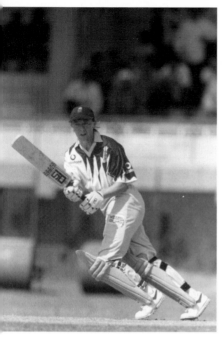

Elegance, craft, control: BB and JB wield the willow.

'That one in the hat':
Jan Brittin, nineteen years an England player.

Smigs: 'Not quite as placid as normal just now, am I?'

Christmas Day: Connie and Romps in the Chidambaram Stadium, Madras.

Liss bowls Kiwi captain Maia Lewis.

Ramel, stumped Cassar, bowled Smithies.

Eden Gardens, Calcutta, 29/12/97.

Australian captain Belinda Clark leads her country to their fourth World Cup.

gate; three blokes were leaning at the counter. Liss looked at the drinks on offer and asked, 'Which one's Juicy Fruit?'

BB nodded towards the three men and said, 'The one on the left,' then laughed wildly. 'Not funny,' she said. 'I'm just hysterical.'

Romps put an arm round Liss' shoulder and led her away, explaining quietly that it got like that when you were thirty-three.

The bus came; the stadium was twenty minutes away and it looked really fine, a cream, three-tiered circle round a pristine field. Despite the earlier downpour, it looked perfectly playable; the wicket was flat and shaved and a bloke was squatting on it with a brush, sweeping away the last grass cuttings, while the outfield was damp but firm. As we headed back for the bus Romps said quietly, 'Game on.'

'And,' BB smiled, holding up a coin, 'I found a lucky rupee.'

Maybe we'd need a bit of luck. Just then Thrasy was talking to Cathryn Fitzpatrick, and she was casually telling him that she bowled at seventy-five miles an hour.

India played New Zealand in Indore for top spot in their group; funnily enough, the first time the Indians had left Delhi. They held the Kiwis to 176 for 9; Debbie Hockley got 44, her combative little opening partner Emily Drumm got 69, but only one of the others got double figures. Then the Indians passed 150 with only four wickets down, and it looked as if they'd cruise it.

The Regency had a five-storey atrium, with rooms on landings all around it; I could hear whoops echoing across it from the English players as they watched the end of the game unfold, but I couldn't find it on my TV. All I could get was an East Zone–North Zone game from the Gymkhana in Hyderabad on ESPN, where they kept cutting away to camels and buffalo wandering about in the road – but I didn't imagine they'd show us the other local wildlife in the toilets and the dressing rooms, and anyway it wasn't the game I wanted to watch.

It was annoying, because the Indians had a fit of the vapours, their bottom order fell to bits, and it finished a thriller. At one point the Indians had two batsmen in one crease; a fielding error allowed one of them to get back to the other end but, panicked under pressure, the wrong one went back. As a result, India got a dot ball instead of a single – which, as it turned out, might have made all the difference. Still, I guess they weren't at leisure to discuss it at the time.

What set the English whooping was Emily Drumm; she was fielding at point, the Indians were getting close to the target but losing wickets all over the shop, and the batter glanced one to backward square. They set off for the single – and as the ball came back to the batter's end it hit the incoming runner's bat, shied off, and they took a second run. It's one of cricket's eighteen billion points of etiquette whether you do that or not, but the batter responsible got run out anyway. So then Drumm legged it from point to get right in her face about it as she was leaving the field. 'I wouldn't want to say what she said,' said Connie, 'but we had a good guess.'

India got to 176 for 9 – then, with the first ball of the final over, New Zealand's Katrina Withers bowled out their last bat to tie the game. The two teams finished their group level on points; New Zealand came top by virtue of a better run rate across their games. Assuming Ireland saw off Pakistan tomorrow, they'd play the Kiwis in the last quarter-final in Bombay; India got South Africa in Patna. As for us, if we beat Australia we got Holland, and if we lost we got Sri Lanka. Seeing we'd surely beat either of those, the honest truth was that losing would be better – because losing meant a semi-final in Madras, which would be nice and warm, and sounded thoroughly pleasant all round. Winning, on the other hand, meant a semi-final in Guwahati, where no one wanted to go in case you got shot or blown up.

Megan Lear, however, was categorically not the type of person who'd throw a game. In the staff room of the school she taught at in Hemel Hempstead, she'd told me before the tournament, 'I'd never play to lose a match for a better draw in the next round, never ever. It's a dangerous game – you want the winning habit every time.'

They had the team meeting at six, then H came to ask if I wanted to go for a beer. She'd been left out again, and was confronting her disappointment with stoic restraint. Bev Nicholson was out too (she was going down with a 'flu bug anyway) and Connie was back in for Laura MacLeod. MacLeod hadn't done badly against the Irish – she'd bowled five overs, gone for sixteen runs and got a wicket – but Fresh had done better. None of the three left out, of course, could possibly be happy – but H looked sorely wounded.

It would have to be masked; we had a birthday party to go to. It was in the basement, in a banquet-cum-conference room called, appropriately enough, Celebrations. Selena brought out the Christmas tree; the players gathered round it to sing carols, sporting Vodafone logos so Craig could get group pictures to wire home for the papers. Carols were sung, lustily, with local variations: 'On the first day in India, my bowels said to me . . .'

Megan sat to one side, watching them enjoy themselves; I asked if she ever felt she had any time for herself out here, away from the game or the players. She said, 'No. But I love cricket with a passion, so I'm thinking about it all the time. I wake up and think about it at three in the morning. It's hard to watch sometimes, because it's always better to play. But I'm all right, I've got mates here. If I need a chat, I can go for a stroll with Pete. He's my mate.'

She slapped Moralee on the shoulder; he looked up grinning and said, 'Sorry? Miles away.'

'I said you're my mate. I can talk to you.'

'Yeah. And we're good on the phone too.'

'When we're back home it'll be two or three times a week, talking it all over. Because you love it so much. Still, look – at the end of the day, it's a game of cricket. My sister-in-law's fighting cancer, and she's my best mate of all. So if we win or lose here, what's that compared to cancer? If we lose it'll feel awful, it'll feel like the end of the world – but it won't be. It'll be a game of cricket.'

She reminded me of Bobby Robson – fiercely committed, fiercely protective of her players, increasingly stressed out, but still always as polite to the press as she was nervous of them – and with it all, thoroughly decent. Knowing how H was disappointed, she was plainly concerned about her; she noted how she stood a shade apart from the group as Craig did his pictures, smiling faintly, sad in her eyes, the smile a bit forced. 'It's not just the selection,' said Megan. 'It's because she's been doing things for other players, getting ready for tonight. Because she's just so nice.'

H left the room to get another beer by herself at the bar; Joce and Fizz went to talk with her. Not playing Australia must have hurt something rotten – and personally, I reckon maybe if she'd played, she might have stuck in against them too. For pure technique, arguably she was the best we had. But who knows? Cricket's a cruel, entirely merciless game; there are few places in sport more lonely and exposed than the crease when you've taken guard against a quick. So maybe she'd have stuck in, maybe not – but it didn't matter because at the top of the order, the way they were thinking at the minute, four into three didn't go.

The food was meant to come at seven-fifteen; at eight-fifteen there wasn't any sign of it. Five tureens of steaming water sat over burning candles on a table along one end of the room; I went to have a futile poke about the table, and found the weirdest bug I've ever seen crawling round among the cutlery. It was a kind of hairy scorpion with fern-like antennae, and it bounced like a grasshopper. So we had an interesting insect, but no waiters, and no food.

JB got up, banged a tureen with a big metal serving spoon, then went behind the table to look into an apparently empty back room. Finally she found someone – and you could see her jaw dropping in disbelief as the news sank in. It seemed the hotel staff and management had been in dispute since three-thirty that afternoon – so there was no food, no room service, nothing. Skip put her head in her hands. I think she was laughing, but I couldn't swear to it.

JB asked, 'Can anybody cook?'

BB said, 'Can't cook, won't cook.'

Lottie shrugged and said, 'Let's eat the cake.'

JB got on the house phone to reception. She told them, 'It's eight-fifteen, we're tired, we're hungry, and there isn't any food. Can you sort something out please? What? Fish and chips?' She held the receiver away from her face and stared at it. Apparently they'd hung up on her.

By now Peter Moralee was in the back room, chasing people in and out saying fierce things like, 'Get on with it,' all this attended by an approving chorus of, 'Pete is *scary*.' Then, mysteriously, pots of curry started appearing. This was either the fastest resolution of an industrial dispute in history, or it was just what happens when a powerfully built bloke from Kent starts charging about in your kitchen.

Thrasy shook his head. After filing from Pune, he'd arrived by taxi at the Centaur in Bombay at quarter to one that morning, knackered, stinking of road fumes, with at best three hours' sleep to look forward to before we flew on to Nagpur. Because there weren't enough rooms, he was sharing with Craig – so Craig was in the room already with the key. Thrasy got to the room with a porter toting his luggage, and the porter said, 'I must knock.'

Not wanting to wake Craig up, Thrasy told him, 'No, no – just open the door.'

'No, no. We must knock.'

'No, it's OK. Just open the door.'

Pause. Then the porter said, 'We must ring.'

'Look,' said Thrasy, 'there's someone asleep in there. Just let me in, OK?'

'We have a problem,' the porter told him. 'There isn't another key.'

'Don't be ridiculous. Of course you have another key.'

Another pause. Then the porter said, 'Give me five minutes. I will go to housekeeping.'

Thrasy thought, five Indian minutes – how long is that? So he stood in the corridor and confronted his choices: either his head exploded, or he gave up and knocked on the door.

And it's all the business like this, one day after another, one hour after another, that wears you down until you want to wring someone's neck. They say, Be patient – but how much patience can a group of people have? The bus doesn't come, or the bus comes but it's too small, or the bus comes and it's big enough but it takes you to the wrong place. The phones don't work, your room bills are all wrong, you order pasta and they haven't got any, or they have but they give you something else, or they've gone on strike so they don't give you anything at all. Meanwhile your belly's falling out of your backside, you're getting up in the small hours every other day, you're flying here, you're getting the bus back to there on a potholed road seething with gesticulating maniacs who all think they're Ayrton Senna – and in amongst all this you're supposed to play cricket as well?

The players drank pop, ate curry, went to bed. Among those of us who remained, a hotel manager scurried about in a fawning lather of desperate apologies. He brought large Indian brandies on the house, which were hugely welcome, but he was in paroxysms of embarrassment because the brandy wasn't in the right sort of glass. We said it was fine, everything was fine, no problem; he could have brought it in a saucepan for all I cared. Joce told him, 'Top banana.'

Fizz looked at her well-filled glass and said, 'I can't drink all this.' She took a sip; it tasted like black treacle. 'Ooh,' she said, 'maybe I can.'

Joce professed herself on the brink of hysteria. 'Ah well,' she said, 'you know why this room's called Celebrations, don't you? It's 'cause we've still managed to get the team fed and off to bed by nine o'clock.'

Peter Moralee, meanwhile, had gone to see about the players' laundry – of which, like the food earlier on, there wasn't any sign. Shirley thought from the look on his face that maybe she'd better go after him; she said, 'We want the laundry back, sure. But we don't want any blood on it.'

Joce left her chair, went to the middle of the room, and did an exceptionally fine impression of a hairy scorpion with fern-like antennae leaping like a grasshopper. Someone asked, 'How long's this book going to be anyway, Pete?'

I said, 'Theoretically, two hundred pages. But I've got twice that much already and we're only half-way through. And who'll buy a book about women's cricket that's eight hundred pages long?'

'They'll buy it if the laundry doesn't come back. 'Cause then you can have pictures in it of them playing in their under-wear.'

Like the Centaur in Bombay, the Regency didn't have enough rooms; I shared with Moralee again, and he put up with it with good humour. His last thought before going to bed was, 'Talent for talent, England can match Australia. But those people, they play serious cricket every weekend. You look at them, and you can see it in their eyes.'

The morning dawned cool, with a gusty breeze; there'd been no rain and the sky was clearing to blue, promising warmth. The bus ride was quiet; we got to the Vidarbha Cricket Association Stadium at eight, and went in to the sound on the boom box of the song that was fast becoming England's theme tune – Chumbawumba. I get knocked down, but I get up again, you're never going to keep me down . . .

The wicket was being rolled. It was flat and brown, with a hint of moisture that'd dry out fast; the outfield was dewy, but smooth and firm. Romper stood at the crease getting her hair up in her lucky ponytail. She said, 'I've been doing a bit of the old visualisation. I'm coming in from this end, it's the inswinger, and it gets that what's her face, Petula Clark, plumb lbw. And as she's on her way I'll say to her, After you.'

From Bombay airport onwards, there'd been a palpable tension between the two sides. With me or Thrasy, the Australian management were more than friendly, but the players weren't talking to each other. The crackling atmosphere had ratcheted up a notch tighter during the surreal chaos of the birthday party, when Belinda Clark came looking for Thrasy to do an interview for him. Seeing a room full of England players, she said (and fair enough) that they'd go and do it somewhere else; England swore blind (or had convinced themselves) that Clark said she wanted to go somewhere else because England were a bunch of bastards. Thrasy was equally sure he'd not heard her say any such thing. But whether she said it or not (and among the lighter-hearted English, there was a spot of semantic analysis as to whether 'bastard' in Australian might actually be a term of endearment) the fact was that these two sides approached what they were about to do with a higher order of deadly seriousness than anything we'd seen yet.

Clark did maintain that for Australia, this wasn't a grudge game to the same extent as it was for the men. Yes, losing in '93 had rankled, and their game against England had been the worst they'd played in that tournament – but losing to New Zealand rankled more, because they played a series with the Kiwis every year, and the rivalry there was more personally intense. So, yes, today was the biggest game so far – but they'd not played each other for four years and for many of the players now involved, the other team was just names on a piece of paper. As an amateur sport, with less documented history and fewer people interested in that history, the main thing was simply that it was good for them to play each other. Having said all of which – sure, Australia did feel they had a point to prove. England were the world champions, weren't they?

If the game was bigger than anything we'd seen, everything about the stadium was better too. The players' area was screened off on both sides with big sheets of material patterned in red and yellow diamonds; the concrete outside each dressing-room was carpeted, and fifteen wicker chairs were set out for each team. Even better – on the sixth day of my continuing condition – there was a decent clean toilet with a fat roll of loo paper, which certainly beat the minging squatholes I'd had to resort to elsewhere. Mind you, it was the umpires' toilet.

Sister Sledge played on the PA. The teams lined up, and a most dapper and charming local official – oddly, a dead ringer for Dirk Bogarde – made the pre-match announcements. Three women in splendid red and white saris dabbed all the players on the forehead with a dot of red paste, decked the captains with floral garlands, and gave each player an orange rose. Connie tucked hers behind her ear, and Craig was on her for a close-up like a shot. Well, a snapper knows a looker when he sees one, but I can see the image now; the blonde hair swept back, the electric blue shades parked on the top of her head, the flower in her ear, the dot on her forehead – and, of course, the logo on her shirt.

The announcer said, 'I will now hand the field to the teams and the umpires.'

England won the toss; Australia fanned out into the field before the empty stands, and Lottie and JB went out to bat. The PA played eerie, atmospheric Indian music, a haunting, blurred drone of string and wind instruments. Cathryn Fitzpatrick came in off twelve paces; Lottie wasn't wearing a helmet. Brave girl.

Fitzpatrick was a raptor; big beaky nose, fierce wide slash of a mouth. She was medium height, lean and wiry, she weighed eight and a half stone – and she was quicker than any woman I've seen. The first ball crashed into Lottie's legs; she blocked the second, played and missed at the third, the fourth beat her onto the front pad again, the fifth and sixth whistled past outside off. She was beaten all ends up for pace. Fitzpatrick said later, 'The minute I've seen she's played me three seconds late, she's out of my mind. Game over.'

Another thing – the Australians had two slips, a gully, short leg. It was a Test match field for one-day cricket; it was sensationally bold, right in your face, electric with confidence. They jogged the over changes, too; this was hurry-up cricket, noisy, fast, remorseless.

From the other end Bronwyn Calver wasn't as quick, but she was tall, bringing it down from a height, and moving it all about. JB got her bat to three or four of them; one ball, the fielder at gully took it, and perfunctorily whipped it back to hit the stumps. Just a little warning, eh?

The third over, Fitzpatrick beat the bat first ball, second ball, third ball. It was so quick, Lottie was still playing the shot when the keeper was giving the ball to first slip. There was a wide, three more dot balls, and a shout for lbw. JB clipped one off her legs for two to midwicket next over, another wide made it four on the board – then Fitzpatrick came steaming in again.

Second ball, fifth over, Lottie's middle and off stumps went flying; she was out for a duck. She came off shaking, telling BB it was moving all over the place out there – but it wasn't just the movement, it was sheer pace that did her. Craig had been watching her through a walloping great zoom; he shook his head and whistled. He said, 'I knew she was going. She wasn't anywhere near it.'

The Australians were jubilant, running screaming together, punching the air. Fitzpatrick would claim later, 'She was just another wicket to me' – but I'm not too sure I believe that. I reckon they'd heard about the scores this girl had been getting, they wanted her scalp, they sent Fitzpatrick out fired up to get it, and she did. As Lottie's stumps splayed back and she turned to leave, Fitzpatrick told her, 'Bye bye, Charlotte.' Game over indeed.

We were 4 for 1 after five overs. The sixth over was another maiden; when JB tried to cut Calver through the gully, the athleticism of the take to stop her getting a run was astonishing. Then BB (wearing a helmet – and I rather think that was wise) clipped Fitzpatrick through midwicket for two, and cut her to deep backward point for a single. Two overs later, she stroked her for four to backward square leg – and of course she could be dealt with, she wasn't Malcolm Marshall – but for all that, the Australian attack was relentless, their fielding urgent, agile and intense. JB and BB were doing a lot more surviving than batting; Australia were so on top, they were putting a silly point in as well.

After ten overs, we were 22 for 1. It was enthralling cricket; the sun was out, several hundred had come into the ground, and they were humming. Australia put on Charmaine Mason for Fitzpatrick, a fizzing little right arm medium; BB got a single to point, JB got one to cover, and the rest was dots. Calver: five dots and a single. Mason went for two again, then Calver bowled a maiden. Mason's third over, two dots, two singles – then she had JB clean bowled with a very, very good ball moving away off the seam, and we were 30 for 2 after fifteen overs. From 48 balls, all JB had to show for it was 7 runs.

Two overs later, BB smashed Mason for four through backward square. H leapt to her feet yelling, 'We'll have more of that.' She sat back down muttering, 'Bounce her again, she'll give her the full monty.'

We got to the drinks break; Thrasy appeared, looking fraught. He was supposed to be getting reports to Five Live; now he said, 'There's nothing wrong with the phone. Except it's in a locked office, and the man with the key is nowhere to be found.'

Brilliant, isn't it? Australia were brilliant too, but how was he going to tell anyone?

They put on a leg spinner called Olivia Magno. She didn't turn it much, but she had nice flight and control, and England were hypnotised. Magno had a slip, a gully, a silly point, only one fielder out on the boundary, and we couldn't do anything about it; her first over was a maiden. Mason bowled a maiden too – then Magno came back and BB fell for it, pulling a catch straight to the deep fielder at backward square. We were 39 for 3. BB had batted bravely to get 23 off 46 balls – so could anyone else get a handle on this?

Magno bowled nine overs. Five of them were maidens, she gave away only 10 runs, and after BB went she had Sue Metcalfe caught and bowled for 14, Karen Smithies clean bowled for 2, and Kathryn Leng lbw for a duck, playing a horrible shot all round a straight ball. Along the way Jane Cassar was run out, called for a daft single by Sue Metcalfe that wasn't ever there. We were 59 for 7 in the thirty-second over, and this was turning into a rout.

Later the Lengster told me, 'I'm disappointed with myself. Very. No discipline. The way I was out, it was a terrible shot. It was straight, I should have played it straight, and I've gone and pulled across it. No brains.'

By the pavilion the Australian manager Chris Matthews, a former player herself, said laconically, 'It's gone marginally better than we expected. We wouldn't expect to get an England side in a position like this. But,' she shrugged, 'we've played bloody good cricket.'

While the wickets tumbled, Liss left the players' area, and went off to sit quietly by herself. Thrasy found her in a dark empty room in the bowels of the pavilion, watching the game through a metal window grille as if she were distancing herself from it – and from the nervy jitters of the other English players too. She said quietly, 'It's different, isn't it?'

She went out to bat; when Leng fell, Clare Connor joined her. They were facing Magno and an off spinner called Avril Fahey, and together they knuckled down and stuck in. Magno was replaced by Karen Rolton, bowling left arm medium; after ten overs, Liss and Connie were still there. They weren't setting the world on fire – their partnership was worth 15 runs; Connie faced 26 balls, and all she scored was one single – but at least they stayed out there.

So the Australians put Fitzpatrick back on. Connie was facing; the first ball screamed down straight, and Connie looked as if she was seeing a freight train bear down. She jumped out of the way, intimidated right out of it; she left her bat dangling in front of the stumps, and they splayed all over.

When she came off, she was refreshingly honest. She said, 'I was sticking at it. We were going to try and launch something later – as best we could, anyway – but I was beginning to feel confident. And I actually prefer quick bowling to slow – but my head wasn't in the right place. She's come on, and I've bottled it. I've done the hard work playing myself in – then I didn't have the temperament or the discipline at that moment to have a look at her, and I've jumped out of the way. It's all up top, isn't it?'

She shook her head, plainly hurt and annoyed. She said, 'Lottie plays county boys' cricket; I've faced better, quicker bowlers than that, we all have. But it's the first time we've faced bowling like that out here – and they're gobby, they're annoying, they've got shrill voices, they stare you out. So,' she said sternly, 'we've got to learn from it. Which I can.'

I went to sit by the boundary, and watched Liss square up to Fitzpatrick; she didn't look intimidated at all. BB came over and said with a smile, 'We like giving you chapters for your book, don't we?'

I asked her what had happened here. She said, 'What you're seeing is that all the games we've had so far aren't adequate preparation to face a side like this. At least it's good to play them today, because next time we'll know what they're about – so I don't want any panic or gnashing of teeth to set in. We can score runs against them – today's just a shock to the system. And it's fair to say that after the last ten days, I'm amazed we're still standing up. But it'll be a different story next time, because it's not her pace *per se*, it's just facing it for the first time – and if you just put the bat on the ball, with the fields they're set-ting, there's runs to be had. Next time, we'll know what to do.'

This time, however, we'd been well and truly rolled over.

She smiled. 'They'll say that. But you're not going to get me to say it.'

Fitzpatrick bowled the final over. Liss cut her for two to cover, then swung the bat to pull four through midwicket. Then she tried to crash it again, and holed out to mid-off. Like BB, she'd scored 23; Thrasy said later, of the moment when he'd found her preparing herself alone, 'It was very clear she understood what she was up against. Then she went out and played the shot of the day – a pull shot for four in front of square off Fitzpatrick that went like an absolute bullet. It took guts, that. But from the first few balls when she was out there, I thought she'd do well.'

But overall, we'd been trashed; with two balls of the innings remaining, we were 95 all out. Not so much of the immense batting today then.

England's defence of the indefensible began pretty well. In front of a crowd grown to maybe 3,000 by now, Romper beat Clark outside off a couple of times, and Skip bowled a maiden. Third over, Clark took a quick single to cover – then her partner Joanne Broadbent edged Romps to Cassar down the leg side. Romps accelerated down the wicket as if someone had set her feet on fire, both arms punching the air; Australia were 3 for 1, and it was noticeable that England's fielding was up a gear, tighter and more aggressive than in any previous game. In the next over Clark cut Skip to point, and Connie got a direct hit on the stumps side-on from twenty yards. Seven overs later she got another one, from more like thirty yards that time – which is a pretty good way to respond when you're annoyed with yourself.

Still, Belinda Clark looked as if she'd just been sizing it up; in the sixth over she nicked Skip deftly for four past Lottie at slip, clobbered four more through midwicket, then slashed two through point to get ten off the over. England tightened up; the next seven overs yielded only eleven runs. But then, Australia hardly needed to swing the bat here, did they?

In the fourteenth over, Skip got some tap again – she went for nine, and four of those came from two misfields by the Lengster. Her head went down; you could see her kicking the grass, peeved and morose. She'd gone, as one of the support staff put it, into 'the fat lip scenario'.

Michelle Goszko was batting with Clark; H watched her carefully then said, 'It's the biomechanics thing. As the front foot goes forward your hands go back, so when you make the shot they're coming through quicker, with more power. Hockley bats the same, and she really drives it.' Biomechanics, of course, was John Harmer's business. As for Clark, H said simply, 'I reckon this is the best batsman in the world at the moment. She moves her feet so well. She seems to have oodles of time to play.'

Drinks came and went; Australia were 55 for 1. Skip put the Lengster on; her first over went for just a single, with a shout as it squirted in from leg onto Clark's pads. Liss came in for the other end – and Clark spooned her to JB at cover. 59 for 2 – and I thought it was a slower ball, I thought Liss had tricked her. Liss said, 'You can put that if you like. But I didn't. She just misjudged it.' It was a big wicket either way.

Karen Rolton came in. Leng's second over went for four; her next over after that was a disaster. She went for three first ball, an edge looping away to vacant fine leg; then she got taken for a single, two, two, two, and another single. There were some rank long hops in there; it was sorry stuff, she argued with the captain about her field placings, and the captain took her off.

H said grimly, 'To beat Australia we'd have to be firing in all departments. And we haven't fired in any today.'

In the twenty-seventh over, Goszko thrashed Smithies for four through midwicket to tie the scores, drove a single to the covers, and that was it. The game was over not long after two-thirty; Australia won by eight wickets.

A big arc of kids in tracksuits fanned out onto the pitch round a table laden with presents; Nagpur plainly meant to be more than generous with its guests. I wandered round trying to confirm whether Sri Lanka or Holland had finished third in the other group, since that was who we'd be playing in the quarter-finals – but if, twenty-four hours after that group had finished, the local executive committee member of the WCAI couldn't say who we were playing next, who could? A bloke in a turban and a dishdash, meanwhile, had got hold of the microphone, and looked set fair to settle in with it for the afternoon. The crowd were merrily boisterous in response to every statement, every gift; they had, after all, been treated to an exhibition. England struggled not to look glum.

There were scarves, garlands, photographers, team shots, and if the organisers could have given presents to everyone in the crowd I think they would have. Karen Smithies looked about at all the applause and good cheer; she said firmly, 'We didn't apply ourselves today, and we've got to learn from it. We knew it'd be very, very different from the last three games, and that step up in class was difficult. It needed someone to be watchful, and get used to the pace of the ball, which no one really did. Still, I'm pleased we've met them in the group. I think we can counter them.'

I found John Harmer coming out of the Australian dressing room. He said, 'I thought we played very well. We bowled tight, and we fielded with real endeavour and enthusiasm. I think a bit of early pace and the pressure fielding worried them, and we didn't allow any partnership to develop. I did think it would be closer, so I'm surprised – but we played with a lot of purpose today. And then, Fitz is quick. It shocks you first up, if you haven't seen it. So she set it up, then the spinners took over. Magno's very accurate, extremely confident, very brisk.'

I asked what he was doing setting Test match fields, and he smiled. He said, 'It speaks confidence, and it gives it. We like to play that way, to attack from the off – and it makes it an exciting game to play. It's good to look at, isn't it?'

It certainly was – unlike the street outside. It was a heaving chaos of bikes and scooters and chubby Humbers; Thrasy and I needed a rickshaw back to the hotel so we could get a phone line and file but, it transpired, there was a rickshaw strike. We stared in vexation at the Golden Pass V.V.I.P. Car Park (*sic*). It was a patch of rutted, stony dirt half covered with a giant puddle.

We waited for England's bus. The Lengster came out of the stadium and muttered at me as she passed, 'Bad day at the office.'

Want to talk about it?

'Definitely not.'

England boarded the bus, frowning, through a circle of policemen fending off a throng of people spilling across the scooter-jammed road. The bus was full of mosquitoes.

Megan said about Australia, 'Not unexpected, in my view. But now my team have seen them, they know what they've got to do.'

When we got back to the hotel, the captain and vice-captain came immediately to Peter Moralee to talk it over. Moralee said of Kathryn Leng, 'She had a monk on from the moment she stepped on the field. I don't mind one misfield, but two in a row, and the body language . . .'

He shook his head, and went off to a support staff meeting. Back in Hyderabad, one of those support staff had said to me of Leng, 'She's a very talented young lady, and talented young ladies are allowed to be stroppy now and then. But she's grown up a lot in the last couple of years. I'm not concerned about her.' They would, however, be concerned what to do about her now.

Down in the foyer, I bumped into Clare Taylor. She said, 'We've played it all wrong. We shouldn't have batted first, for a start. A track like that's going to dry out for the afternoon, and we should have put them in on it. But the fact is, we've been beaten by a better side, and you've got to hold your hands up. And that Fitzpatrick, she's quick, no doubt about it.' She laughed and said, 'I'll tell you, my fucking knees were knocking together when I had to go out there. That's why I kept running twos. I didn't want to face any of that.'

Then she said, 'People are saying we can beat them when we get to the final, and maybe we can – but we've got to beat the Kiwis first, and they're no slouches either.'

11

The Opportunity of a Lifetime

England and Australia were due to fly back to Delhi together that evening. England, however, didn't even want to sit with Australia, never mind fly anywhere with them. We had a while until the plane left, and Fitzpatrick told Moralee they had to go to the bar together ('We go to the bar after every game') – but when they went there, the two squads sat apart.

Jane Cassar did speak at some point with Michelle Goszko – the two had played together at Bankstown in Sydney – and Megan spoke with Fitzpatrick. Generally, however, people kept a pretty frosty distance. At one point Connie went into the bar with Cassar and the Lengster behind her, turned in the doorway, and came straight back out again. She said, 'I'm not going in there. Australia are in there.'

It was pretty childish. From an ordinarily sociable and intelligent young woman, I'd take it as an indicator of how badly England were thrown – and if you did talk to the Aussies, you got looked at as if you were some kind of traitor. When Thrasy was speaking to Fitzpatrick in the foyer, a group of England players who saw them went quickly into a huddle. Fitzpatrick just laughed. 'I think they want a team meeting.'

Huffy tempers were further inflamed when assorted players' bills came out wrong. Sue Metcalfe scrumpled up a drinks tab and threw it back across the counter. 'I've paid it, mate. And I'm not paying it again.'

At the bar, assorted horrible Scandinavian industrialists were being rude about India; the remarks made by one of them were nakedly racist. I looked on disgusted, thinking, How dare you? It's an extraordinary place, fascinating, wonderful . . . at which point Fresher came to tell us the flight was delayed.

'Right,' said one of the English grimly, 'I'll have three more pints of lemonade then.'

Megan sat alone, looking weary; she was beginning to go down with something. She said, 'I've spoken to their coach today, and he's a nice guy. I take back anything I've said earlier. And he's told me some days they're focused, some days they aren't. Today they were, and we were outclassed. Fair enough. We'll learn from it. We have to. Like their fielding – it's everything I want us to do. We've come on miles – but the Australians play competitive cricket all the time, and I hope some of ours learn a lesson. You have to play with passion and belief, and there's a few of ours who didn't today. Or didn't look like it, anyway. People who smile when you're losing?' She shook her head. 'I can't deal with it.'

Then she told me about the Second Test against Australia at the Adelaide Oval, at the back end of 1984. She was opening; first innings England were poor, and got all out for 91. Australia got 262; England did better in their second innings, and got 296. It came to the last day, all Australia needed was 125, and they had six hours to get it.

Megan said, 'We got them 1 for 1, 4 for 2, 4 for 3, 4 for 4, 6 for 5 – sort of sticks in your memory, that. Chaos. Then they got away a bit. So it ended with them needing five runs, us need-ing one wicket, and we got it. It was Chris Matthews, their manager here now, caught behind. It was a good ball but it was outside off, she didn't need to play it. But she did, and we got it. My best memory ever. I can remember JB jumping up and down . . .'

JB went by the table now; she had a little side glance and a smile, wondering what we were talking about. She was a sys-tems manager at British Airways, working in a great hive of office blocks out by Heathrow – and, thirteen years after Adelaide, she also had 1,485 Test runs from twenty-four matches, on an average of 42.42.

Megan sighed, remembering, 'It was Christmas Eve. *Big* cel-ebration.' But there were no English celebrations tonight. She said, 'For a year and a half, I've based all our preparation on climbing Mount Everest. The graph goes up, through winter training, and the first peak was South Africa in the summer. Bit of a scamper there, you make it, you keep going – then this one today was a sharp one. OK, we failed – but we haven't stopped climbing the mountain, have we? We'll just take a different route. And,' she shrugged, 'we haven't got to go to Guwahati, have we?'

Later I found her at the bar, sat alone and looking miserable. She said, 'I think I've got a problem with the team.'

She'd tried to sit with a few of them, and it had instantly become a conversation about the game. People were asking why we didn't bowl first, they got into it, and Romper took umbrage at something Megan said – as in, What are you saying? That I can't take wickets like Fitzpatrick can? Then it got made pretty plain that Megan wasn't welcome, and the players were in a tizz with her, and Romper was all wrathful, and Megan looked heartbroken. Oh, but it's shite losing, isn't it?

On another day Clare Taylor would say of her coach, 'Look, she gets stressed, OK. She gets tense and uptight. But it's because she loves the game, and we all know her. She's one of us, isn't she?'

Meanwhile Joce and Fizz (the Dynamic Duo) were at the airport five minutes down the road. They'd gone there on the bus to check in all the baggage while we waited for the plane to turn up – big kitbags, heavy coffins, fifty items in all, a lot of them twenty-five kilos apiece. They unloaded the bus, loaded everything onto a relay of wonky trolleys, and pushed it to the security scanners. Then they offloaded it all again, shovelled it through the X-ray, reloaded the trolleys, and pushed them on to the check-in desk. It took over an hour. During this process, the contribution of our local Nagpur helper (I don't know what his name was, but they called him Bubba Rock) was to carry four handbags, and otherwise to poke them repeatedly in the upper arm saying, 'Hurry up. Hurry up.'

Then he went off and stood with a group of thirty or so blokes, and watched. None of them raised a finger to help. When they finished, these blokes all came over and started asking for autographs.

'So we're sitting there knackered,' said Fizz, 'and we're thinking, at least all we've got to do now is wait for the others to arrive. But you don't arrive. And then we find there's no boarding pass for Craig. And they don't tell us the plane's arrived until they tell us it's leaving, and you're still not there.'

The plane was sitting on the airstrip from soon after nine. Bubba Rock phoned the hotel, who said the teams were on their way; how they thought we were on our way I don't know, because they omitted to tell us to get on our way. None the less the plane was boarding, and its departure was announced, until at nine-forty-five someone started getting lippy with Joce and Fizz, saying they were going to offload all our baggage.

At this point Mr Pillay popped up, maintaining his remarkable, Dr Who-like ability to materialise wherever we went all over India. 'Where,' he inquired, 'are the teams?' So now he phoned the hotel.

Meanwhile, Selena was in an office somewhere having a stand-up communication gap with someone because Craig had a ticket, it was paid for and confirmed – but, no, he couldn't get on the plane. In India, having a plane ticket that's paid for and confirmed did not, it would seem, necessarily mean all that much.

Back in the hotel bar, at about ten o'clock the message got through – and suddenly it was, Go! Go! Go! The two teams streaked to the airport, grabbed boarding passes as we spilled off the bus, and tumbled through the security checks towards the departure gate. In the entrance hall, Craig found he was getting left behind. He threw a major wobbly featuring extensive use of the f-word in the general direction of the luckless and undeserving Selena – who at some point in this nightmare had ended up crawling round the hold of an Indian Airlines jet trying bravely (but failing) to retrieve Craig's luggage. And I doubt, when she started out in public relations, she ever imagined she'd end up doing that on a dark night in Nagpur.

Craig was left behind with nothing but the clothes he stood up in, a camera, and an imprint of Selena's credit card. To give him his due, when he caught up with us, he put in a major, full-on grovel to mend his fences there – but meantime, the possibility was arising that the rest of us might not be leaving either. We sprinted through the gate, dived onto a bus, zipped five seconds across the Tarmac to the foot of the airplane steps – and they wouldn't let us on. The pilot had the hump, England and Australia had kept him waiting all this time – and now he wasn't going to let us on the plane.

We stood staring at the steps in disbelief. Peter Moralee was grinning in an alarming manner, and being held back by assorted women who feared he might lead a hostile boarding party. But what the hell were we to do?

By very good fortune – and, no doubt, good planning on

their part – the Australian team doctor was Indian by birth. He led a diplomatic mission to the cockpit – and finally we scrambled on, to be greeted by the frowning faces of many disgruntled businessmen. 'Oh,' sighed Joce, collapsing into her seat, 'but we've had fun tonight, haven't we?'

Selena hadn't. By the time she got on the plane, she was in tears.

At 12.15 in the morning of Friday 19 December, England stood by their trolleys in the baggage reclaim of Delhi's domestic terminal. Romps read a fax she'd got in Nagpur: 'Emley beat Lincoln on pens in the McAlpine replay. They now meet West Ham at Upton Park. First snow yesterday, didn't last long. Best wishes for the rest of the tour. Maintain line and length and don't drink the water. Father (& Mother).'

She smiled, tickled. She said she'd send him one back and sign it, Daughter.

Liss sighed, and stared about her. She said, 'That airline meal hasn't sat down very well.'

Metcalfe told her, 'I just spit half of mine.'

'Thanks for that, Sue. I think I'll put ten rupees in that cancer charity box. As an investment for the future.'

Metcalfe watched the empty carousel going round. 'It's like a very disappointing Generation Game, isn't it?'

Joce and Fizz gaped happily at the bizarre spectacle of a luggage trolley revolving in an ornate gold and glass case. 'It's like, Yes we have trolleys. Shiny new ones. Just not in the real world beyond the display case, unfortunately.'

The baggage came – Australia had extremely natty red Coca Cola coffins – and the two teams lugged it out wearily to their respective buses. How nice, I thought, to niff once more that fragrant Delhi air. We got everything on board; Fizz called out, 'Anyone want to look out the back and see if we've left anything behind?'

Joce said, 'That'd just top our evening, wouldn't it?' She

laughed, with a distinct edge of hysteria – as, at one in the morning, the bus pulled away. She said, 'Go on, mate. Toe it.'

No chance of that – Delhi, once more, was shrouded in a dense, clammy, grey-white fog. It took seventy minutes to get to the Mela Plaza. We lurched into the foyer and Selena said, 'Everyone looks in shock.'

'Well,' Shirley told her, 'we've been up twenty hours, haven't we?' And we'd got tonked by Australia in the middle of it too.

'Room service.'

'Morning. Could you bring me up some coffee, please.'

'Yes, sir. What room number?'

'Four-oh-eight. Thanks.'

'You're welcome.'

I put the phone down; a millisecond later it rang, and I picked it up. 'Sir, this is room service. Why don't you come downstairs and have your breakfast?'

I stared at the phone. I said, 'Because I'd like to have some coffee in my room.'

'But you can have some coffee downstairs with your breakfast.'

In the past fortnight I'd watched seven games of cricket, taken two seven-hour train journeys, five plane flights, and one five-hour cab ride that I'd prefer to forget. Three days had started in the middle of the night, three days had finished in the middle of the night, including yesterday – yet now I had the chance for a lie in, room service was telling me to get out of bed.

The worst cricket injury Fizz ever dealt with was a ball on the fingertip that split the nail open like a butterfly's wings. The worst injury generally was an inferior fracture dislocation of the shoulder, with nerve damage that paralysed the arm for three months. It was a skiing accident, the victim was her husband, and it happened in the run-up to their wedding. So, she said, 'You wait months to see if the man you're about to marry has a paralysed left arm for the rest of his life. And he's left-handed.'

More than that, he was an orthopaedic surgeon. They lived in Cardiff; they were going to Australia for a year three days after she got back and, she said, 'He's very tolerant really, 'cause he's packing. But I did that last time too. We bought a house, and I went to the Himalayas for six weeks to do the Skyline Marathon, and left him to move in. Now, our first married Christmas I'm here. That went down like a lead balloon with his family.'

She did it for the experience; she'd been with the team since May, but while Steve Bull and Joce Brooks were paid, all Fizz got was an honorarium of £500 a year. That's how it is in a lot of sports, especially women's sports – a team can always find a young physio who wants it on the CV. She didn't think it was ideal, because a physio on that basis couldn't ever commit long-term – but she did it because she enjoyed it, and she liked the people.

Steve had gone home from Bombay to be with his children for Christmas; Joce and Fizz were now minding their side of the shop on their own. On the injury front, things were good; apart from Leng's ankle and a few tender shoulders, there'd been no real problems. It was attitude she was worried about right now, not fitness. She said, 'What's gone wrong here? And can it be put right in a week? Because New Zealand might not be as good as Australia, but their attitude will be.'

Trying to help put England back on track, she and Joce were in the middle between players and management; they got stuff from both sides, and acted like a filter system. It could be difficult – did you pass things on or didn't you? She said, 'If Joce and I didn't get on as we do, it'd be a lot more stressful. But we're the United Front. The United Front for the Liberation of Sports Scientists and Physios. And we need to be, 'cause imagine doing all this on your own. Besides, cricket – you're sitting there waiting for someone to have their face smashed open. Do I want to do that alone? No thanks.'

I asked how she was in herself and she said, 'I'm fine. I have a very high stress tolerance. Or at least, I can categorise what I should or shouldn't worry about. In India, that tends to help.'

The selectors for the Indian men's team, apparently, had a very low stress tolerance; after their débâcle in Sharjah they axed six players, among them Rahul Dravid. Since Dravid was everywhere on TV at the time telling us excitably, 'More cricket, more Pepsi', I'll bet that went down a bundle at Fizzy Pop HQ.

It was on the front page of every paper. Never mind Geoffrey Boycott (who said, more or less in as many words, that the selectors were barmy) – this was the stuff of leader columns. It was also a relief; ever since the government had fallen, the front pages had been an endlessly tedious parade of politicians delivering high-flown utterances while leaping from one party to another with a positively dizzying promiscuity. It was a fantastic kaleidoscope of factional mischief-making – but then, I read somewhere that the previous election had involved no fewer than 513 political parties. If even remotely accurate, this only confirms my (admittedly cursory) impression of Indian politics as a crazy cockpit of rampant egos shuffling acronyms around, while wretchedness of staggering dimensions went untended outside the window.

All the interesting stuff – bus plunges, forest brigands, the busy naxalites of Bodoland – was relegated to the small print. Only cricket got past politics – and that's India for you.

Our own cricket involved a quarter-final with Sri Lanka in Chandigarh; now Selena was on the phone to find out how many train tickets we had, and it turned out we were going by bus instead. Fine, we could get up a bit later. She was dealing with this because Shirley had gone down with the same 'flu-type thing that had got to Bev and Megan; Selena was twenty-seven but today, she said, she felt more like fifty.

There was another thing – Anuradha Dutt wanted payment for all our extra people. The Indians were hosting squads of seventeen so Joce, Selena, Cath Harris, Pete Moralee, Thrasy and I were all extra. The original deal had been that we'd get billed for travel and accommodation in one lump through the WCA when it was over, but of course it hadn't turned out that way. We'd paid our hotels as we'd gone along; now they wanted money for the plane flights too.

Fair enough – they weren't brimming over with money here – and I was more worried about getting a ticket out of Calcutta after the final, so I could catch my plane back home from Delhi. On the day I'd arrived, Dutt had said they'd sort me one out, but there wasn't any sign of it. Meanwhile, I rang Gulf Air to reconfirm my ticket home.

'Lunchtime, sir. Call at one-thirty, please.'

'It's one-twenty. Why can't we do it now?'

'Please hold.' She put on some tinny electronic music – the Mogadon version of 'Home On The Range'. This was more surreal by the minute. I hung up and went to training.

The weather was dank, grey and cold. The roadside people huddled round tiny, guttering fires. They had on ragged bala-clavas, or scarves wrapped round their heads, or blankets round their shoulders. Ox breath steamed.

We went back to the pitch at the brewery; there weren't any nets. Megan thought they should do some fielding, because there were people in the field who didn't give it the max yesterday – but then she'd told them that at the team meeting so they knew all about it, and she wanted them doing something that they wanted to do as well. Trouble was, what they wanted was to face some fast bowling.

'I'll bowl quick at you,' said Moralee. 'You want quick, I'll give you quick.'

Except there weren't any nets – and anyway it wasn't perti-
nent, Sri Lanka wouldn't have anyone like Fitzpatrick. Megan
was thinking that if they got to the final in Calcutta, fine, she'd
get a bowling machine there, or some local lads to sling down
some quick stuff – but could we think about Sri Lanka now? Sri
Lanka were all tiny little stick people, it'd be spin – but they
wouldn't be mugs.

They warmed up, then a few went jogging round the boundary. Connie, Laura, and the Lengster padded up to bat to
throwdowns, other people wandering off to field what they
hit – and OK, it was better to be here than sat about. But it was
desultory, disorganised stuff.

Romps said, 'It's just getting it out of your system, isn't it?'
She'd done three circuits, a round of presses and stretches. 'At
home we'd have had three or four straight fitness sessions, but
there isn't ever the time, is there? And I just feel like a right
good burn-up, 'cause I've eaten so much shit these last two
weeks. Only that third lap, my throat started burning – I don't
know if it's the pollution, or the curried cauliflower.' She went
off to bowl at Jane Cassar; I wandered about gathering stray
balls behind the people batting, dodging dog turds and scaffold
poles round the perimeter.

The Lengster said, 'I'm going to work on my fitness when
we get home. They could beat every one of us for that. But we
can beat them. That Fitzpatrick, she's quick – but she's all
over the place.'

Lottie was rooming with Romper. I asked her, If you could
have one thing . . .

'A roast dinner. Beef.'

And if you could be one place . . .

'In my room at home asleep. Going to sleep listening to my
music.'

Are you missing home?

'Probably more than I thought. I don't miss it too much. I

miss Mum and Dad. But I don't think about it too much, 'cause I'm enjoying it here. It's better than I thought. I was worried about the food, but I've been living on chip butties, and that's OK. And ten slices of toast and jam for breakfast.'

Romps was lying on her bed writing her diary. She looked up grinning and said, 'Fat knacker.'

On TV, England were playing the West Indies in Sharjah. The West Indians were steaming along, 60 for 0 off 9 overs, but Stuart Williams was rolling about in pain after a return throw hit him in the face as he dived for the crease. Lottie said idly, 'Bad luck, me old china.'

I said, You're enjoying it?

'Well, it helps to score runs. But getting on with everyone's really nice. They just help, they encourage you, they make you feel at home. And Romper the Roomie's brilliant. Roomie of The Year. She's cool. Like a mother. She cleaned me bottle out the other night.'

Romper: 'It's murder trying to wind her after her bottle, mind.'

Lottie said India made her laugh. 'It's so funny. I love the roads.' Then she had a look at Mark Ealham bowling. 'He's nice, isn't he?'

She said, 'All the begging and that could get to you, but you've just got to leave it alone, haven't you? Here, them Vodafone tops they've got are nice. Oi, Selena –' Selena'd just come in to nick a large brandy – 'see what you can do, eh? Go on, Hicky.'

She did an excellent Alec Stewart impersonation. 'I like that one, Crofty. Boooow-ling . . .'

I asked how she felt about the way she'd turned eighteen. She said, 'Oh God, it was weird, wasn't it? I was a bit knack-ered. But I'm not bothered. I don't think it's December at the moment anyway. I think it's about June. Lost the plot with the month, really.'

Of the world record that never was against the Irish she said,

'I didn't have a clue if it was a record. I didn't know how many I'd got anyway. People kept going on about it after the game, but I wasn't bothered.'

Does anything bother you?

She laughed. 'Not much. Yesterday bothered me. I don't like getting beat, especially by them, and they probably think we're shit now. But we'll give a better account of ourselves next time. Be an interesting summer, won't it? But oh, that rent-a-gob at short leg . . .'

What's been the best thing so far?

Romper said, 'Sharing with me, come on.'

Lottie said, 'Yeah. Romps.'

'Don't feel under any pressure to say that, Lottie.'

Lottie said, 'No, everything. Everything just makes me laugh here. It's just India, innit? Like, when they went on strike. That was funny. Or last night, when they wouldn't let us on the plane. You'd cry if you didn't laugh, eh?'

She worked for Hunts County Bats in Huntingdon; with the possible exception of pop music, I doubt she thinks about anything much but cricket. If she was a bloke, she'd have a massive future; she ought to have one anyway. The girl's a star.

Two doors down, JB was writing to a mate who used to play for Australia. She'd been there on three tours, they'd been to England – she couldn't count how many times she'd played them. I asked if there was always that tension between the two teams and she said, 'It was worse when I started. It's got a bit more amicable off the field more recently – but we're never going to be buddies.'

She felt the Australians got an edge from playing regular international competition at a decent standard with New Zealand; England had to go a lot further afield to find anyone to test them. She also suspected they'd got nearer to their men's association sooner than we had – but, she said, 'For all that, they're not untouchable. No team is. They're obviously fitter than we are – but pound for pound, player for player, we've got the ability. They've obviously got a useful strike bowler – her movement early on, it made you wary, and you can get a bit shelled up. Thankfully I wasn't down there too much, it was Lottie and Barbara who got the brunt of it. I did cop a few bruises. But if you can survive, the quicker it comes, the quicker it goes – and once you start getting the bat to her, the bubble could burst, couldn't it? How deep is their belief? 'Cause they haven't been tested too much, have they?'

I asked if it was a useful wake-up call for England; she said it could go either way. 'We could lose all confidence, or it can act as a spur. I think most people, even the young ones, have been around long enough to see the ups and downs, so it should act as a little reminder of what we're here to do. 'Cause there's nothing that grates more than your coach telling you the Aussies have a better product than you have. Anyone that's got pride'll take note, won't they?'

I asked how she was coping otherwise. She said, 'It's easy enough on tour. You're closeted from a lot of the hassle, someone else worries about that. And actually, compared to the past, and considering what they've taken on, they've done very well. It's been remarkably well organised.'

Some might say this was taking forbearance to the point of saintliness. But JB said, 'If you've been here before, you just know things are done differently. This is India. Ultimately, all they want is to be hospitable, and to see some good cricket. So I'm tired, yes, and I feel I haven't quite got my teeth into my own game' – this from a woman who'd just scored 238 runs in five World Cup innings, for an average of 47.6 – 'but India doesn't faze me. It's a bit odd, 'cause I hate dirt and uncleanliness. But I find it a bit of a fantasy, and I like it. And then, only fourteen people have this opportunity. I'm just fortunate to be one of them.'

*

I went down to the foyer to catch sight of Lara being most cannily stumped by Alec Stewart, to a chorus of aggrieved West Indian women in tracksuits wailing, 'Him out!'

'What I tell you,' said their coach in his bomber jacket, shaking his head, ''bout keepin' behin' dat line?'

The TV cut to more tourist shots of Dubai Golf Club. BB had said the other day that it was good to see the men doing well in Sharjah; she'd said, 'I like watching them, and there's a lot we can learn from them. How it's about keeping calm all the way, working through the phases of the game, playing positive but sensible. It's nice to see them doing that – not headless hitting, but planned aggression – and it's interesting to see how they do it.'

Via Selena, the women faxed the men a good luck message for the final. They got back some puerile doggerel about how that was the first women they'd heard from in ages, they'd been away for many moons and their balls were like balloons . . . I'm not sure the women were too impressed.

England beat the West Indies, who should have won, but fell to bits. They bowled so many no balls and wides that they gave England about three extra overs' worth of batting; that's daft. England's women, by contrast, hadn't given away a single extra against Australia, and Jane Cassar said that in the last two games, Romper had bowled as well as she had in a long time – so as defeat receded, you could start to see things in it that were worth hanging onto. As for Sri Lanka, from the way Cassar talked, you got the feeling they were going to find themselves on the wrong end of an exorcism.

Some of the players stayed up late to watch the men win; it was fun at the time, but it didn't seem so wise when the alarm went off at six the next morning. The bus left for Chandigarh at seven-fifty; sitting at the back, Connie discussed the relative merits of the Mel Gibson/Kenneth Branagh Hamlets. Movie star horniness ratings were also mulled over; Connie gave de

Niro a no contest win over Antonio Banderas, the Lengster was a Tom Cruise fan, and Smigs kept her counsel. They offered me Sandra Bullock for the male vote; I suggested Kristin Scott Thomas. Connie said, 'Hmm. More your age really, isn't she?' Ta for that, Con.

Some of the others were less up for conversation. Shirley'd beaten the flu thing by spending twenty-four hours in bed while Selena took up the management baton, but Megan had it bad; she was shiverish and freezing. BB and the Lengster were off colour too, and Leng was further smarting at criticism of her performance against Australia. She and Connie talked that one over quietly at the back, and that was interesting – Connie, though only twenty-one, three years Leng's junior, sounding supportive but firm, advising her on what to do to make it right.

She came from Hove in Sussex; her father was MD of an electronics company and she'd been privately educated, though she resolutely denied that she was posh. Her father played for Preston Nomads up on the Downs; one of her mother's earliest memories of her was as a toddler, dragging a bat twice her size round the boundary pestering people to play with her. She joined the Colts when she was eight or nine; she played at prep school, and eventually for Brighton College 1st XI.

There was a bit of doubt about it when she got to the sixth form, with the boys getting stronger and quicker – but she ended up vice-captain, opening the batting. A couple of the sports masters at other schools weren't happy about it when they went to play them, and some of the lads she played against were, she said, 'Quite rude. It's to be expected, but I got lots of comments. I'd hear it in the slips, or square leg. I suppose it'd just be called sledging, if it was men to men – it never bothered me, anyway.'

She first heard about the women's game when she was about thirteen. She was in a net at Roedean, and a woman with a clipboard told her, 'If you carry on batting like that, young lady, you'll play for England.' The woman was Ruth Prideaux, who coached England to their world title in 1993.

She opened the batting with Lottie for Junior England; she was in the senior side for her bowling. She played for Brighton & Hove Ladies, and for Sussex; neither club nor county were among the country's stronger sides, and that gave her a dilemma. If she went to one of the top women's clubs – the Redoubtables in Surrey, Invicta in Kent – or if she played in the men's game (she'd been approached to go to nets at the Nomads) she'd get a better standard of cricket, and her game might improve faster. On the other hand, 'You want to support your home team and your county.' So she did.

When she got to university, she was presented with different problems. The winter of her first year, she netted with the lads' university side at Old Trafford. Then the summer came, and she wasn't allowed to play for them. The British University Sports Association said there was a women's equivalent set-up, and she should go and play in that. But how, when her own university didn't have a women's team? The captain of the club, the secretary of the club, and the secretary of the university athletics union all wrote letters about it, but they wouldn't budge.

She said, 'I was pretty cheesed off. I could have played in the second XI, maybe in the first a few times – and all my friends said I really ought to do something about it. But I was going to India, I had so much work to do to compensate for missing seven weeks of term – I just never had the time.'

When BB heard about it she said, 'I'm not surprised, but it's not great. If people can hold their own, what's the problem? There may not be hundreds of women who want to play in the men's game – but someone like Connie would easily be too good for a BUSA women's team. And if she's good enough, she should be up for selection – simple as that.'

At university, meanwhile, Connie had other problems. She said, 'They've not been supportive about my cricket at all. My first year, OK, I had seven weeks off – but I still came out with a 2:1. But they didn't offer any help – all they said was, if you want to do it, you sort yourself out.' She went to India, dislocated a finger, went to hospital with dysentery – great tour, eh? She smiled and said, 'At least I got a lot of reading done.'

BB said, 'She was trying to fit in reading *King Lear* between matches, when she was just nineteen – it was a huge task for her, to take her course work on a Test series. Well, I know universities have changed in their nature since I was there – but this is another thing where merging with the ECB might help us. We'd have that much more authority; we'd be able to write to people like Connie's tutors, and maybe it'd make a difference.'

For the World Cup, she had to write a signed letter saying that she knew what she was undertaking; she had to get several essays finished before she left and, she said, 'They haven't helped. There's been no extra notes to cover what I'm missing, and I've got to do it all early. I talked to each tutor on the individual courses, told them what the story was – and one of them, the reaction basically was, I'd be a lot more understanding if it was football, but I hate cricket. It's shocked me, all the way through. A couple have been interested, one wished me good luck – but I'm sure if I was a boy going to play cricket for England it'd be different.'

In the end, it didn't matter. She said, 'You can't do any more than play for your country, can you? I do it because I love it. OK, we get a bit of coverage with the sponsorship now, and that's great; the change in the two years I've been involved has been incredible and I'm very aware of it, I feel very lucky and grateful that I'm coming into it now. But if we still had to pay to do it, I would. And because we've worked so hard for it, this trip right now is the most important thing in all our lives – so if people don't know about that, I'm too busy to get angry about it. We're doing this to defend the World Cup, and it's got to be the highest pressure cricket any cricketer, male or female, could get – a World Cup in India. It's the opportunity of a lifetime.'

I'm not alone in thinking that Clare Connor has the potential to be a future captain of England. Her advice to Leng, in a nutshell, was that if she said she was trying her best, she wasn't copping off in a strop, fine – but it had to look like it.

The two players were close. Leng told me later that when her mother had died, it had been Connor who had known all the right things to say. Leng said, 'It's funny. She's three years younger than me, but she's twenty years wiser.'

From Delhi to Chandigarh was 160 miles; the bus journey took over six hours. It was another video arcade experience, veering past the rolled and rusting carcasses of trucks littering the roadside; you had the choice of sitting up front where you could see all the things you were about to crash into, or sitting at the back having your internal organs rearranged by the potholes. Outside, it was freezing; pitstops were huddled, teeth-chattering affairs.

Chandigarh is 'the city beautiful', so the roundabouts were well tended. It was designed in the fifties by Le Corbusier; imagine Milton Keynes with rising damp and a litter problem. We were staying at the Hotel Piccadily (*sic*); we were greeted with more garlands, more dobs on the forehead, and a bloke with a machine gun. Not for the first time, six single rooms for the extra members of the party (booked and confirmed by Selena the day before) weren't available, so the assistant coach of the England cricket team found himself sharing with a rodent again. We were also sharing our landing with two blokes sat by the lift sporting turbans and rifles.

Moralee went to check out the Mohali Stadium, and came back reporting it the best we'd seen yet. 'First class facilities,' he said. 'Reminds me of Newlands in Cape Town. It's so good, it might be a bit of a culture shock.'

The people at the stadium told him Sri Lanka weren't much good, 'So we ought to roll them over. But then, Coventry probably thought Woking weren't much good, and look what happened to them.'

He went to the team meeting; when it was over, Skip said Bev was twelfth man, and H was back in for Fresh. It was hard on Fresh but they were going for an extra bat, they wanted another look at Laura MacLeod, and H was a better fielder. As for Leng, she was out. Smithies said, 'I'm not happy with her performance on Thursday. Hopefully, it'll give her a kick up the arse.' Then she ran upstairs with a plate of pasta to do an interview with the World Service.

I found Sue Metcalfe at the bar. Of Leng's omission she said, 'She didn't bowl as well as she could have done. We've already got a leg spinner in Lottie who's doing equally as well. And we're . . . well, I can't comment further because it wouldn't be fair to Lengy. It's very difficult to get the balance between being honest with somebody, and putting across criticism in a constructive manner. You have to respect people's feelings, but nobody's daft – and it's a really hard thing to tell someone she's not playing in the quarter-final of the World Cup. She'll be absolutely gutted.'

I said, it's because she had a 'mare against Australia.

'We had a 'mare all round. We're all to blame, not one player.'

So why her?

'She didn't bowl well. She didn't field well. She didn't bat well. Look, I'll hold my hand up – I fuckin' grafted, I got into double figures, then I got out to a poor shot. But when I fielded I worked my fuckin' guts out. Because you can't do anything about what's gone, and you have to do every next part of the game as best you can. And unfortunately it was felt . . . well, if you've got someone kicking the grass, looking at their feet – that can affect people.'

So out she went – and it's a hard, hard game. Metcalfe's first tour was in Australia, when she was nineteen years old. A quick came in, someone quicker than she'd ever faced, and gave her a bouncer. She hit the deck. Two balls later, another bouncer – so she hooked it for four. The bowler snarled at her, 'You fuckin' lucky Pommie bitch.' Metcalfe just laughed – what was that? No one had ever talked to her on a cricket pitch like that.

When she was young, Metcalfe was a bowler – so the next innings she was sending it down at this same woman, and she got driven for four. The Aussie told her, 'That's how you enjoy hitting a fuckin' four, girl.'

A couple of overs later, Metcalfe took out her middle stump. 'And that,' she told her, 'is how you enjoy a walk back to the fuckin' pavilion.'

Moralee on sledging: 'It's you against the ball, isn't it? It's not you against the chirp.'

BB said the Australians hadn't gone in for it much at Nagpur. 'It was just that Magno at short leg. Looks like Morticia out of the Addams family, sounds like a canary in a cage, wittering away.' She put on a nasal, whiny Australian accent – *c'mon Aussies, c'mon Aussie girls* – and shuddered. 'As for that Fitzpatrick, she's mad. She's bounced me with one, it's gone off my gloves, I thought it was hitting my head – and she's down on the ground getting it, staring at me like she's absolutely mad. I'm shaking like a leaf, trying to look cool – and I'm thinking, Well, at least I'm *normal*.'

We were talking in the restaurant, Thrasy, BB, me, and Craig (who'd caught us up and duly grovelled). There was a band tuning up on a little dais, drums, electric keyboard, two guitars; they all looked about fourteen. Skip came in; she'd been trying to get a line to the BBC that didn't sound like snap, crackle and pop for two hours. Now she finally got one on the hotel portable – and the band started playing. She rolled her eyes and ran out again.

Craig looked aghast. He said, 'They're playing the Shadows.'

12

Clearing Out the Chaff

'I asked for this bill last night. I asked for it at seven o'clock this morning. It's now quarter to eight. We have an international game of cricket to play. We're going to the stadium and you can bring the bill to me there, correctly made up, with a swipe machine. Goodbye.'

Shirley walked out of the Piccadily to the bus. She said, 'It's the same as it's been everywhere. I'm just snapping earlier.'

The blokes with the rifles and machine guns got on the bus with us, wearing furry-collared windcheaters. They looked pretty dozy; I can't say I was filled with confidence in their ability to protect us from any passing naxalites or forest brigands. Sheryl Crow sang on the boom box that all we wanted to do was have some fun.

The morning was chill, damp, and grey. My heart went out to the organisers; they'd done so much work with so little backing, and for their pains they'd been rewarded with this unseasonably foul winter. Here we had this absolutely gorgeous new stadium – a ring of open terracing coloured pink, yellow, white, green and blue, with a splendid five-storey pavilion, all arches and colonnades – but the bird-flecked sky above it was a dank and sodden blanket, the field was silver with dew, and wide puddles of water lay on the terrace in front of the dressing rooms. Control the controllables, they said – but you began to wonder if there were any.

Two blokes in hooded anoraks painted the sight screen black, covering over the Pepsi logo – and I guess forty minutes before we were due to start was as good a time to do it as any. Not that there was the faintest chance of starting on time. Less cricket, less Pepsi.

Romps came off the terrace muttering, 'Miserable old gits.' The blokes with the guns wouldn't let her have her picture taken with them. She wandered off saying, 'It's an issue of national security, right?'

The air was wet with a freezing mist. At eight-thirty, one of the umpires said we couldn't take the covers off the square when it was like this. He was a distinguished gent with a warrior's visage, a hooked hawk's nose, a small red turban, thick black gloves, and a heavy gold watch. It turned out he'd played for some years with Meltham, one of the better club sides around Huddersfield; he and Romps had a natter about his mate who had a restaurant back in her home town. He said sadly, 'This weather is like England.'

Two motorised whales puttered about squeegee-ing the outfield. Liss sat quietly on her own, listening to dance music on her Walkman. Thrasy appeared, and told me to go look at the press box. It had six phones, faxes, you could get calls in and out – media heaven. We stood hoping we'd get something to report so we could actually use it.

At eight-forty-five, the covers came off the square. They left one over the wicket; Skip and JB were out there, sticking their hands underneath it for a feel. They came back and said it was damp, but hard; JB said we'd be OK. Skip told them, 'Warm up at nine, we're starting at ten.'

I had a look round the stadium. Five years ago there'd been a ravine through here – then they put this up, and inaugurated the pavilion in 1996. The floodlights were set on low, stubby little towers, because the air force had a base down the road; sometimes, said one of the officials, you'd get MiGs popping in over a game, wiggling their wings to take a peek at the scoreboard as they passed.

In the grandly dim foyer there was a tidy exhibition about the history of the game – about the establishment of Lord's and the MCC, the original use of the word 'test' on England's first tour of Australia in 1861–62, and the first proper Test match (eleven men a side) in Melbourne in 1877. The earliest record of cricket in India was dated at 1721, when traders pitched stumps for a game at Cambay to loosen limbs after the long sea voyage. The Parsees in Bombay took it up, forming a club in 1848 on Esplanade Maidan; they first beat an English side in 1877, and toured England in 1886. In 1907 the Hindus joined in, the Muslims in 1912, and the pentangular competition between the communities began in the thirties, before anti-sectarian policies put paid to it after the war.

In 1911, the first All India team to visit England was captained by the Maharaja of Patiala; it was related how another Maharaja of that ilk, batting against a touring MCC side at Lahore, edged a catch to slip, and the bowler didn't appeal for it. One of the fielders asked him why he hadn't done so and the bowler told him, 'Don't be a fool. We'll be staying at this chap's palace later on. I don't want to be poisoned.'

Two stadium officials found me some coffee; they were, as ever, entirely charming and hospitable. Of the inexplicable slaughter just wrought among the Indian men's one-day team by their selectors, one of them said sadly, 'Merit is given a back seat in this country.'

Fizz said of the Lengster's omission, 'You've got to be hard, 'cause people have got to pull their weight. How would it look if someone came to me for treatment and I told them I couldn't be arsed? Mind you,' she grinned, 'someone did come to me last night. And I told them I was watching *Mrs Doubtfire*.'

It was announced that the game would start at ten-thirty, with 46 overs a side. On a damp wicket, it was going to seam out there big time; it was an ideal opportunity for England to bowl first, for the first time in the tournament. Now the bowlers had started finding some bite, they needed to be given someone to go at – and the batsmen needed to get used to the idea of chasing something, too.

Skip came back from the field with her arms wide, shrugging; she said, 'I lost the toss,' as if to say, what d'you expect? The Sri Lankans opted to bat anyway; Pete Moralee said, 'We'll have an early doors finish then.'

A local journalist asked him, 'Have you seen Sri Lanka bat?'

He shook his head and said, 'They've got a flight out of here tonight. Maybe they just want to pack up early.'

Skip said if she'd won, she'd have fielded first; it looked as if we all wanted to get it over with. England were heading straight back to Delhi on the bus after the game; I suppose they wanted to be on their way as soon as possible.

Someone got hold of a Sri Lankan team sheet. Their average age was twenty-one; their oldest players, the vice-captain and the keeper, were twenty-five, and two of them were schoolgirls. One of their players who'd been left out, Kalpana Liyanarachchy, said she was from Colombo, like nearly all of them; only two came from 'outstation'. She was twenty-four, and helped her mum in a flower business; she'd played club cricket for six years, but the national team had only been in existence for a couple of months.

They had BA T-shirts promoting the Colombo–London route, so presumably they had a little backing there; they'd got together for this tournament. Their first international matches came in a three-game warm-up series with the Dutch, who (having a Sri Lankan coach) had come to India via Colombo to acclimatise. The Dutch won the series 2–1.

Sri Lanka got to the quarter-final by sharing the points with India when their game was rained off in Delhi, then beating the West Indians; they bowled them all out for 79, and won by six wickets. Then they got hammered by the Kiwis, bowled out the Dutch for 138, and lost that one as well when they were all out themselves for 91. Liyanarachchy said, 'It's all very new to us, but we've enjoyed it. It's good experience for us.'

Then she said, 'England should be good, shouldn't they?'

At ten-fifteen we went up to the press box; the view was brilliant. 'What a stadium,' sighed Thrasy. 'It's such a shame there's no one in it.' He went into the back room to get set up for his hourly reports to Five Live on the all-singing, all-dancing telecom clobber – and came back seething. The Jobsworth manning the phones wouldn't let him have incoming calls – which you need when you're doing radio. You want them calling you, so you can report when they want it; you can't report on the game if you're calling out to them each time, then sitting there waiting for them to come to you while the game goes on, and you can't see it. But Jobsworth didn't want incoming calls – because he didn't get to charge you money for those, did he?

Thrasy went to find someone to sort it out. We ended up staring bug-eyed at Jobsworth across his desk as he told us he couldn't allow it, it was government telecom rules. While the endlessly polite local official looked on embarrassed and agonised, desperate to help us but not looking as if he knew how, I lost it. Not having incoming calls didn't actually matter to me – I could easily just file from the hotel – but you go through enough days and weeks of this rubbish together, and it starts to feel like trouble for any one of you is trouble for you all. This was the media centre at a Test match ground at the quarter-final of the World Cup, and this noddy-headed little bugger wouldn't give my mate a phone line? Struggling not to scream I told him, 'I don't care if you're a government body, a private company, or a bloke flying upside down in a hang glider in his underpants – WE WANT INCOMING.'

The local official was trying to stay calm, but his eyes looked frantic and his feet were paddling madly underwater. He told us he'd talk to someone on the next rung up the bureaucratic ladder, he promised he'd get it sorted – and Thrasy said later that he was altogether a mild-mannered young man, but just at that moment he'd wanted to lean forward over the desk, take Jobsworth by the shirt, and smash him against the wall.

I suppose I can only say, in tribute to India, that on all previous occasions when things hadn't worked, it was down to incompetence or malfunction, and in the end it always got sorted. With the notable exception of all too many rickshaw drivers, this was the first guy in three weeks who'd been genuinely greedy and obstructive – which is actually pretty amazing. All the same, be patient, they say. You try it.

Romps got the outswinger working; her first over had six dots and a wide. There would, in the end, be twenty-six wides, which was pretty icky – but Romps said later it was moving about so much out there that she was actually trying to rein it in. 'It was so unpredictable, it was weird.'

It was, said Thrasy, 'Swinging like a banana.'

Her second over she took out the opener, spooning a catch to Connie at point. At the other end, Laura MacLeod bowled five overs; she went for sixteen runs, no maidens, no wickets, and got called for seven wides, four of them in one over. The first one sprang wildly away off the seam, I thought the second was a bit harsh, the third was well wide, and by the fourth one I was just shaking my head. She had all kinds of promise, a nice clean action – but this was all over the place.

The Lengster sat down beside me and said quietly, 'If I was bowling, eh?' Then she added, in a genuinely sympathetic tone, 'She's nervous. And she's cold.'

She turned to look at me, half sad, half vexed; she asked, 'You know why I've been dropped?'

'Attitude.'

'Yeah. Disciplinary reasons. I feel it's totally unjustified. I've upset the captain by disagreeing with the field placings. I thought it was wrong. I needed a conventional field and I didn't get one. Which resulted in me getting in a huff. I accept me body language was bad, but it's in me nature, and it's difficult to change, and it feels a little bit harsh. It's pretty ridiculous, 'cause they're not going on me cricketing ability. But it's not like I'm Phil Tufnell, is it? And one little glip's condemned me. I'm well pissed off. So,' she shrugged, 'I've got two options. I can sulk and take me bat home, or I can do something about it. So I'm going to have to do something about it. Better start looking keen, eh?'

The trouble was, she said, 'It's difficult to keep going twenty-four hours a day. We've had that bus journey yesterday, you're tired – and now I feel I'm being watched all the time. If I go round the boundary clapping me hands and saying, Come on girls, will that be right? Or will it be construed as I'm trying too hard?' She sighed. 'Make an excellent headline back home, wouldn't it? Bad Girl Of Cricket.'

She got up and said firmly, 'Right. I'm going to do some scoring. 'Cause the sooner I've done that, the sooner I can get in the nets.'

Out in the field, the umpire was calling another wide – the eleventh, in nine overs. Thrasy enquired idly, 'Is it too cold for them to function?'

Romps got another wicket; the second Sri Lankan opener wafting about round the outswinger, snicking a little tickle into the safe hands of Jane Cassar. The over finished a wicket maiden; Sri Lanka were 27 for 2. Thrasy said of Romps, 'I'm pleased for her. She's not had it easy, and she's bowled the best of anyone.'

Liss came on; her first two balls were wides. Then she got a handle on it, and put in six dot balls; her next over was a maiden, and so would the next one have been if she'd not been unlucky with a streaky edge that ran away for four. Next over after that she got a wicket, JB stooping at slip to snatch a fine catch round her ankles. It was 39 for 3; the bat just out had been there an hour, and all she'd scored was that streaky four.

Romps bowled her ten overs; five maidens, two wickets, just 17 runs. It was exactly what was called for – not just the figures, but turning them in when the match was still live and we needed wickets – and she was chuffed. With the World Cup semi-final in view she said afterwards, 'You can't relax and think you're in just 'cause you've been there ten years. If you want to stay in, you've got to bowl well. And people don't think of us as a bowling team – so it's nice to go out and prove them wrong.'

Connie stepped up in her place – two dots, and then a long hop pulled for four. The batter who did that was the Sri Lankan captain Vanessa Bowen, who'd be sticking out there gamely to knock 38 off 100 balls – only now she went for a completely daft single. JB fielded cleanly at midwicket, got in a sharp throw, and the other bat was run out by a furlong.

Liss bowled a maiden, then a wicket maiden, skewering a seventeen-year-old schoolgirl leg before. They were 47 for 5 off twenty-four overs; it was getting pretty obvious that we'd not be long delayed in the city beautiful. Now Connie bowled a maiden, then Liss another one; by the time she was finished, five of her nine overs were maidens, she'd put two wickets in her pocket, and she'd given away only ten runs. Just to cap it, she went back in the field – and narrowly missed a run out with a direct hit to the bowler's end from point.

Up in the press box, Thrasy came back from the phone room with his head on fire. The local guy had finally sorted him out a phone on which Five Live could call him; he'd called in, and they'd told him what time they'd call back for an update. The time came, he went to get the call – and there was a local guy sitting gassing on his line. This may have been the occasion on which BBC listeners were told that the programme couldn't get through to their man in India – on the other hand, there were more than a few such occasions. 'Next time,' Thrasy snarled, 'if I find someone on my phone, I'm taking it out of his hand and I'm cutting him off.'

Lottie came on, bowled seven overs which she herself admitted were unremarkable – but she got three wickets anyway. All three were stumpings; Smigs didn't miss many of them. Afterwards, Lottie shrugged. 'It was turning a mile. That first match with South Africa, I was really surprised when Karen gave me the ball. But I'm getting used to it now.'

Another Sri Lankan was run out, trying for a crazy third run; the fielding was oiled as a machine, the ball slinging inch perfect from Liss via Skip at the bowler's end to the keeper, bails off, bye bye. Connie finished it off; in the forty-fourth over Vanessa Bowen, the only Sri Lankan who'd managed to stay there, sliced a wild swing to Lottie at backward square. They were all out for 104, and I could hardly see us being stretched much to beat it.

The Sri Lankans opened with two seamers who, especially given the conditions, were actually pretty handy. I suspect one of them had Lottie nicking a faint edge to the keeper in the second over – but she dropped it anyway. They did get H, caught behind for 7 – but when you've scored 87 against Denmark, been Eve of the Match and got dropped, what does that do for your confidence? It hadn't been high in the first place; even after she'd anchored that innings, she'd described her batting style with a dry little smile as, 'Cautious. Verging on the negative.' Now the Sri Lankans got her out.

She was the only person they did get out; Lottie and JB strolled to 105 for 1 in 22.1 overs, and we won by nine wickets. There were 17 extras, JB got 24, and Lottie 57; she spent a short while weighing up the seamers, then in the eighth over she drove a four through midwicket, four more through cover, and off she went. She was watchful and sharp, calmly waiting for the delivery, holding still and poised – and I only regret to say I can't tell you more about this knock, because about now

an enormously friendly fellow came into the press box to hand
out traditional woolly caps, and to promote with pride the pion-
eering development of kiwi fruit cultivation in the Punjab.

Much politeness was therefore required during the next ten
overs or so. In between discussing innovative agriculture with
clenched teeth, I did manage to note that an unfortunate spinner called Rose Fernando came on, H took a single off her, then
Lottie bashed her for three fours and a two. So that was the only
over Rose Fernando bowled – and there's not much point saying
she was only seventeen, because how old was Lottie?

After H was out, JB got off the mark with a single that
involved both batsmen running backwards and forwards, apparently trying to arrive simultaneously at first one crease and
then the other, while the Sri Lankans threw the ball about at
each other in a similar state of high flusterment. Once past that
initial palaver, JB and Lottie got the job done untroubled;
Lottie's 50 came up off 57 balls, JB saw us home, and – for the
third time in five World Cup appearances – Lottie was Eve of
the Match. She got a gigantic plastic cheque from Hero Honda
for 2,000 roops – a shade over thirty quid – and looked at it
uncertainly, wondering how she was meant to cash it.

Pressed for a quote before they scarpered back to Delhi, she
said, 'Their seamers bowled well, they made it difficult early
on – until I started knocking them about, anyway. But they're
enthusiastic. They'll be a good side in a few years.'

They were indeed a spirited outfit, quick and noisy in the
field – and they may well get better very soon. Right now, however, they weren't good – spirited, yes, but largely inept. You
had one side here that played its first international cricket in
1934, and another whose first match was two months ago. It
wasn't exactly a balanced contest.

There were only five women's cricket teams in India that you
could genuinely call capable all-round units, squads that could
send out eleven who all knew what they were doing. These

were Australia, England, India, New Zealand, and South Africa – so the quarter-finals, ultimately, were about clearing out whatever chaff had survived from the group games before we got down to the real business.

England duly got shot of Sri Lanka; the day before, Australia had beaten Holland in Lucknow by 115 runs. They rested Belinda Clark from the top of the order, played two bats who'd not got into the side for their game against us, and they still ran up 223 for 4 in 50 overs; bowler Bronwyn Calver showed she could bat a bit too, hitting 74. Holland did at least survive 50 overs – but all they could score in them was 108 for 6.

In two days' time in Bombay, New Zealand would do a similarly straightforward job on Ireland. They scored 244 for 5 – Hockley got 70, Drumm got 60 – then they held Ireland to 105 for 9.

The fact that the Dutch and the Irish both batted their full 50 at least confirmed they were better sides than Pakistan or Denmark. On the other hand, I'd imagine the Australians were hardly less tired than the English; they'd had to play a day earlier than us after the delayed escape from Nagpur, with no time to rest before they moved on to Lucknow. In the circumstances, once they'd made sure the Dutch weren't going to catch them, the fact that they gave eight players a bowl does suggest they took their foot off the gas a bit.

As for the Kiwis, their failure to remove a stubborn Irish tail hinted that their bowling might not be too special; the *Hindu* reported that they 'did not appear particularly threatening'. England could take heart from that; news that they were smart and lively in the field, on the other hand, wasn't news to us anyway.

The only quarter-final that looked a genuine contest was the India–South Africa game in Patna. Patna's the capital of Bihar, one of India's most backward and impoverished states, and by all accounts it's a pretty dispiriting place; 'noisy, crowded, polluted, and chaotic', as the *Lonely Planet* enticingly puts it. The South Africans said later that they were locked in their hotel there for forty-eight hours; it was in Patna that England were driven from the field under a hail of missiles two years earlier, barricaded in their dressing room while the police went in for a bit of lathi charging, and then subjected to a bricking on their bus when they finally left the ground.

An intimidatory environment like that might count in the hosts' favour; on the other hand, India had shown themselves wobbly under pressure against New Zealand, while the South Africans had that massive spirit about them. Putting my faith in the inspirational Conrad Hunte, I duly tipped South Africa for an upset – which just goes to show that you don't ever want the backing of a rodent. Come the game, Linda Olivier was lbw first ball, India's spinners had the rest of them in all kinds of trouble, and they folded for 80 all out. India beat them by five wickets, and for their pains they earned a semi-final against Australia.

Back in Chandigarh, England got on the bus as fast as they politely could, and headed off to Delhi. The rodents stayed behind to file match reports:

England stroll into semi-final
Edwards puts Sri Lanka in spin

Interestingly, this other one appeared in the *Telegraph* from Mihir Bose:

England hang Sri Lankans out to dry

I don't know where Bose wrote it from; none of us saw him in the press-box. Still, I knew where I was. I was a long way from home in a hotel bar in Chandigarh with a bottle of Kingfisher and a barman who looked like Bela Lugosi. It was 21 December; Bela put on a hauntingly ethereal version of 'Silent Night'.

13

Happy Christmas

The alarm went off at five-fifteen; I reached for the phone. 'Room service.'

'Morning. Could you bring me up some coffee, please, and a plain omelette?'

'I'm sorry, sir, an omelette is not available.'

'I'm sorry, but an omelette *is* available. I'm leaving at six o'clock, I checked with the front desk last night that you could do me some breakfast before I went, they said that you could, and I'm telling you now that you will. A plain omelette, OK?'

'Yes, sir.'

'Thank you.'

The omelette arrived half an hour later. It wasn't plain, but stuffed to the hilt with sliced green chilli. I managed about half of it, by which time my throat resembled the lava pipe of an active volcano. And that, I guess, was the Revenge of the Room Service People.

Incredibly – seeing it was designed by a Frenchman – Chandigarh has an orderly road system. After the usual chaotic kerfuffle that passes for checking out of a hotel in India, the rodent troop cabbed down broad avenues to the station through the chill and foggy dark. The express train back to Delhi was on time and comfortable; better yet, first-class air-con chair-car tickets included a brilliant relay of tea and biscuits, mango juice, mineral water, hot spicy veg things, bread and jam and more tea. So I hadn't needed the magma omelette after all.

At the station in Delhi, I went to the STD booth to call Selena at the Mela Plaza. It was 22 December, and England had been scheduled to fly to Madras that evening; unfortunately, it seemed no one had got around to booking them any plane tickets. There'd been a suggestion that they might have to sit about in Ghaziabad until as late as Christmas Eve, when the semi-final was on Boxing Day; Megan wasn't having it. Madras would be hot; she wanted to get down there, and get the players rested up and acclimatised. The rodents, therefore, needed to know if we were going out to Ghaziabad now, or making straight for the airport.

At the STD booth, the queue was big enough to populate a fair-sized town. I went directly to the head of it. By now there were no second thoughts about doing something like that, no guilt, no shame, not a flicker; you just did it. At the end of the game the day before, Thrasy'd gone to his phone to take a call from London so he could give his final match report; the phone rang, he picked it up, and the call was for an Indian journalist. He looked at the phone a moment – then he hung up. You just do.

It turned out we were stuck in Ghaziabad until tomorrow. We got a cab out there; another hour's ride that involved sightings of elephants, camels, and a beggar child whose patter was delivered in more than passable Italian.

Three days earlier, I'd been promised that a plane ticket to get me from Calcutta back to Delhi after the final would be delivered to the Mela Plaza before we left for Chandigarh; now we were back from Chandigarh, and there was still no sign of that ticket.

The invaluable Selena, however, had discovered a travel agent called Mr Wilson. His firm was Dolphin Travel, he was on the first floor of an unfinished tower block on a bleak spread of waste ground just down the road, and this guy was incredibly efficient. He got me a confirmed plane ticket back from Calcutta in five minutes flat, and conducted an exceptionally well-informed discourse on the madness of the Indian men's selection policy while he did it. When you meet people like this, you want to hug them and break into song.

Back at the hotel, the players were organising a shopping expedition; with a gleam in her eye and a credit card in her wallet Romps said, 'Plastic *melts*.' I wanted to join them, but couldn't; the WCAI's travel agent was supposed to be turning up any moment to take payment for the extra members of England's party. After a few more hours and no sign of him, I gave up; passing on the shopping I could live with, but we also had invitations to the bar at the British High Commission, and that I couldn't possibly miss.

I went into town with Joce, Fizz, Thrasy and Craig; the hotel organised a car to take us there and back, told us the price for the ride, and then the driver started renegotiating the price upwards the instant we set off. One minute you've got Mr Wilson, the next you're back dealing with this. It gets to where you're living in a permanent black fog of fury and fatigue.

Stepping out of that fog, the High Commission was an oasis of bliss. The bar was done out like the smarter breed of pub; it had a snooker table, proper Christmas decorations, cans of Boddington's, Walker's crisps, and – oh heaven – Mr Porky pork scratchings. We fell on two-week-old copies of *The Times* and the *Telegraph* like people finding water in a desert; our hosts were all completely bats for cricket, fantastically generous, and I didn't so much drink large quantities of gin and tonic as absorb it osmotically. When the first one came it had ice in it, and in India, ice is normally a no-no – then I thought, what the hell. This is *British* ice.

Connie, Bev, Romps and H pitched up. They were pretty happy already – they'd tossed caution to the winds and been to Pizza Express – but this was even better. Wanting photos, Connie said, 'Girls, get round the Christmas tree. This is the dog's bollocks, isn't it?'

Fizz said, 'I haven't stopped smiling since I came in here.'

Naturally, our driver spoilt it on the way back. He pulled into a garage for petrol, and tried to get us to pay for it. I came close to losing it; I told him fiercely that a fare had been agreed, and that fare would be stuck to. In the back Connie said mildly, 'Don't be harsh.' I thought, How many of these mercenary buggers have you had to deal with then? – but I managed not to say it.

I felt wired, frayed, close to burn-out. I had a gin-fuelled conversation with Fizz; we argued about where you might start if you wanted to sort out India. Sooner or later you're always going to have that debate, by turns enthralled and enraged as you are by everything you see all about you – but apart from the fact that it's none of my business how India lives its life in the first place, the bottom line is this: As long as a billion people keep on having babies, it isn't ever going to get sorted out anyway.

In the Mela Plaza, Romps wandered up and said, 'I brought Karen a present.' She'd come back with a can of High Commission Boddy's. She smiled and said, 'Got to keep in the skipper's good books, eh?'

Thank God for someone with a sense of humour. Then I went up to my room, and found that my shampoo bottle had burst inside my sponge bag. I could have wept.

The evening wore on; Shirley was still waiting for tomorrow's plane tickets to Madras. She'd been waiting all day. The first we'd heard, the agent had been supposed to turn up at eleven in the morning; in the end, he arrived at nine-forty-five at night.

And yet the crazy thing is, you don't mind. So long as you're not in a phase of inner rage and despair about rickshaw drivers, malfunctioning phone lines, or shampoo all over your sponge bag, you can put up with it. You can even forgive it. You can, for goodness' sake, even *defend* it.

Someone was wandering round with a copy of a piece date-lined 'Mihir Bose in Calcutta' that included some pretty derogatory stuff about the organisation of the Women's World Cup. How much of it he'd seen I don't know – there hadn't been any games in Calcutta yet – but for those of us who'd been going through it all, who'd seen how much they'd laid on with such threadbare resources, how much effort and charm and courtesy had been expended on our behalf, the fact that this guy was running them down felt outrageous.

It made you want to say, OK, sure, the World Cup's a mess, and I'm so knackered and crazed that I'm spitting blood half the day – but for all that, this had been an experience like no other in my life, and I knew I'd look back on it and think it was brilliant, utterly brilliant. Because it was; now I'm home I really do look back and think that.

It also made you want to take the travel agent and clasp him to your bosom. So he was the best part of twelve hours late? Hey, no problem. At least he came, didn't he?

He had bills for me, Selena, Thrasy, Joce, Cath Harris, and Peter Moralee of £513 apiece. That was for plane tickets Delhi–Hyderabad, Hyderabad–Bombay–Pune, Bombay–Nagpur, Nagpur–Delhi, and Delhi–Madras–Calcutta. The WCA were picking up three of these tabs, the rodents and Selena were picking up theirs, and it struck me as bloody good value. Only thing was, how were we going to pay him?

In the dim hotel foyer at ten-thirty of an evening he took our credit cards, and he used a Biro to rub imprints of them onto payment slips like a bloke in a church doing brass etchings.

And that has to be the oddest way I've ever parted with five hundred quid.

Shirley said, 'When you look at the logistics of this, actually, probably only India could have pulled it off at all.'

A pot plant went up and down in one of the lifts bearing a message requesting decoration for Christmas. Leaves and fronds were taped to the ceiling of another lift, with another message proclaiming that they were mistletoe. The departing Dutch and Danish squads were in the hotel, and having a serious party. The Danish had a top dance routine, performed to their own version of a disco song:

I need a superhero
Honda Hero
Ah-ay-eeh-ah-yeah

This involved much carefully choreographed revving of imaginary scooter handles. I joined the party, got absolutely bladdered, and about thirty seconds later the alarm went off at three-thirty in the morning. Thanks to heroic work by Thrasy I just made it on the bus, and off we went to the airport for a six-thirty departure to Madras. I stumbled through check-in quietly wishing I was dead. Then someone told us the flight was delayed; the fog outside was as dense as cotton wool. Dirty cotton wool.

Thrasy was in blazing-head mode again; Megan was trying to get him (and me) to stay in a different hotel again when we got to Madras. He growled, 'I'm perfectly happy not to speak to her ever again.'

It was announced that the flight would be delayed until nine-fifteen. I went to stand in a queue for a complimentary breakfast with Lottie and Laura. We stood in the queue for an hour, with no idea what might be at the end of it. Laura said wearily, 'I don't like being away from home at Christmas.'

Lottie sighed and said mildly, encouragingly, 'Well, don't keep moaning about it, eh?'

We got tea and toast, then went back to the departure lounge; we read match reports of the Indian win over South Africa in Patna. There was also news that the Australians had refused to go to Guwahati on security grounds, and that their semi-final with India would be in Delhi. Meanwhile, it was announced that the flight was now delayed until ten-thirty.

The bloke at the coffee stand gave up in the face of a milling horde of the frustrated and delayed, and disappeared. Romps caught up on her diary. Outside, planes were just beginning to emerge from the grey-white soup in the air, vague shapes in the murk on the Tarmac. I wandered about aimlessly, and came on a suggestions box. I could think of a few suggestions.

Lottie's suggestion, at nine-forty-five, was to plough with impressive determination through a mob of people, change the TV to the Ireland–New Zealand game in Bombay, then plough back to her seat waving fiercely at the crowd until they got out of our way and we could watch the cricket. Megan hunched forward, intent on every ball. She said thoughtfully, 'Hockley doesn't like the slow stuff, does she?'

We eventually got off the ground just after midday, and were served an airline meal involving quite the most acridly vile baked beans I've ever come across in my life. It's hard to get your head round that one. How can you get baked beans wrong?

The approach into Madras perked things up, with truly heartening views of sunshine, seaside, and palm trees. The plane stopped outside the terminal, we started easing out of our seats – and the bloke who opened the overhead locker where Skip and Sue Metcalfe were sitting spilled a large, heavy, sharp-cornered briefcase out of it onto their laps. He gave them not a look, not a gesture, not one word of apology. The idea of losing your captain or vice-captain felled by flying luggage three days before a World Cup semi-final was a pretty dismal one, and it was a narrow shave. Sue said grimly, 'I could have slapped him.'

Outside the terminal, the organisers had a separate van for our baggage; a welcome sight. They said the bus ride into town would be twenty minutes; a spectacularly optimistic estimate, though they couldn't have foreseen that we'd be held up by a king-size demonstration. Romps watched them march past and said quietly, 'Must have heard I was on unpaid leave.'

We sat cooking gently in the snarled-up traffic, with a sound-track by M People and Alison Moyet – but the city didn't seem to wear quite so filthy an aspect as we'd got used to. It had a bright, tatterdemalion air; there were (of course) thatch-roofed shanties along rancid ditches, and we passed one foul patch of waste ground strewn with garbage, picked over by fat black pigs, on which (of course) ragged boys were playing cricket. But overall it felt pleasantly heat-stunned and leafy, and the Hotel Savera was big and shiny, and it actually had all the rooms we'd booked. After the Centaur, the Regency, and the Piccadily, that was definitely a result.

Peter Moralee had taken doubling up with a rodent in those places with a patient good grace – but I could well understand why Megan wouldn't have been happy about it, if it had happened in the build-up to the semi-final. She hadn't liked having to double up with Shirley herself, and it was fair enough that she should want and need her own space.

On the other hand, if we all had rooms of our own, why couldn't Thrasy and I stay here? I suspect she'd have added Craig to the list of ejectees too, if he hadn't been paid for by Vodafone; maybe Cath Harris as well, who, for all that she was supposed to be the WCA's press secretary, said she was often made to feel no more welcome than a genuine rodent. Anyway, Thrasy and I weren't having it; we'd been through all this together, and we were going to stay with it now to the end. Fortress England wasn't going to be much of a fortress anyway, when the Kiwis were booked into the same hotel.

It was great though, wasn't it? Here we'd carried bags and boxes of mineral water, tipped porters, bought aerogrammes, generally helped out wherever asked – and now we were being made to feel about as welcome as a bout of *E coli* in the tandoori.

As a gesture of goodwill, we changed our rooms onto a different floor to the rest of the squad, and stumbled off to settle in. I fell on my bed, and scanned the room service menu. It suggested I go down to the pool and 'bask in the sun with a crunchy munchy snack'. What a thoroughly sound idea.

A polystyrene Father Christmas was riding a polystyrene sleigh pulled by polystyrene reindeer across the lobby. The speakers in the lifts played the Bing Crosby brand of Christmas song – and, these being the slowest elevators in the known universe, you got to listen to loads of them. I've seen glaciers move quicker than those lifts.

Still, it was very sweet – unlike the phones. They claimed to have a direct dial facility; it didn't work. So you called the operator, gave him the number of the sports desk in London, he said he'd connect you, and then he didn't. You stared at the phone for a while then you called him back, and now he said he couldn't connect you, because there wasn't a line. So you shouted at him and – hey presto – he connected you.

I moseyed down the corridor to find Thrasy near the end of his rope because his phone didn't seem to be working at all. Two small men in brown coats appeared, and stared silently at the phone in his bathroom. Then they picked up the phone by his bed and went away with it. He gave up and moved rooms again.

England had now been in India for twenty days. They'd played eight games of cricket, and spent nearly all the other twelve days (and/or nights) travelling. The three-thirty alarm call this morning was the fifth time in a fortnight that we'd started in the small hours. What was worse, we could actually have flown into Madras the night before – Mr Wilson had said that Jet's service that evening had twenty-five free seats on it – but instead we'd lost a day that could have been spent on practice and recovery sitting about for six hours at Delhi airport.

We had two days left to get ready for New Zealand. The Kiwis, meanwhile, had played one game fewer than us in their truncated group; the first two of those games had both been in Delhi, so their itinerary had been markedly less grievous. Between their game with India and their quarter-final in Bombay today, they'd also had a gap of five days. I'm not saying they'd been having some easy doddle of a time – but work it out for yourself.

Karen Smithies said, 'To say the schedule's not had an effect would be the biggest understatement ever. How have we kept going? I think as long as we're here we will keep going, because we've got to – and when we get home, we'll all completely collapse. This is the first place we've actually unpacked since Hyderabad. It's incredible – twenty-hour days, battles with the laundry, team meetings, seeing players that aren't playing, it never stops. Then there's meeting the press.'

She gave me a big grin on that one – but she'd been very good about it, given her original wariness. In Pune the night before we played Ireland, she was still talking to an Indian journalist at quarter to ten in the evening. Now she said, 'These players have done really well – and I just hope people in England know what we've been through. 'Cause if we do lose, and people have a go at us . . . obviously they'll be disappointed we've not won, OK. But they should think what we've undergone – and as long as I know we've given it our best shot, that's what matters. Because I'll tell you – I've got fourteen here who've given everything.'

At nine-thirty on the morning of Christmas Eve, the bus was supposed to take us to training. At ten-fifteen, there wasn't any sign of it; players started organising taxis. Then the bus arrived; it was late because they'd used it to bring New Zealand from the airport.

We left at ten-thirty, an hour behind time; the players were gone already. Departure involved reversing into three lanes of cycles, scooters, and rickshaws. We drove down to the beach road – and the police had blocked it off. We turned round, and took another route down clogged-up sidestreets. 'Ten minutes,' said our guide and helper. Right, and I'm the King of Buganda.

Thirty minutes later, we were creeping and jolting down a dirt lane strewn with rotting trash and bony-hipped cattle. This, it turned out, was the approach road to the M. A. Chidambaram Stadium – which, despite its unpromising ingress, was an imposing and pretty well-equipped arena. There were two sets of nets, one inside the ground, and one in a walled yard by the outer gates.

The squad had split into two groups of seven; in the walled-off area Peter Moralee was among the bowlers, giving Lottie some quicker stuff off twelve paces. It was pretty game of him, seeing he had the trots; he'd been sick twice on the plane the day before. But then, he'd been a solid presence throughout. Now Lottie hoiked him out of the nets, away over the wall and beyond the dirt road into a minging ditch, and the local helper barked (helpfully), 'No lifting, hey. Tell them to play it on the ground.'

Moralee turned to look at him in dry disbelief. He told him, 'She plays the right shot for the ball, yeah? If it's a six ball, then that's where it goes.'

Thrasy joined in. After a while I asked him if the players were treating his leg breaks with proper respect, and he grinned. 'They haven't broken yet.'

Connie retrieved a ball from a dirt strip between the fencing and the wall behind us, then jolted back scared. She said, 'There's something moving in there. There's snakes in that grass.'

Moralee told her, 'Better bowl tight then, Con.'

Crows barked in the dense green trees; Liss said her back

was a bit tight, so Fizz contorted her into an assortment of unlikely shapes. More balls flew over the wall, disappearing among a pack of barefoot boys on the road outside.

Connie collapsed in a chair, and said she was missing home. 'I've been thinking about it all morning. Christmas is the same every year, and you know exactly what they'll be doing at any time of the day. It's hard not to think about it.'

Craig nipped about getting pictures. They were wearing white T-shirts with the Vodafone logo on the back; he got them all to turn the T-shirts round. So when Connie appeared on the back page of the *Independent* on Boxing Day morning, bowling towards the camera next to the semi-final preview with Vodafone on her chest, she was wearing her T-shirt the wrong way round. There's marketing for you.

The session finished at one-thirty. Inside the stadium, JB stayed on her own in the nets, throwing balls up and clouting them away as they fell. Liss did a lap of the boundary; Lottie chatted with two of the groundstaff, a pair of cheerful, dark-skinned, barefoot little guys in khaki shirts and shorts. One of them said, 'Twenty-five Christmas?'

Romps murmured, 'Don't we know it.' Then she picked her voice up and said, 'C'mon, Lotts. Stretches. Warm down.' Lottie groaned; Romps said, 'As your former roomie and mother, I'm telling you.'

BB walked over, smiling, holding her arms wide to the high sweep of the empty stands in the sun. She said, 'I'm happy to be tired from playing cricket, instead of tired from travelling.'

Australia's semi-final with India was shortened by the dismal weather in Delhi; two and a quarter hours of the morning disappeared in the fog, and the game was cut to thirty-two overs a side. India won the toss and put Australia in; Belinda Clark and Joanne Broadbent put on 66 for the first wicket, but once those two were gone, the Indian spinners put in some tight and tricky stuff, slowed up the Australian middle order, and got three of them out for ducks. Australia finished on 123 for 7.

It was eminently gettable, even though India were penalised two overs for not getting their own overs bowled quickly enough. Between Australia's quality in the field and their own nerves, however, the Indians couldn't do it. One of the openers fell to an absolutely blinding catch at midwicket by Melanie Jones; it was cracked really hard at her, flew up out of her hands, and she dived backwards to take it one-handed at the second attempt. That was off Fitzpatrick's bowling; Fitzpatrick got three wickets and was Eve of the Match, four of the Indians were run out, and they could only falter haltingly to 104 for 9 at the death.

I watched their hopes slowly evaporate through the afternoon on TV; Jane Cassar came and watched some of it with me. For Cassar it wasn't just Christmas Eve, it was her birthday too – but she shrugged and said, 'I'm not so fussed about it. I do sometimes want to be home, because it's Christmas – but I can't do anything about it, so there it is. I'll just treat it as another day.'

She turned twenty-five that day; she was five foot seven, a quiet, placid woman who didn't let anything much get to her. She came from Ilkeston in Derbyshire; the nickname Smigs came from her maiden name, Smit. Her grandfather had come over from Holland, and started a business making bedspreads and quilts; her dad had taken it over in his turn, and he'd also taken up cricket. From childhood she'd played with him and her brother; one day when she was thirteen they were at a game in Stanton, they were one short, she played, and she'd been playing boys' and men's cricket ever since.

She was a regular with Ilkeston's second XI on a Saturday; on a Sunday she played with Skip for Newark & Sherwood. I asked, if the women's side played on a Saturday, did they get first call? She laughed and said, 'They do now. A couple of years back I told them I was ill, then went and played a men's game – and one of the girls knew one of the guys I played against, and he mentioned that I'd played. I got a bit of a bollocking then.'

She worked as a part-time secretary at an engineering firm, where they were good about giving her the time she needed for cricket. She was two years out of Nottingham Trent University – she did sports science and administration – but it didn't sound as if she'd made the greatest of efforts to find full-time work, or a career-type job, because the cricket was more important, and what she wanted more than anything was a long time playing for England. In the run-up to the tournament she'd been in the gym six nights a week, and she'd been netting on the bowling machine at Derbyshire at the weekends; with her husband playing there she got to use the facilities a bit, and a few of the other players helped out too, with a spot of coaching or shadow batting.

After the game at Taunton, when South Africa beat England on the last ball, Sky's Charles Colville had given her the award for the game's quickest 50 – then (seeing we'd lost) he asked if her husband would be giving her some practice in the garden when she got back home. That had struck me as pretty crass (and their garden's pretty tiny, too) but Smigs just laughed. 'He's a prat, isn't he? I thought, here he goes again. Charles Colville.'

She'd always kept wicket; when she was a kid she couldn't bowl, couldn't even get it in the net, so they gave her the gloves. She won her first cap in 1992, when she was 19, at the back end of a tour down under; the cap came when England played the first ever five-day women's Test against Australia in Sydney. She'd gone as the second-choice keeper, and barely got a game before that in New Zealand, just a couple of friendlies – but when they went to Australia, three of England's fourteen had to fly home to go back to their jobs. Seeing there were only eleven left, she got a game then, but not much of one; she batted at eleven, got one run in each innings, and it didn't last five days – Australia won by an innings and 85 runs. Still, you've got to start somewhere.

Now she'd made the gloves her own; at the World Cup in '93, she didn't give away a single bye in the whole tournament. When JB caught the winning catch it was, she said simply, 'Joy. We all had to run over, to be together. It's being in a team, isn't it?'

Two years later, before the first tour to India she'd been dreading it, really dreading it – then it turned out she enjoyed it way more than she'd expected. Before this World Cup now, she'd told me she couldn't wait to get back – so while India crumbled on the telly, I asked how she was coping.

She said, 'I don't particularly like what you see sometimes. You get stared at all the time, that can make you a bit uneasy – but you carry on, you don't feel they mean you harm. I suppose they're intrigued, white women walking about, they're going to be inquisitive – I'm not bothered. And I've scored a few runs, got some stumpings and catches, so I'm happy. It's nice not to be travelling now, too – I was getting a bit sick of it.'

So could we beat the Kiwis?

'They're a good side, but nothing to be scared of. The bowling's looked a bit ragged on TV; we've a good chance to beat them. I'm rooming with Connie and we've talked about it a lot, because this is a different game now – and we want it so badly. You're thinking, if we lose, we'd have five more days here and nothing to do except watch someone else in the final – that's a frightening thought. If we lose we'd be distraught, I'd be heartbroken. I want to win so badly. I want to win the World Cup. We've done it before and I want us to do it again, because there's nothing that compares to it. It's such a high, I've never felt anything like it, and I want that feeling again. So I'm thinking about cricket, not Christmas. Christmas can wait. Boxing Day's what matters – to win that and get in a World Cup final, that'll be fantastic. You couldn't get a better present, could you?'

She smiled and said, 'Not quite as placid as normal just now, am I?'

Skip said her keeper was, 'A very focused person. Very quiet, but one hundred and ten per cent. If she wants it, she'll go for it.'

She and Smigs batted together for an age in Madras two years back, came off absolutely dripping – but they'd had six weeks acclimatising that time. Still, she liked the place; it was warm, friendly, organised. OK, not this morning with the bus – but, she shrugged, 'There's always something.'

She was confident about New Zealand; she reckoned they weren't the same side they'd been in England eighteen months ago. They'd lost a couple of players, among them the captain on that tour who'd retired, she'd been a big character – and, she said, 'If we keep in containing mode, they don't like the slow stuff. As fielders, they're similar to the Australians – but if you get on top of them, they can feel it. The bowlers have mediocre days – but even if they're having a good one, we can bat to eleven. So we're much better prepared. And then, we remember losing 3–0. They came gunning for us, after '93 – and we'll do that to them this time. It's tight, it's close – but we've a very good chance. We know them, and we've played this ground before. I'm pleased we've got them and not India, that's for sure. But if all of us have a good day, we're unbeatable whoever it is.'

On selection, she was pondering whether to go for strength in the batting as they had against Sri Lanka – which meant H played again – or to put in an extra bowler instead. She said, 'I think one seamer's probably enough, 'cause using Lottie's been a revelation. I turned to her in that first game against South Africa 'cause the wicket was turning, and she was more focused than I've ever seen her – so I thought, let's give her a go. It was just a hunch. She looked at me a little strange, I must admit, especially when I gave her the ball last over – but I knew she'd be OK, and she's kept at it. And this track sits up nice for seamers, it comes through OK; I'd rather use spinners on it and make New Zealand hit the ball.'

In sum, she reckoned on bringing back the Lengster in place of Laura MacLeod, and no other changes. Of Leng she said, 'She's reacted appropriately. We've talked about it, and I'm happy with what she's said. I've always told her her leg spin's vital, and if her head's right, she's a class act. Lottie bowling well gives her a shove up the arse, too.'

Her own bowling, by contrast, had not been good; normally as economical as anyone in England, she'd been unusually expensive on this tour, and apart from the two crucial early wickets against South Africa, her only other scalp had been one of the Irish. She readily admitted, 'I'm not right by a long chalk. It's the first time in my career I've had to think about my bowling. There was a lot of pressure before coming here, people saying I'd be the most crucial bowler, and maybe that's had an effect – but the little teams have been swinging the bat at me. Thinking about it's probably not the best thing to do, but it's bothering me that much that I am thinking about it. Still, I rise to big games. Come Friday, all I'll see is Debbie Hockley's wicket.'

Besides, we had other bowlers who'd found their line. England were the only team here that were playing out of season, and it had taken time – but she said of Clare Taylor, 'I'm really proud of her. She had a rotten summer against the South Africans but she's really worked hard, and between that and her experience, she's come up trumps. She's got a very big heart.'

On Reynard: 'Top notch. If you had eleven like Melissa, you'd be happy.'

On Connor: 'Her figures have been tremendous. She's very steady. She doesn't do much with the ball, but she puts it on the spot, and in one-day cricket that's what you want. Then she's an aggressive fielder, a thinking cricketer, and a great bat to have going in at nine. She's got a big future.'

With that and the batting, it was good enough. All round, she said, 'This game means more than anything in the world. We've worked so hard – and all of a sudden it's the last two steps to the mountain top now. Playing in a World Cup final at Eden Gardens – you've got to go for it, haven't you? It's a knock-out situation, it'll be tough – but you're playing for England, and you've got to go out and give it everything you've got. So I'm confident, I can't wait for the day to arrive. OK, getting beat by Australia like that wasn't good at the time – but we lost to New Zealand in a group game in '93, and it gives you a kick up the arse. You think, Right, you bastards, you're not doing that to me again. And it showed in the field against Sri Lanka, the noise was unbelievable. So we'll be up for it. If anybody isn't, what are they doing here?'

The corridor outside the players' rooms was decorated with a chain of Christmas trees and snowmen cut out of newspaper. In Selena's room, a pre-dinner drink was on; me, Joce, Fizz, Cath, Craig, and Thrasy, now renamed Thorax Metropolis. Splashing out for the festive season, we ordered Indian wine on room service; it came with a metal screw-top which entirely defeated the waiter. He stood turning it round and round and getting nowhere in a mounting frenzy of embarrassment; ever resourceful, Selena rescued him with a Swiss army knife the size of a Sherman tank.

The wine was Bosca, from Maharashtra State; the white said it was a riesling, and the red a cabernet. The white was the colour of a poorly man's urine, it smelt like aviation fuel, and it tasted like sherry. Oddly, the red tasted like sherry too. More oddly yet, when you mixed them together you got rose-coloured sherry, and then it tasted like Martini. Oddest of all, after a couple of glasses you could get quite fond of it.

In the restaurant, the hotel battled gamely to lay on a Christmas dinner, theoretically at seven-thirty. This consisted of a green soup of indeterminate character and, by eight-thirty, nothing else. We weren't bothered. Connie had a Christmas karaoke tape; Selena got in the beers. The turkey arrived at eight-forty-five, and appeared to be a mix of lamb and nut rissole. Well, they'd tried hard; the roast potatoes were good. The players pushed it about a bit on their plates, then sang some carols. Skip said she had to go on the radio tomorrow after the Queen. She'd begin, My subjects . . . people smiled, but for a little while it was a bit quiet, a bit sad; we were definitely a long way from home. Smigs was called away on a hotel mobile to talk to her family. Romps tried to keep it going: *We three kings of Orient are, one in a rickshaw, two in a car* . . .

Then a truly amazing band turned up. On keyboard, Salman Rushdie with a ponytail. On bass, Manuel. On rhythm guitar, Igor. On vocals, Margarita Pracatan in red satin, ruched up to the left hip with matching shoes and American tan tights. They gave us Boney M, a reggae version of 'Silent Night', and 'Jingle Bells' in amphetamine-disco style. Bop, said someone, for tomorrow we train. The band started in on M People: *Search for the hero inside yourself* . . .

Connie said quietly, 'This was playing in the dressing room when I went out to bat in the Test at Hyderabad. JB was in there and I was only nineteen, she's my secret hero, it was my first Test match – and she just said quietly, You can do it, kid. We had to bat three hours to save it, with three wickets left, and we did. Your first Test. Sticks in the mind, that.'

Connie got 13, stayed in a while – and I remember Romps coming home from that tour, talking about that game. It was the last in a three-Test series, England were 1–0 ahead, and it finished with her and the Thames Valley spinner Debbie Stock staying out there for the best part of two hours for the final wicket to save the match. There's a photograph of Romps at the crease, a thicket of close fielders all about. She shook her head and smiled, 'I'm supposed to be a slogger, me.' And then you realise, when you think about how those two hours must have been, that these people will have memories like these for all of their lives that aren't available to the rest of us. Men or women, money or no money, that doesn't matter; what matters is that they've played for their country a long way from home, and done well at it – and you or I will never know what that feels like.

At nine-fifty, the phone was brought back in; a call for Sue Metcalfe. It was her boyfriend, and he proposed. She accepted, the band struck up with 'I'm getting married in the morning', and the party swung a lot better after that. Everyone danced, including a few wildly optimistic Indians in *Saturday Night Fever* shirts with gold chains and flashing white smiles. Shirley said later, whatever happened come Boxing Day, 'We definitely won the Christmas party.'

Even so, I am absolutely not covering for them when I tell you that the players drank moderately and, in some cases, not at all; there were more pop bottles on the table than Kingfishers. Being a rodent, on the other hand, I myself got – to use Joce's immortal phrase – 'as lashed as a lashed thing on a lashed night in Lashville'. I remember the Lengster singing along to 'Hotel California', I remember a slow dance with H, I remember inquiring of Connie in the best traditions of investigative journalism, 'Just how posh are you then?', and I remember telling Fresh dolefully that I was missing my children. Then, unsteadily, I went to bed – and that was Christmas Eve in Madras.

At nine-thirty on Christmas morning I was woken by a goddess in a green sari standing by my bed with a box of complimentary biscuits saying, 'Happy Christmas.'

If possible, at that moment I'd have crawled into a dark hole somewhere and waited quietly for death to take me, but unfortunately it wasn't an option. Builders appeared to be dismantling the room next door, someone was testing the world's loudest PA system immediately outside my window, and anyway I had to get up and write a preview for the paper.

Given the mood I was in, I reached somewhat creakily for a touch of the old epic tone, concluding, 'Spare a thought, then, for these women of England doing battle far from home on Boxing Day.' To my surprise, they didn't sub that out; more surprising yet, for the second time it made the back page. In the end, I filed a dozen stories, something I'd never have expected to find myself doing, and something I've never done while writing any book before; at first I was worried, thinking it'd get in the way of the book, but the more they asked for, the better it felt. I'd thought I was off to write about something no one was interested in, just out of a stubborn cussedness that I thought they should be – but instead it felt, at last, as if these women were being taken seriously for what they did, and that was a very good feeling.

When I was done, I went downstairs and found Joce by the pool. She grinned. 'Had a visit from the beer monkey then?' I stared, uncomprehending. She explained, 'He steals all your money, beats you round the head with a stick, and shits in your mouth.'

'And,' said Fizz, 'he throws your clothes all round the room, eats half a kebab, then leaves the other half under your pillow.'

Oh, *that* monkey . . . I went to the bar for a bottle of mineral water, and enjoyed the spectacle of five waiters taking ten minutes to get it. Outside, there was a bright pastel sign painted on the wall saying, 'Get Mugged Here' – meaning that they had draught beer. They didn't have any now; the rodents had seen to that.

I bumped into Megan in the foyer, and asked how she was feeling. She smiled, friendly and content; she said, 'We didn't want to lose to Australia, but it couldn't have worked out better. Everything here is perfect. This hotel, a good party last night, time to relax and to train – I'm happy.'

The ride along the beach road to the stadium was lovely; a wide strip of orange sand ran down to the sea, tankers and freighters lined the blue horizon, and on a bare field across the road from the strand, men in whites and helmets were playing cricket. It looked pretty hot work, mind.

At the stadium, New Zealand were in the nets on the out-field. A couple of blokes clambered about on rickety bamboo frames, setting up Hero Honda logos over the sight screens; when the screen was behind the bowler's arm, they'd simply draw black curtains over the logo. Shirley wandered off to hang a few pairs of socks out to dry on the perimeter fencing; DIY laundry. Fizz strapped the Lengster's ankle; BB chortled quietly to JB that she'd got a dancing injury.

Megan drew them all together and said, 'Right, girls. It starts from here. We've had a brilliant night last night, and now we're going to be up for it right from the warm-up. Off you go.'

While they jogged and stretched Joce moved among them, martial with her instructions. To one side, Fizz talked to Megan about organising a trip an hour up the coast to Fisherman's Cove on Saturday, the day after the game; Megan told her, 'If we win they can go. How about that?'

They started working in pairs, crouched low, zipping the ball back and forth quick and hard, fifty catches left hand, fifty right hand, fifty two-handed. Then they knocked each other catches off the bat, striking it firm, pushing each other along; Megan walked among them as the ball thocked off the willow, fiercely encouraging. 'Great catch, Liss, great catch, Bev, good work, Lengy, way to go.' Then she rounded them up for fielding drills: 'We are *going* to hit that stump, and we are *going* to back each other up. Let's look sharp, let's *attack* it.'

An Indian photographer roamed among them; Megan and Skip shouted, applauded, urged them on – and I confess at this moment to a welling of emotion, a stark realisation of how much this meant to these people. In the broiling afternoon sun of Tamil Nadu on Christmas Day, all they wanted to do was run out a Kiwi, and get to the final of the 6th Women's Cricket World Cup. As Shirley Taylor fielded the local press, and skinny men swept the concrete terraces, and barefoot boys hung spellbound over the neat white picket fence in front of the pavilion, at that point I wanted them to win so badly that the thought of it not happening was an abyss. It had been such a long way to come, such a draining investment of effort and desire, that to fall at this point now would be utterly crushing.

A spectacularly big hawk settled on the Bharat Petroleum board on the roof above the terraces. I wondered how we looked from up there, dots of white darting and calling across the gleaming green field in this massive ring of concrete. From on high you could say, It's only a game of cricket – but we weren't on high, we were down here and in amongst it, and all perspective was narrowing to that fierce and clenching point of 100 overs tomorrow. And then we would know.

Fizz and Joce came back from an amble round the boundary, and pointed out something they'd seen at the foot of the terracing fifty yards away. I went to have a look. It was the carcass of a dog, headless, fly-blown, the skin picked off, the flesh liquefying in the heat; the flesh was orange. It was the most minging thing yet.

I went back and Joce said, 'You're telling me it hasn't got a head? You mean you looked *closely* at it?'

I was, I said, a fearless investigative rodent.

'You,' she told me firmly, 'are a sad, sad man.' She made as if to throw up.

Shirley wondered if it was as horrid as the dead rat in the toilet at the Gymkhana. Close call, I'd say.

England took on water between each drill. After seventy minutes, Megan called them together for the last one. 'Let's have a dazzling finish now, shall we?'

A ball got lost down a storm drain. Megan decided not to put her hand too far in there after it, after catching sight of the toad. The toad, at least, was alive.

They did ten more minutes and, watching them work,

Megan professed herself pleased. 'It's very hot out there, but they've kept the quality. They've done very well.' She told them that was it, unless anybody wanted to do more – and every one of them did. The bowlers went to turn their arms over at Lottie, Smigs, and BB in the nets; I went to where Debbie Hockley was packing up after the Kiwis had finished.

She was thirty-five years old, a short, stocky, strong-shouldered woman who'd been playing for her country for eighteen years; she was a physio at a hospital in Christchurch. She said, 'Tomorrow's pretty huge. If you don't win, you're not there, are you? But it's too close to call. It's difficult, when you've not had much tough competition – it starts here, really. Games like Pakistan,' she shrugged, 'are a waste of time.'

The women's game in New Zealand had merged with the men's game already; the national side had had sponsorship for several years, and the majority of their players still got their wages while they were away, their employers more positive and enlightened than most of ours tend to be. Hockley said, 'We're strong all round; our fielding's sharp, we're looking for disciplined bowling, and we can score runs.'

So, I asked, what did they have to do to beat England? She smiled, but not in her eyes. She said, 'Score a lot of runs, and get them out for fewer.' Then she turned to one of the others and said, 'Are you watching Lottie bat?' And so they were.

14

The Missing Over

During the night, a fax from Radio 4's *Today* programme was shoved under Shirley's door; they wanted reports phoned in for their two sports bulletins. At breakfast she said contentedly, 'We've made the big time.'

We were sitting with Megan and Craig; we asked four times for a pot of coffee. Eventually, a pot of tea came. I said, 'We didn't order that.'

'Yes we did,' said Shirley. 'Craig ordered it yesterday.'

I got up, roamed the room, and found a waiter puttering aimlessly about with a big Thermos on a tray. I asked him, 'Is that coffee?'

He said, 'I don't know.'

I thought about killing him. I said, 'I tell you what. Let's have a look inside and find out, shall we?' I unscrewed the lid. It was coffee. How could he wander about with it and not know that? There was, you might say, a certain tension in the air.

The bus left at seven-forty-five. It was hot already, with

bright sunlight. The bus was quiet; H lay on her own across the back seat, eyes shut. She was playing; so was the Lengster. We passed along the shorefront, the beach lined with nets and sharp-prowed fishing boats, the cargo ships silhouetted against the shining rim of sea and sky. We passed people living in thatch and plastic lean-tos along the pavement; they waved and smiled, and a woman stooped to brush dust off the kerb.

When we got to the stadium Liss went to sit alone, chugging carbo-drink, plugged into her Walkman. Romps covered herself with moz repellent. There were TV cameras on the boundary, and on rickety bamboo scaffolds behind the sightscreens. Someone pointed out the press box for me; fifteen yellow desks in the stand over the pavilion, and plastic chairs with armrests. A crew of little skinny guys in khaki padded barefoot about the wicket; one of them had a kettle in a wicker basket for their chai. The stumps were laid out ready at each crease, the words 'Hero Honda' stencilled down each one. A photographer took a picture of them. People put boards up round the perimeter saying Bridgestone, Konica, the Bank of Maharashtra, AIDS – Be Aware, Take Care.

I went back to the area in front of the dressing rooms; fans were turning in the ceiling, stirring the hot air. I felt as if I was going to go at the knees. Thrasy said, 'There's nothing like the morning of a big cricket match. All the people doing their bits and pieces, and you can see it in the faces of the players. Put a crowd in here, you really would go at the knees.'

New Zealand arrived at eight-twenty. Connie blew me a yellow sunblock kiss, and went to jog with England round the boundary. Thrasy said under his breath, 'These guys have *got* to get to the final.' Still, on one front he was happy; the good and efficient people of Madras had given him a dedicated private line in the Honorary Secretary's office.

Fizz sat in front of the dressing room, using a ruler to cut a clean edge into a rubber, and sharpening her pencils. During games she'd get too nervous to watch, so the past few matches she'd been sketching a picture of a sadhu, a holy man, from a postcard she kept in a room service menu in her medical notes. The rendering was precisely detailed, and remarkably good.

So too was the deep fielding practice, as Peter Moralee knocked up high balls and ground balls to be returned to Jane Cassar. They sent the ball back to the top of a single stump from thirty yards or more, over and over. The Kiwis, meanwhile, were doing busy little drills, running and catching, whipping the ball about amongst themselves, and like the Australians they looked like athletes. If they were as able as they were fit . . . I tried not to think about it.

The Lightning Seeds played quietly from the boom box amid a pile of Vodafone kitbags. It was five past nine; the players went back to the dressing room. A TV commentator came to Cath Harris and said, 'We're going live in five minutes.' She went off to help him put names to faces.

Officials called towards the dressing rooms, wanting the teams out. 'They're changing,' someone called back, 'they're changing.' An echoey hubbub of voices drifted up under the stepped concrete ceilings. News came that we'd lost the toss, and were fielding. Studs clattered down the steps as the players went to line up and shake hands with the Indian Minister of Sport, and the British Deputy High Commissioner. Then, to a polite scatter of applause, Skip led England running into the field, Debbie Hockley and Emily Drumm walked out behind them, and the World Cup semi-final began.

Romps opened; Hockley let the first one go by outside off. The second hit her high on the thigh pad; the third, she played forward and blocked it. Then a single went through cover. Drumm took guard, squared up – and pelted four through backward square off her hips.

Skip took the job at the other end; after the tap she'd been getting, a brave captain's decision. Hockley got a single, then Drumm spent three balls poking about outside off. She hit the next one hard to midwicket; BB fielded sharply, slung it back in. Another dot ball, and there was only one off the over.

Romps bowled five dots to Hockley; cries rang out round the field, 'Well bowled.' Liss was on the boundary at deep cover, everyone else was in the ring, the fielding was tight and aggressive – then Sue Metcalfe let one through at backward square, and the Kiwis ran two.

Skip bowled to Drumm – and the second ball she played round a straight one, the shout went up and the finger followed it, she was leg before and Skip was spinning, screaming, both arms punching air. Everyone sprinted in around her; New Zealand were 8 for 1, and Shelley Fruin came in.

They might have lost Hockley in the next over. The first ball she went forward uncertainly, it popped up low towards H at short cover, and fell too short as she dived. Near enough the same thing happened with the third ball too, it carried further, again H dived – and spilled a tough chance, stretched out full length.

Still Skip and Romps stayed tight and controlled; still the fielding was sharp. Romps took out middle stump with a direct hit from backward square – but Fruin was well in. She and Hockley nudged it along, but slowly, slowly; after ten overs they were 21 for 1, and the two of them spent a long time talking in the middle.

A single to Connie – the runners hesitated, looked panicky, the throw was on the button and Smigs took the bails off. Hockley was in, but only just. You could see them edgy, wanting to go, deciding against it as the fielders zipped in. BB pulled off a fabulous diving stop at short square leg; several hundred were in the ground now, and little spurts of applause sounded round the hollow stands like the noise of tearing paper.

Then they got away a bit, seven off an over from Romps, four off Skip – so she took herself off and put on the Lengster. It was the big temperament question now – and she answered

it. One wide, one single, five dots; she had both batsmen looking distinctly uncertain. The game stayed tense, balanced, not
knowing which way to teeter.

Leng's second over was nearly perfect – one wide, but nothing else. The applause that came now, however, wasn't for her;
it was an ironical ripple for a limping dog meandering onto the
outfield. It stopped at deep point, and sat down.

Romps bowled her tenth and final over; in all she went for 29
runs, one maiden, no wickets but a tough chance dropped –
against bats like these, a tidy job. At the other end, Leng had
Hockley flummoxed; again, six dots only marred by a wide. A
second dog, meanwhile, now wandered on and off, while the
first dog moved to do some fielding in the covers. This was
absurd. New Zealand were 52 for 1 off 20 overs, and around
and about it we had the poor man's Cruft's.

Liss came on for Romps; a third dog appeared in the outfield. Liss went for one run from her first over while now a
fourth dog appeared, most likely the third one's puppy. I suppose at least they were alive.

Leng stayed on the button; Liss bowled a maiden. At the
halfway point New Zealand had only 63 for 1 and in the press
box, doing the scoring for the WCA's records, Fresh said quietly, 'If I were New Zealand, I'd be rather narked with this.'
Then she added nervously, 'Let's not say anything yet, eh?'

Fruin tried to sweep Leng, and missed by a mile. England
cried and groaned, hands in the air as the spin had her foxed.
Hockley cut Liss for two through backward point, then went
for a sharp single – it was well taken, but it had a little bit of the
desperate about it. H took out middle stump from close range,
but Fruin was just in. Next over, another sensational stop and
throw – by JB this time – had Hockley scrambling for her
ground.

The Lengster had bowled seven overs, and given away only
fifteen runs. It would have been ideal, if not for five wides –
though the umpires were pretty strict on that front. With three

overs still to come from her, Skip put on Connie in her place. The first ball went for a single and an unlucky overthrow, and here's how good England's fielding was – the overthrow came when JB got a direct hit on the stumps at the bowler's end, and the ball ricocheted away. So the next fielder got to it – and scored a direct hit at the other end for good measure.

The rest of the over, Connie bowled five dots. They'd been right; Hockley didn't like the slow stuff. After 30 overs, New Zealand were 80 for 1 – and England's claim to be an attack whose virtues were containment, consistency, line and length, was beginning to look well vindicated.

Craig came up from his monster zoom on the boundary. He said, 'I'm not very convinced by that Fruin,' as she played and missed outside off against Liss. So the next over, of course, she thrashed Connie for four high over the covers; it only bounced twice before it was away over the rope. And this was desperately tense; eighteen overs to go, and if we could keep them pegged back like this, then surely the game was ours.

But Liss had gone for eight off an unlucky over – three of them had pinged up past Hockley's face off bat and pad before squirting away to third man – so now Skip gambled, and brought on Lottie to bowl to Hockley. Now my take on Lottie's bowling to date had been harsh; I thought it was lollipop stuff. You'd get a good 'un turning sharp, then the next one would be a full toss or a dolly drop long hop – and that was OK against the little teams, 'cause they got out to the bad balls as easy as the good ones. But set a part-time bowler just turned eighteen years old onto someone like Hockley . . .

Including the previous games in this tournament, Hockley had 4,521 runs in international competition, more than any other woman on earth. She'd played 108 one-day matches for her country, 33 World Cup games, she had 1,229 World Cup runs – only JB had more – and she had two centuries to her name in India already. Let Lottie give her anything duff, in other words, and this was someone who'd bash her halfway to the Himalayas and back.

So here's what happened. Second ball, Hockley swept it to square leg. The Lengster was out there; she ran to her right, picked it up one-handed as it raced by her, threw it back in one movement, and got a direct hit from side on, only one stump to aim at. Fruin was well out – and just as they'd looked as if they might be starting to motor, New Zealand were 93 for 2. Fruin had taken 84 balls to make her 29, which shows how tight we'd been already – but nothing yet had been as wonderful a piece of cricket as Leng's run-out was.

It wasn't a lot to do with Lottie, obviously. But there's me worrying she might not be good enough? She looked at the new bat, Katrina Withers, a big tall woman who opened the Kiwi bowling – and she bowled her four more dots for a maiden. She wasn't finished, either. Her second over, second ball – oops, a full toss. Withers stepped back, had a look at it, then thrashed it though the covers for four to bring up the hundred. Two balls later she took a single to mid-on, so now Hockley was facing – at a time when, surely, she was going to have to cut loose.

The sixth ball of the over was short, and Hockley lashed out at it – against the spin. She swung the bat so hard, and so misjudged it, that bat and ball together went spiralling up away in the air. From square leg, the Lengster ran in to take the high falling catch sweet and simple as the bat fell to earth before her – and Hockley was out. New Zealand were 101 for 3 with only fifteen overs remaining, the gamble had paid off, and England were surely, definitely on top of this one now.

New Zealand's captain Maia Lewis came in. She and Withers needed to accelerate – but when forty overs were gone, they'd still only got to 118, a run rate under three an over. Lottie went for six off her fifth over; the next over, Liss pinged Lewis' off stump clean out of the ground, and New Zealand were 125 for 4. Kathryn Ramel joined Withers; Skip put Leng back on for Lottie, and she stayed tight. In the end, she was our most economical bowler; ten overs, twenty-six runs.

Nine wides was a blemish, but never mind – New Zealand still couldn't take it up past two or three an over. With five overs left they were on 136, a run rate only a whisker above three an over, and we looked good. Obviously, they were going to thrash out now – but still, letting them get 39 off those last five overs was a bit of a whoopsie.

Ramel and Withers clattered everything; Skip bowled three of those last overs, and got bashed for 26 runs. That was painful. Leng went for 6 off her last over, Liss went for 7 off her last, and inevitably it was pretty frantic and clumsy. H dropped another catch – again, not the easiest in the world, the ball dropping behind her as she turned and ran for it – and in the last over Romps dropped Withers in the deep. Smithies bowled her next ball anyway; Ramel had gone by then too, stumped by Cassar three balls earlier.

It was a messy end, but not a calamitous one. Overall, England's performance in the field had been their best of the tournament, stepped up against decent opponents to a whole new pitch of concentration – with the result that New Zealand had been held to 175 for 6. The Kiwis' scorer Maria McElroy muttered warily, 'Semi-respectable – but probably not what they wanted.' And with the batting we had, how could we not catch it? Three and a half runs an over? How could we not make it to Eden Gardens now?

Word came that umpires Muralidharan and Venketesan were docking England an over. The rules allowed you three hours to bowl your fifty; we'd taken three hours and five minutes, so we'd be allowed to bat for only forty-nine. Megan went to the umpires to point out that they'd not allowed time for the drinks breaks (or for interruptions while the groundsmen chased assorted mongrels round the outfield) and she came back to say that we had our fifty overs after all, and that they'd shaken hands on it.

Lottie and H went out to bat. Katrina Withers was medium-quick, but nothing like Fitzpatrick; she looked ungainly, and not greatly threatening. In the first over Lottie cut her to point for a single, H worked another off her legs to backward square, and Lottie guided a third to backward point; good start.

A tall, gangly off spinner called Clare Nicholson came on and bowled Lottie a maiden; worse altogether, Withers had H lbw for 1 in the next over. So much for going with an extra bat – but she'd been uncertain of her place from the start and twice now, here and in Chandigarh, that uncertainty had shown. So JB went out, had a look at Withers – and the over finished a wicket maiden. We were 3 for 1 off three overs – not such a good start after all.

Lottie clouted two fours off Nicholson; a textbook cover drive, and a shot driven back past the bowler so hard that though it deflected off her feet and was slowed a bit as it did so, it carried to the rope anyway. At the other end, Withers was plying a line outside off, but she wasn't consistent; she bowled a wide, a no ball, JB took a single, the next over Nicholson went for six, and it began to feel as if these two were picking up, that we were setting off OK after all.

Withers traded a shade off her pace for a shade more accuracy; her next over, she only gave away a single. Scoring beside me in the press box, Laura MacLeod asked, 'What d'you think the press will be like at Heathrow?'

She was a strong, handsome blonde from Cheshire; she'd turned twenty a few days before we got on the plane. She'd not had much luck in India, but she'd taken not playing many games in good part, and was certainly one for the future. I told her, if we lost this game there'd be nobody there. If we got to the final and lost, there might be a few – and if we won the final there'd be loads, but it wouldn't matter 'cause they'd be friendly. Why, anyway? Was she nervous?

She smiled and said quietly, 'Nah. I just want to get into Burger King when we get off the plane, that's all.'

Out in the middle, Nicholson was tightening her line; she bowled a maiden. Kelly Brown came on, bowling right-arm medium inswingers, and she looked steady too; after ten overs we were 27 for 1, a whisker ahead of New Zealand at this point in the innings, but not looking too comfortable. The next few overs went for two, one, three, one; we were getting penned in here.

Skip came and sat by my desk. She said, 'We bowled and fielded brilliantly – so it's up to us now. We wanted them below 180, and as long as we've got wickets in hand we'll pull it off. Eighteen wides is annoying – a couple were harsh, maybe, but most were correct. But otherwise everybody kept with it, if somebody had a bad over we stayed together, and the fielding was superb.'

She was chewing her nails, tensed up, giving them a real good gnaw. I remarked on that and she said, 'I can tell you, I'm playing every ball. I'm a hopeless watcher.'

Lottie swept Brown for four; she bowled a wide, the batsmen running it to no purpose, then JB belted four back past the bowler. Nine off the over, that was more like it – so they put on another off spinner, Catherine Campbell, and she pegged us back in again. The New Zealand field was tight all about, stopping singles, squeezing up the pressure. Frustrated, Lottie hit out at Campbell across the line – and was bowled for 25. She'd faced 71 balls, then played a poor shot born of mounting impatience; England were 43 for 2, and BB walked out to the wicket.

In the twentieth over, she knocked Campbell for seven; that took it to 54, still staying just a shade ahead of New Zealand. Like Skip said, as long as we'd got wickets in hand . . . all we had to do was stay in, build it up, keep nudging along.

Down by the boundary, bizarrely, a military band struck up, a rackety noise of drums. The crowd was around 2,000 by now, and they liked it – but I don't think I'd have liked it if I was batting. Still, BB didn't look bothered, she was going nicely; she slammed two back over Campbell's head, then whacked a glorious drive for four through midwicket. Again, that irritating band struck up; they had skirly pipes now too. Dogs, bagpipes – what next? Campbell put it in the air for BB again, so once more she stepped up and said ta very much, sent four more zinging to the boundary. Ten off the over.

The Kiwis had another medium pacer at the other end, Sara McLauchlan, and she was tidy; now she put in a maiden. Every little burst, they reined us back. We got to the halfway point on 69 for 2 – keeping, still, just a whisker ahead of them. The game, as it had always been, was too close to call; the run rate required to get us home was now 4.28 an over. I was beginning to find it painful to watch – and how can people say cricket is boring? Every time the bowler starts her run-up, the batter taps the willow at her feet and the fielders come striding in, there's a world of possibilities waiting on the turn of a ball . . .

Katrina Withers came back; BB stood lounging on her bat in an attitude of casual nonchalance. She looked good – but all that came off the over was a leg bye. Behind me in the press box, Romps wrote her diary with an air of strung-out and furious concentration. McLauchlan bowled to BB; they took a sharp single to point, the fielder's throw back crashed the stumps, and BB was only just in. She did her lounging act again between the overs as if to say, no problem. You take your time, 'cause I'm here all day. Withers gave her a loose one, and she pulled it over square leg for four; the next one she hoiked inches above the straining fingertips of short midwicket for three. New Zealand were shunting the field about virtually every time we scored a run now – but one of the dogs was back, so maybe they were just trying to avoid getting bitten.

McLauchlan bowled to BB. Dot, dot, dot, dot – and down below me a gang of kids were chanting, 'We want four, we want four.' I can tell you, they didn't want it as badly as I did.

But she didn't get four; McLauchlan had her leg before, and we were 78 for 3. She'd got 30 off 45 balls; now she was gone, and Sue Metcalfe joined JB. As long as we'd got wickets in hand . . .

After 30 overs, we had 81; at this point in their innings, the Kiwis had 80. McLauchlan sent down more precision-oiled stuff; dot, dot, dot, an lbw shout, more dots, a maiden, another lurch in the stomach. She was New Zealand's best bowler, unfussy, straight, hard to get away. They kept chopping and changing, too – now Campbell was back in place of Withers. JB took a single, Metcalfe struck four through midwicket, a wide, a single – seven off the over, and it swings back your way. This innings, it was like living on a pendulum.

Kathryn Ramel came on, bowled two overs, went for one off the first then five off the second, and Maia Lewis took her off again; it was hard to tell who was under more pressure here. There were fifteen overs to go, the Kiwis were fielding with four deep now, we had 98 for 3, level pegging all the way – and beside me at the scorebook Fresh said firmly, 'It's less than a run a ball. It's perfectly gettable.' It was, in fact, 78 runs required off 90 balls. And as long as we'd got wickets in hand . . .

Campbell stepped up – and Sue Metcalfe was run out. It was an electric bit of fielding by McLauchlan, a direct hit from mid-off, and we had 100 for 4. OK, OK – we had fourteen overs left – or did we?

While she was batting, Sue Metcalfe heard something said between Maia Lewis and the umpires that made her realise they were only giving us forty-nine overs after all. She went to the boundary to tell Megan that, and Skip ran on to talk to the umpires. Then Metcalfe was out, and Smigs joined JB in the middle; Kelly Brown came on, bowled three wides, and Fresh said grimly, 'You can keep on bowling them.' Campbell went for five off the next over, Brown went for five more off the next – while down in the pavilion, an outbreak of bafflement, consternation, and plain point-blank rage spread through the

England camp – because how could we only have forty-nine overs? What was happening here? Didn't the coach shake hands with them on fifty? And someone somewhere was complaining to an IWCC person – but how much power did they ever have?

Out in the middle, Smigs sliced a deft two to backward point. Quick running had her back in, the bails were off, she was given not out, the Kiwis were round the umpire – and now Skip was back out there too with the drinks bottles, clearly arguing with the umpires about the missing over again, gesticulating, trying to fathom how fifty could turn into forty-nine in the middle of an innings. Next over, she was out there again – with her bat this time, because now Jane Cassar really had been run out. It was the speed and agility of the fielding again, a one-move pick-up and throw from mid-off to the bowler's end, and we were 116 for 5. JB hit a four and a single; the over finished 121 for 5, we needed 55 more, and now we only had nine overs to get them instead of ten.

Control the controllables, that was what they said – and, enraged in the heat of the moment by the mystery of the missing over, Karen Smithies didn't. The first ball she faced (from who else but Debbie Hockley) she aimed an angry heave at it, got it all wrong, and lofted it to Maia Lewis at midwicket. Lewis took the catch calmly above her head, England were 122 for 6 – and the World Cup was tumbling in fury and confusion from their hands.

In the press box a knot of Indian journalists pressed round Fresh at the scorebook, demanding the numbers; she snapped the answers back sharper and sharper. The next over JB was stumped; Liss and the Lengster were out there now, we needed 51 off 42 balls, and it was all sliding horribly away. They were getting singles, it wasn't enough, we were scrambling, things were falling to bits; Leng dobbed up a catch to Nicholson and she spilled it, they ran a single through, then another, then another. Liss dived full length to make her ground; the keeper fell sideways as the bails flew, rolling over on the back of Liss' head. She got up spitting out a mouthful of dirt.

Dogs, bagpipes, a missing over – but don't worry, there's more. McLauchlan was bowling, and the forty-fifth over went like this:

First ball, Liss got a single.

Second ball, the Lengster swung out and looped an edge for four straight behind her.

Third ball, she hit a single.

Fourth ball, Liss fine cut to third man for one more.

Fifth ball, dot.

Sixth ball, a single for the Lengster.

Seventh ball, a wide.

Yup – seventh ball. It was a seven-ball over. Laura MacLeod shook her head and said angrily, 'This is *crap*.'

When it was all over, Fresh and Maria McElroy both agreed that that wasn't all of it either. They had me look back through my notes to the fourth over, the one where Lottie hit two fours – and sure enough, that one only had five balls in it. Great. You're running a World Cup semi-final and you can't *count*? It was, said McElroy, a disgrace.

Seeing McLauchlan's seventh ball was a wide, she had of course to bowl an eighth ball, and Liss got a single off it. England were 146 for 7 with four overs left; we needed 30 off 24 balls.

Nicholson bowled to Liss; she got a single. Then Leng hoiked it back high behind the bowler; Nicholson turned and ran, caught it falling, diving, spilled it, bobbled it, and finally made it safe in her outstretched hands as she landed flat out. 147 for 8, three overs remaining, 29 required, and all hope fast fading.

Chasing the increasingly impossible, Liss was run out, Connie was run out, and we were 155 all out in 47.5 overs.

New Zealand won by 20 runs, and England's World Cup was over.

Ever honest about the game she loved so much, outside the dressing-room Megan Lear put the missing over in perspective. She said, 'We should never have been docked any overs. I've been in there and shaken hands with them on that, that we had fifty to bat – then they've told the Kiwis it was forty-nine. Now in the end, it didn't make any difference – we've lost because we didn't bat well enough, and that's the bottom line. But it might have done – and you just don't need that sort of confusion.'

Personally, I think it did make a difference – it certainly did to Karen Smithies. Like Thrasy said, 'You can't bat when you're angry.'

New Zealand had finished their forty-first over on 124 for 3. We finished our forty-first on exactly the same score – but with 6 wickets down, because Skip was out in that over with steam jetting from her ears. We'd found out about the missing over a short while before that – and a dozen overs to go with the chase still on is absolutely no time to find out that you've been penalised, when your coach had previously returned from the umpire's dressing room entirely certain that you hadn't been. In short, to say that this was a messy and controversial exit from a messy and controversial tournament is to express how I feel on the matter with the greatest of restraint.

For all that, like Megan, Karen Smithies was not prepared to use it as an excuse – and in truth, forty-nine overs or fifty, a batting line-up like England's should have beaten a total of 175. Amid a knot of local pressmen in a little foyer outside the dressing room, Skip said, 'Fair credit to the Kiwis – they bowled well, and they fielded well. We knew we had to build a foundation, but we lost wickets when we didn't want to. We threw it away.'

She said, 'I lost in the final nine years ago at the MCG, and it's not a very nice feeling. And I'm feeling that way right now.' As soon as she decently could, she got away from the notepads and back to her team.

I went to see the umpires. Muralidharan was adamant that the time allotted to bowl your fifty overs was three hours, that no allowance was made in the rules for the drinks breaks, and that during the lunch break they'd told Megan that England would have forty-nine overs.

I cannot believe for one minute that Megan Lear would have left that room saying she'd shaken hands on England having fifty overs, if she wasn't absolutely sure that that was how the issue had been settled. Very obviously, I cannot call an umpire a liar either. We must, therefore, ascribe these events in Madras to another of Mr Pillay's communication gaps.

But I will say that Mr Muralidharan's English seemed very good to me.

Megan said, 'It's obviously disappointing, because I still believe we're the better side. And I'm disappointed for the girls, because they've worked so hard. We've played superbly well, there's no comparison to how we were against them in '96; we put in a really professional performance in the field, and I was really happy at the end of their innings. And we should have got those runs – with the batting we've got, we should be able to get that. It's just on the day, isn't it? It's just on the day. And it'll take time to get over this, it'll really take time.' She sighed and asked, 'Will that do for you then?'

Of course it did. Any further questions would have been pointless cruelty. So at five-thirty we went and got on the bus. 'Well,' said H, collapsing into the seat beside me, 'that's brought an abrupt end to your story, hasn't it?'

15

The Hardest Thing in the World

When I found Sue Metcalfe's house in a tiny village in a gorgeous stretch of the Yorkshire Dales, I asked her how many people lived there. About eight, maybe? She smiled and said, 'Is it as many as that?'

There were in fact about twenty houses, and the obligatory pub. The front of the cottage looked out across the wide sweep of a valley, with green hills rising high on the far side; the back nestled beneath the rocky slope of the near side. That, said Metcalfe, was handy for training; she only had to pop out the back door, and she was straight into a hill sprint. She was doing a fair bit of that, too; it was late September, two months before departure for India, and she was training four nights a week. She did the running, put in time in the gym, and she had one night a week with her rugby club.

The cottage was part of a converted barn; she'd been born in the house next door. Her grandad was a farmer; she had two brothers, and she grew up playing rugby and cricket with them on the farm's open land in any spare moment they had. Since she was nine or ten, she'd played cricket with the lads' side at the village club in Kettlewell; as for the rugby, she started training with the ladies' section at Wharfedale Rugby Club to get fit, and finished up playing scrum half. Now in National Division Two, they're one of the top sixteen women's sides in the country.

She was thirty-two years old; she went to India with thirty-nine caps for England. She won the first when she was eighteen, against New Zealand at Headingley; she got the call on a Sunday morning, and she was shocked rigid. She reeled into the next room and told her dad she'd been selected; being a Yorkshireman, he barely looked up from his paper and just grunted, 'That's good.' He was, of course, thrilled to the core; he went to watch her every day. A fast bowler then, she had Debbie Hockley caught behind in the first innings, and ran her out in the second – a notable double scalp on her debut.

Nowadays, she played in an evening league for the ladies' club at Pateley Bridge, she played for North Riding at the weekend, and she'd captained Yorkshire to their string of area championships. When she wasn't playing cricket, she was a blood coagulation specialist for Bio Products Laboratory, a branch of the National Blood Authority. They made plasma products for haemophiliacs; Metcalfe travelled to hospitals all round the North, from Liverpool to Hull. But if she fitted it all together now, in earlier days work and cricket had collided uncomfortably.

She'd left home in her late teens to study sports science for four years at Crewe & Alsager College; the next six years she lived in Leeds. She went to work for Bio Products – but in the winter of '91–'92 she was picked for a tour down under, and to go on it she had to give up the job. Looking back she said, 'I just wanted to go and play. I didn't really consider the consequences, unfortunately. It's turned out all right – but when we came back, I really struggled to settle down.'

She worked in her dad's business for a bit, she did some medical repping, and a spot of debt collecting round Leeds. She did some time in an office with a sports and leisure company – she hated it, being stuck indoors – until an opportunity arose to go back to Bio Products. So now, if she had to choose between the job and a tour again, she'd not go on the tour. She liked her work too much, and at thirty-two, it was a career; she couldn't afford to chuck it in.

When I asked how she felt about that, she said if the situation ever came up, it would be her decision to make; she could understand the company's point of view and so far, they'd been good to her. Since she used all her holiday allowance to play cricket, in four years she'd only missed eighteen days' work anyway. I said, if she'd been a man . . .

She shrugged. 'I'd be a professional.'

I asked if she'd want that, and she paused to think about it. Then she said, 'If I were sixteen, yes. With sponsorship now, with lottery money coming in, who knows what'll happen for youngsters in the future? And of course I'd like to be paid,' she laughed, 'I'm from Yorkshire. But it's not going to happen, is it?'

When I wondered if this didn't seem unjust, she betrayed no hint of resentment. She said, 'I'm a realist. It's just the way the situation's been for us. Yes, you could complain – but it's not going to get you anywhere, is it? You've just got to get on and get the most you can for the ladies' game, and contribute as much as you can yourself.'

Including every day of your holiday . . .

'OK. I represent my country, and sometimes it does seem unfair. But I enjoy playing cricket; it's what I want to do. So I can have some other sort of holiday when I'm older, can't I?'

To ask how much cricket took out of her life was meaningless; the point was, how much did she get out of cricket? She said, 'I'll travel anywhere, play anywhere. The hardest thing is the winter, if you've got to go somewhere like Eastbourne to train – it's a bit of a way. But when there's a game on the end of it, I'm never bothered.'

She'd never tried working out how much it had cost her. With another shrug she told me, 'You spend your money on what you want, don't you?' She did concede that sometimes her boyfriend found it hard at a time like this, when she was forever away training, playing, preparing – but on the other hand, she said fondly, he supported her absolutely. Indeed, just now, he was probably backing her more than ever – for the simple reason that in the previous two World Cups, she hadn't been selected. I asked how it felt to have made it this time, and she laughed out loud. She said, 'About bloody time.'

In the Dales, no one raised an eyebrow at a woman playing cricket. A lot of lasses in the night league would be farmers; they'd work as hard as the men, and they could play their games too. 'Up here,' she said, 'cricket's just cricket. It doesn't matter who's playing it.'

Further afield, she'd met her share of chauvinism down the years, and her reaction was amusement. She said, 'It's entertaining. Men that haven't seen a woman play before, initially it's, Huh. I'll smack this about. Or if you're batting they'll say, Shall I bowl underarm? But it's just their own embarrassment, isn't it? Really they're thinking, What if she bowls me? What if she hits me for four? Because it threatens them, doesn't it? Still, once they've seen you can play, most'll say, Fair dos to you.'

Where she lived, if it was OK playing cricket, there were still a few souls unbudgeably convinced that rugby was too rough for women. Metcalfe said, 'I'll talk with them. It's their view, isn't it? They're not nasty about it, and they're entitled to their view – and as long as they don't actually try and stop me, it's not a problem.'

About this time, in a wave of puffy-cheeked media indignation, two thirteen-year-old girls who'd been scheduled to have a boxing match were pressured into backing out of it. Metcalfe said simply, 'If two people want to get in a ring and clout each other, it shouldn't matter whether they're men or women. It's not my cup of tea – but I wouldn't stop someone doing it just because she's a woman.'

Women in boxing may be broaching a male realm too far for a lot of men yet – but for the cricketers, at least a little respect and recognition had come in down the years. When she was a teenager first playing at Pateley Bridge Ladies they were, she said, very much second class citizens; this year, by contrast, she'd been asked to speak at the men's club dinner. She was disappointed she couldn't do it, because of being in India – but as she said, 'Things change, don't they?'

Her own game had certainly changed. She'd started as a right arm quick, but in her early twenties she tore her inter-costal muscles, and she tried coming back before they'd properly mended. It made it worse; she tried changing her action, she went all round-armed, and she couldn't get it back. So – plainly not a person inclined to give up – she turned herself into a batsman instead. Now she opened for her club, batted 3 for Yorkshire, 4 for England; against the South Africans in August, Vodafone made her England's batsman of the series.

It was obvious that she was a woman of stern determina-tion; it wasn't hard to see why they'd made her vice-captain. When I asked what she thought about going back to India she said, 'I can't wait. It's fantastic. I loved it, absolutely loved it. What a place. The bad, you learn from it – and the good, that's what you're there for.'

Apart from the money, I suggested that another difference between the men and the women was that the women won.

'Bit harsh, that. Bit harsh. We win, we lose – and when we lose, we don't get as much publicity as the men do. We don't get ridiculed, we don't get shredded – so we have an easy time of it in that respect. But look, you have to have it in perspective. It's a game of cricket. It may be Michael Atherton's job in a way that it isn't Karen Smithies' job, so it may be easier for us to have that perspective – and if we win, fantastic. Everybody's out there to do that, and you won't find fourteen more competitive people. But it's still just a game of cricket; nobody dies if you lose.

'So we're going out there as professional as we can be, within our limits, and we all want to win more than anything – but I think we'll be able to put it in perspective if we don't. If we give one hundred per cent, then somebody must have played bloody well to beat us – and if they did do, you shake their hand and say, Well played. It's the hardest thing in the world – but it's what you have to do anyway.'

16

Calcutta

England shook hands with New Zealand, and went back to the Hotel Savera. The sun hung low over the shore-front; a cow roamed the edge of a dirt patch, watching kids play cricket. I wondered if the rules allowed time for cow breaks. Out to sea, the humid sky was an ugly grey murk, and the water had a matt, gunmetal sheen. We turned a corner where a big sign offered us a Happy '98 – but there wasn't anyone too happy just now. H said quietly, 'I think JB's just retired.'

The bus pulled up outside the hotel; Megan stood up. She said, 'Before we get off the bus, I'm not going to make a big speech – but I just want to say that I'm extremely proud of every single one of you for everything you've done over the last year. Whatever's happened, you're still a great bunch of crick-eters and, more important, a great bunch of people. And we'll be back.'

Applause broke out as she turned away. Skip said a few

words too – then Romps said, 'C'mon, Helen the Plim. Let's go and get a beverage.'

I got in one of the ponderous lifts with Thrasy. We were wondering what we could say about the umpires. 'I know I can say,' said Thrasy, 'that I've got in the lift without my room key.'

I filed my match report and went down to the bar. A small group of players sat with their beers looking numb and exhausted. Connie said, 'I've got two essays to do by the middle of January.'

Sue Metcalfe sighed and said, 'At least I've still got a job.'

'Right,' said Connie, 'at least we've still got roofs over our heads. Except Fresh. Hers has blown off in Derbyshire, hasn't it?'

They played a Q & A game. 'In the second week in June,' Liss said, 'how many rats run from the river outside the ground into that shanty town?'

Connie asked, 'Per house?' Then she asked, thinking of the barefoot boys we'd seen playing cricket everywhere we went, 'On a Saturday in August, how many wickets fall in Madras?'

Romps said, 'Ninety-three thousand.'

'Don't be so stupid,' Liss told her. 'Twenty-four. They're all very good bats.' She had a big graze on her face, red-raw from where the Kiwi keeper sat on her head. She said, 'I think I swallowed half the pitch.'

'On average,' someone asked, 'how many minutes would your average English tourist spend arguing with your average rickshaw driver? And to the nearest rupee, how much of a reduction would they get?'

'On average,' someone asked, 'how many beers has H consumed?'

H said, 'Ask that one again in two hours.'

Liss: 'In a normal week . . .'

Romps: 'Bzzz, interruption. Define normal.'

Liss: 'In a normal week in India . . .'

At some point Romps said, 'It's too late to have a sense of

humour failure now, isn't it?' But like a lot of them that evening, when it came to talking about the game, she had a moment when she looked close to tears. When we talked about the missing over she shrugged and said, 'It's not just one over, is it?'

Shirley came in. She stood before our table and announced, 'I have to inform you that there are seats on the plane from Madras to London at eight o'clock tomorrow morning. Seats for everyone.'

There was a brief pause, then Romps said, 'Nah. Let's stay here.'

It turned out that BB had been working the phone to England (with, I think, the assistance of BA systems manager Jan Brittin) and she'd swung changes in their tickets for all who wanted to go. So those two were going, as were Laura, Bev, Connie, Smigs, Sue, the Lengster . . .

Megan frowned and said, 'Have we got enough left for a six-a-side then?'

Fizz was staying. 'My deciding factor,' she said pensively, 'is that I can't be arsed to get up at five o'clock in the morning. I just can't be titted to do that.'

Connie said, 'Eh, Fresh. Are you going home?'

The stout Derbyshire lass looked up steady and told her, 'No way. I'm staying.'

'Big points for that,' said Romps, 'big respect.'

Fresh said firmly, 'I love India, me.'

Cue gales of laughter. Romps asked, 'On average, on Boxing Day, how many English tourists say they love India?'

That evening, she'd had thirty quid in cash stolen from her room. But she was staying; so was Liss. I told her, 'Merit points there. Terminal diligence.'

She laughed and said, 'Terminal something.'

'Are you staying,' I asked, 'on the grounds that you might never be here again?'

She fell serious and told me quietly, 'I might never have the chance again to be in Eden Gardens. And I hope there's a big crowd. Because I would just love to sit in there with tens of thousands of Indians, watching a game of cricket.'

I stumbled to my room about one in the morning, and found Ben Okri being a pretentious twerp on BBC World, spouting twaddle to Tim Sebastian about 'the wisdom of tribal dance', and 'the tide of great difficulties'. He said airily, 'You see why one despairs.'

I snarled, 'Try getting room service in India, mate.' Then I turned him off and passed out.

In the morning, only six players were left – Skip, Romps, Liss, Lottie, Fresher and H. Despite saying she was staying because she couldn't be bothered to get up early in the morning, Fizz did get up to see them off, as did Joce – then they saw that Connie'd left her bag behind. So they jumped in a cab and took it to the airport for her, still in their pyjamas.

Rodents, management and support staff all stayed too – with the exception of Peter Moralee, who'd been pretty ill – but it didn't feel good. On the one hand, I understood why they'd gone; they'd been through a debilitating month, they'd lost, they were shattered and heart-broken, they wanted to get home to their families for the tail-end of Christmas, and Sue Metcalfe had the additional, not inconsiderable reason for returning that she'd just become engaged. On the other hand, I don't think they should have been allowed to go; it made it look as if England had fallen apart.

Probably Megan and Shirley didn't feel they could stop them; probably they couldn't have stopped them anyway, with BB acting unilaterally and going to work on the phone. But when we got to Calcutta, it was plain that our Indian hosts there – though far too polite to say so directly – were pretty hurt that half the England squad had cleared off before the final. The players who stayed didn't like it either; Skip was angered, Lottie was upset, it made a sad end to England's story more sad – and Romps was left holding BB's sixty quid phone bill to boot. Succinct as ever, Liss said, 'It's crap, isn't it?'

They'd talked a professional game all the way – but in the end, they were amateurs. The coach and the manager weren't paid to do what they did – they were teachers, with a new term waiting for them when they got home – so in effect they just shrugged, said it was over, and if you want to go then fair enough, off you go. But it looked bad, when India were hosting the four semi-finalists right through to the end. It looked bad, when Ireland and South Africa stayed on too because they wanted to go to Eden Gardens, and played a fund-raiser for the Missionaries of Charity while they were at it. As I say, I do understand it – but it shouldn't happen in future, if you want people to say that you approach the game as a professional unit.

We flew to Calcutta late in the afternoon; conversation was stilted and weary. People spoke of how hard it would be to settle down when they got back home; how it was difficult to decide on even a simple thing like what to wear in the morning, when you'd had that decision made for you by Shirley every day for a month. Or you'd go back to work and people would ask, 'Did you have a nice holiday?' And how could you ever say what it was like?

Then there was defeat, and the struggle to absorb it. 'The worst thing,' said H, 'was waking up in the morning. There it was, staring you in the face.'

'It's gone,' said Megan, 'that's one-day cricket. So you try to put it out of your mind – but it keeps coming back, what might have been. Then you're reflecting on it, and it gets you all over again.'

The flight was two hours; in the dark of the evening we crawled onto a bus, and were escorted into the city by a Jeep with a wailing siren. They put us up at the Oberoi Grand, the best hotel in Calcutta, a palace of luxury and efficiency; the foyer was an ocean of marble, and tall palms rose round the swimming pool in an inner courtyard painted gleaming white. Iron balconies adorned the windows, and the red tile roofs looked spotless.

In the morning I padded on piled carpet to the Rotisserie for breakfast – sausage and bacon, hash browns and vegetable cro-quettes, sautéed mushrooms and scrambled eggs. The tea was loose leaf, in a silver pot – it was very heaven. You had only to take a cigarette from the packet and before you'd even raised it to your lips, a bloke in a crisp white jacket with gold epaulettes and a black bow tie materialised at your shoulder, a match already lit in his cupped hands.

Another guy was set up behind a pair of gas rings, cooking omelettes to order; he had little bowls of diced ham, chicken, cheese, onion, chilli, tomato, and coriander. Craig had an omelette *and* scrambled eggs, 'Because I can.' Through the doorway, I could see a cricketer in a swimming cap, lean and tall, idly stroking lengths of the pool.

We went out from this oasis of comfort – Selena, Craig, and I – and walked into the other realities of Calcutta. The exterior of the hotel, so pristine within, stood fume-smudged in air so wreathed and stinking with exhaust fumes that it was grey-black, viscous, tangibly foul. Across a wide avenue on the edge of the Maidan, men were washing in water gathered from a rancid pond in paint cans. Two grimy boys rested on their haunches, eating rice by hand from a plastic bag. Huge crows with stained beaks picked at piles of indeterminate refuse. One man squatted in the rough grass to have a shit; another man squatting had no trousers on, and between his ankles his scro-tum was the size of a handbag.

Half a dozen kids ran past clutching stumps, a bat with ragged bindings, and a keeper's glove. 'Hello,' they cried, 'hello.'

'Hello, sir,' said another voice beside me, 'how are you?' He wore a dirty shirt and trousers, and ancient scuffed shoes; he was unshaven, and smiling a nervous, uncertain smile. I said I was very well, thank you, and he told me, 'You can get to the museum quicker through the park.'

'Thanks very much.'

'Where are you from, sir?'

'England.'

'I am British. My father is from Manchester. I have an uncle in Croydon. My father's father is from Glasgow, in Scotland. I am from Bihar. I am new here in town like you. I work in plastic, in mouldings and injections. Are you working here?'

'I am, yes.'

'Can you get me a job, sir? I am unemployed. I am pushing cars.'

I said I was sorry I couldn't help, and we walked on to the Victoria Monument, wondering what it paid when you pushed a car. The Monument was a hulking pile of pollution-tinged white marble; kids called out all round the gates, 'Hey coffee coffee coffee. Chai coffee Nescafé teabag.'

Inside, the building breathed an extraordinary, ghostly aura of British power, confidence, and self-righteousness, preserved incongruously at the centre of a litter-strewn park. Giant Romanesque statues of most noble Marquesses stood in dim and dusty halls, contemplating the scope of their dominions. The First Queen Empress herself sat beneath a dome, the walls around her bearing inscriptions from speeches to her Indian subjects; a massive painting showed the Prince of Wales riding past a palace on an elephant with the Nizam of Hyderabad. It seemed to come from another universe entirely – yet the building was only ninety years old.

We took a cab to the Khalighat Temple. It was in a warren of streets and narrow alleys jammed with people selling vegetables, jewellery, and livid-blue religious paintings. In a little yard, a boy practised his leg spin by a pile of rotting green leaves. Just beyond him, people clustered round a man cutting up fresh-killed goat's meat to take as offerings to Kali's shrine.

Inside the temple, I went barefoot on a stone floor dotted with petals and globs of red spit. There was a sharp scent of burning candles and herbs, and a hall where people sat cross-legged on mats on the grimed marble, doing ritual-looking things with flowers and bowls of fruit. At the gate to the inner temple, a throng of people with flowers in small baskets on their heads wrestled and jostled in a turbulent scrum to get in, reaching over their heads as they went to swing at the clappers of bells strung across the top of the doorway. The place was a ringing hubbub of unfathomable activity. Smoke drifted from tapers smouldering by piles of leaves and rubbish in the corners; at the far end, a body lay motionless on the floor by the portal, sheathed entirely in ragged and filthy dun material, covered in flies.

I went to stand in the portal, surrounded by children begging for chocolate. Outside was a walled yard maybe five yards square, into which a man led a goat. He stood behind it, reached forward over its back to seize its front legs, and jerked them sharply backwards, breaking the shoulders. The goat screamed, and slumped forwards. The man put his left arm round the goat's flopping front legs and chest, and pulled the back legs out behind him inside his other arm so the goat was now an arrow, a straight, quivering line.

He thrust it forward, driving the head between two wooden struts rising from a chopping block scattered with red petals and gore. A second man brought down a blade a yard long in one clean, fierce swing; the goat's head dropped off, and blood jetted from the neck. The headless carcass was thrown to the floor, still spraying blood; it kicked and writhed about the corner of the yard for minutes. The floor was thickly smeared with blood and dirt; a dog lapped at the severed neck.

I thought, no wonder the umpires make decisions we don't understand, if they're growing up with stuff like this going on around them.

*

We went for coffee at the Tollygunge Club, where the rich are the same as they are all over the world; loud and self-adoring in brand-name sportswear. Then we walked round the corner to try Calcutta's metro line, which is said to be spanking clean and super-efficient. It was just past two o'clock on a Sunday afternoon, and the station had just opened; we were at the head of a queue forming already at the ticket counter, but there was no one behind the counter to sell us tickets. The man in front of me said he had a brother on the Isle of Man; on the more immediate matter of getting a ticket for the tube, he shrugged.

I jumped over the ticket barriers, wandered down the platform, and found a bloke doing nothing in an office. I asked if they were going to sell any tickets, seeing there were fifty-odd people waiting already, and he said there wasn't a train until three o'clock. 'Please wait.' So I can tell you that Calcutta's metro is indeed very clean; whether it's efficient or not I don't know, because it wasn't running.

We got a cab back to the Oberoi to drop off Selena, then Craig and I went to gawp at the Writer's Building on BBD Bagh, a vast red affair somewhat in the style of a Loire chateau put up by the British to house their hordes of clerking bureaucrats. You should always remind yourself, Shirley once said, whenever you're getting peevish with Indian bureaucracy, who taught them how to do it – and here was the evidence in stone of our penchant for imperial paperwork. It is, today, the seat of the government of West Bengal.

In the middle of the tram terminus across the road, boys were playing cricket. We walked away towards the Howrah Bridge across the Hooghly, and came – within a city block of the state's government – upon more people living in the street than I could count. Down sidestreets and along the main road men sat on wooden boxes, giving other men a shave with cutthroat razors. People slept under blankets on wooden boards. On pavements of black dirt and broken stone, home for an entire family was a sheet of black plastic pegged to the wall and stretched out to the kerb, held up on sticks. There was one sheet after another after another. Laundry and cooking pots were washed in buckets; drying clothes hung from the walls of buildings, or on strands of rope strung up on poles. Children struggled down the road with paint cans full of water; those that weren't toiling at their chores put their hands out for money. They got some, until my pockets were empty – but all the small change in the world couldn't sort this out.

We came to a stone walkway over a railway line; it was a couple of yards wide, with a narrow kerb on either side. Along the length of both kerbs all the way across the bridge, each stretch of paving the length of a body appeared to be someone's home. People slept there, or just sat staring, amid a perpetual mass of humanity walking to and fro. Across the walkway we found a concrete deck on the banks of the Hooghly, and this too was overflowing with people, each with a mat or a blanket on the ground. By the shore, in the shadow of the cantilever bridge with its bulky lacing of massive girders, people washed themselves and their clothes in the grey and sludgy water.

Just along from here was a teeming shanty, wedged onto the bank between the river and the road to the bridge. Where the bridge rose across the river, a huge pile of garbage and vegetable detritus stood at the shanty's edge, picked over by cows and pigs and people. On the pavement above this, from their squares of cloth the street vendors offered pop music, padlocks, plastic combs, belts, scissors, screwdrivers, switchblades, knuckledusters, sandals and flip flops, wallets, cigarette lighters, eggs, apples, pineapples, limes, potatoes, coconuts, bananas, bracelets, lanterns, pens, sunglasses, inflatable cushions, kindling wood, everything under the sun. Not that you could see the sun, in the smeared and filthy sky. Even on a Sunday afternoon, the traffic across the bridge was a deranged and heaving scrum, belching a noxious murk so emetic I started feeling as if my lungs were coming out of my nose.

I've had the good fortune to travel a lot in my life, and in

Africa and Latin America I've seen some sad and grim stuff. But I've never seen anything like Calcutta. It was, on the face of it, the most awful place I've ever been – yet given the chance (and this applies to India all round) I'd go back there tomorrow.

17

Bolling Bolling

The final of the 6th Women's Cricket World Cup between Australia and New Zealand on 29 December 1997 was the ninth time the two sides had met that year. They played each other annually in the Shell Rose Bowl series; preparing for the World Cup they'd played the series twice, contesting five games in February, and three more in November. Australia won the first set 4–1, the second 2–1, and while Megan Lear always said Australia would be strong, why no one else seemed to have taken more notice of those results I don't know.

We shared our flight from Madras to Calcutta with the Kiwis; while we waited to board, I spoke with Debbie Hockley. She said Fitzpatrick was quick and aggressive, and Charmaine Mason was too; that both were everything you'd want in a fast bowler. 'They're prepared to stick it up your nose, no problem.'

For all that, she said, 'More than their bowlers, their principal asset is Belinda Clark. The bowlers are quick, but we can cope with that – whereas Belinda's a magnificent batsman, and you have to respect that. But then, we respect all of them; they're all tough competitors.'

By contrast, she said that she'd heard – and she'd heard correctly – that the English thought if they got her and Emily Drumm out, they'd won. With a fierce smile she said, 'Well sorry, boy – but that's no way to approach a contest, is it?'

She said of the final that games between these two were generally pretty even; whoever won, they didn't win by a lot. But as we came towards the game, I'd have to say that if anyone was betting on New Zealand, I never heard about it.

The final was due to start at nine-thirty; at nine o'clock in the foyer of the Oberoi Grand, there was neither word nor sign of a bus for the England party. I left for the stadium in a taxi with three of the players, and we found it sealed off with roadblocks and mounted policemen.

We also found Craig and Thrasy being denied entrance to the ground by a uniformed Jobsworth possessed of the most almighty self-importance. True, they didn't have tickets – but there'd never been press tickets at any of the previous games, so not realising you'd need one now was understandable. The production of press cards didn't do them any good either; the Jobsworth eyed them with magisterial disdain and announced, 'You have not followed the official procedure.'

Thrasy wailed, 'What official procedure? There's never *been* an official procedure.'

The Jobsworth was immoveable; the gate was a teeming chaos of people. At this point the Australian manager Chris Matthews appeared through the scrum and, in an act of heroic decency – when her team was due to commence playing the World Cup final in ten minutes' time – she tried to help out by barging towards us and calling out as she went, 'Let them through. They're part of our team.'

Unfortunately, this didn't get Craig and Thrasy any further.

Luckily, thanks to Shirley, I did have a ticket – so, obeying the First Law of Rodent Solidarity (if someone gets left behind, sod 'em) I ducked into Matthews' slipstream and went in. Next thing I knew, I was in the players' area by the boundary – so on the one hand my colleagues were marooned on the pavement, while on the other I'd arrived at a place to which my ticket gave me no right of access whatsoever. But since when did logic apply?

Looking about me, I saw that Australia were making ready to field; I said to Matthews that in that case, I assumed they'd lost the toss. She said they had, and agreed that they'd have preferred to bat first. Then she smiled and said, with a hard and absolute confidence, 'But it doesn't make any difference, does it?'

And if that doesn't tell you all you need to know about the mindset of this marvellous cricket team, what does?

Around and behind us, all manner of milling, bawling chaos was going on. I don't know quite how you achieve that condition in a stadium that was, at this point, virtually empty, but they'd certainly managed it. With barely minutes to go before the game began, an Indian journalist was yelling at the Kiwi manager to get their captain out of the dressing room for a photograph; when Hockley and Drumm got out to the middle, and Fitzpatrick set herself ready at the start of her run-up to open the bowling, someone started shouting over the PA system.

Thrasy and Craig, meanwhile, had got inside the ground, only to find another Jobsworth denying Thrasy access to the press box, and Craig ditto to the boundary. After much intensely beetle-browed study of their press cards, he then announced that Craig (but not Thrasy) could go up to the press box – prompting more anguished wailings because the press box, high in the stand behind glass, is the last place a photographer wants to be.

At this point I didn't even know where the press box was; I'd just sat myself down to watch Fitzpatrick beat the bat. In the huge and empty arena you could hear the fielders – *c'mon Aussies, c'mon Aussie girls, that's the way, Fitzy* – and you could see the vicious swing Bronwyn Calver was putting on it at the other end. With the second ball of the sixth over, she had Emily Drumm clean bowled through the gate with an absolute Jaffa; New Zealand were 14 for 1, and Australia were on their way.

How I was going to write this up if they wouldn't let us in the press box so we had access to the scorer, I didn't know – but it was entirely typical of India that during these first overs, a journalist from the Calcutta *Telegraph* saw the plight of the hapless English rodents, and somehow magically got it sorted in no time. That's India – one minute you're flummoxed by enraging sticklers, the next you're saved by someone whose every word and gesture speaks courtesy and consideration – and thanks to this guy's help, the three of us were eventually installed in our places. After an inauspicious start to the day, moreover, everything that followed was magical.

I shall be glad all my life that I was in Eden Gardens that day. It's an awesome arena, a gigantic flat bowl, double-tiered for most of its circumference, with a capacity of 110,000 – and as the day progressed, so the people streamed in. Estimates of the crowd varied from 50,000 to 65,000; they were virtually all women and girls, and they'd been brought in from miles around by the Sports Minister of West Bengal in a commandeered fleet of 1,600 buses.

Some saw the hand of electioneering in this, but why not? That's what politicians do – and the result of the Sports Minister's work, however much of an eye he may have had on his vote, was to produce a spectacle the like of which can never before have been seen in women's cricket. The best team in the world was out there, moving remorselessly towards a title they richly deserved, and taking the women's game onto a new plane in the process – and having so many there to see it was nothing short of wonderful. As the stands about us steadily absorbed more people, so Eden Gardens filled with a lively, immensely cheerful buzz and chatter. It was vividly colourful, and a triumphant finale to a tournament that may sometimes have been chaotic, but which succeeded in the end in being every bit as big as it had set out to be.

There was a quote from Swami Vivekanandi on the back of the tickets: 'There is no chance for the welfare of the world unless the condition of woman is improved. It is not possible for a bird to fly on only one wing.'

In a country where the condition of woman still leaves much to be desired, if the 6th Women's Cricket World Cup went even a tiny part of the way towards helping achieve the ambition expressed in those words, then everything – every stomach cramp, every rickshaw driver, every battle with room service, every broken phone line, every bus journey, every alarm call in the small hours – will have been absolutely worth it.

Debbie Hockley was magnificent. She batted for 165 minutes, scoring 79 runs off 121 balls; she hit seven 4s, and one huge 6 pulled over square leg off medium pacer Karen Rolton. Against an attack as fierce as the Australians, this was surely the finest innings of the tournament; unlike the hypnotised English, she moved her feet to Olivia Magno until Magno didn't seem to know what to do with her, and she steadily pressed those Test match fields back away from her. But while she cut and drove and blocked, watchful and strong, at the other end the wickets were steadily falling.

Only two other Kiwis made double figures. Captain Maia Lewis made 10 before Magno had her lbw, a decision she greeted with pretty evident disgust; she'd shared a partnership with Hockley of 38 for the fourth wicket. At the death, a brave and bold knock of 18 off 24 balls by keeper Rebecca Rolls put on 30 for the eighth wicket – but by now Hockley was tiring. She fell in the forty-seventh over, swinging a horrid lunge across Fitzpatrick as she tried to find a few more last runs; her off stump keeled over, and the Kiwis were done for. Their last bat Kelly Brown was run out in the final over, and they finished on 164 all out.

'Ironic,' said one of the South Africans over lunch. 'We got about that score against them too. And then they smashed us.'

In the press box, meanwhile, we were being aided with the numbers by the best scorer of the competition so far. I was subsequently told that this guy was something of a legend among the Indian cricket writers' fraternity – a short, proud, excitable man, he was prone to fits of comic irascibility when unduly harassed by the local pressmen – but with Thrasy and myself, he was the soul of kindness and patience. Early in the innings I asked him a question and he told me, 'Anything you want, sir, anything you want.' When I thanked him he said simply, 'It is my duty.'

Thereafter, whenever a wicket fell and he was calling out the runs, balls, and minutes, he always turned towards us to call out those numbers one extra time, going that little bit slower to make sure we'd got them. Then, when the innings was over, he ran through the batsmen's figures, came to the bowlers, and shouted, 'Bolling bolling!'

The Australian bolling bolling had been predictably excellent. Partners in pace Fitzpatrick, Calver, and Mason did the best work; Fitzpatrick got Hockley, and gave away only 23 runs from 10 overs, while Calver took out Drumm and the No. 3 Shelley Fruin at a cost of 29 runs in 10 overs. She wasn't as quick as Fitzpatrick, but her movement was lethal; Mason was aggressive too, and her reward came with the wickets of Katrina Withers caught behind, and Rebecca Rolls skying to deep mid-wicket at the end. As for the spinners, offie Avril Fahey was the tightest – no wickets, but only 18 runs off 8 overs – and it was another mark of Australia's single-mindedness that John Harmer should later say that he'd been working on her (no doubt with the World Cup in mind) for three years.

Where the Australians really excelled, however, was in their fielding. Melanie Jones brought off a string of diving stops with electric agility; the sizzling direct hit from thirty yards with which Michelle Goszko ran out Kathryn Ramel was similarly ruthless in its speed and panache.

Thrasy would later spin a line that this Australian side had revolutionised the women's game in the same way that Sri Lanka turned men's one-day cricket upside down at their own World Cup in the subcontinent two years earlier. I suspect that's over-egging it a shade; Australia's batting was still conventional, in the sense that they didn't launch an all-out assault over the top of the fielding restrictions from the first ball of the innings (something New Zealand did to England in the summer of '96, Hockley leading the way, and rocking us back on our heels in stunned surprise when she did so).

But in the fielding and bolling bolling departments, I'd say Thrasy's right. No one had ever played women's cricket with this degree of urgency, intensity, athleticism, and sheer in-your-face confidence as this side did. As Harmer would later contentedly remark (with his biomechanical hat on), 'What I'd like to work out next is how come Fitzpatrick can bowl seventy-five per cent as quick as a bloke, when she only weighs fifty-four kilos.'

Whatever the mechanics of it, I'd reckon the plain answer is that she wanted to. That evening she told me, 'We don't think about anyone else. We have our own standards, we think about what we can do – and nothing else matters.'

It wasn't just Fitzpatrick, either – all of them had that attitude. Harmer said, 'If a ball's going to the boundary and you're chasing it, there's only one way to field it, and if they don't do it right they get their knuckles rapped. Because I want them to perform their skills.'

I asked him about the Test match fields and he said, 'Hey – you can always surrender, right? But you want to be positive. When I took over I looked at it, it was seventy per cent dot balls. Now how are the players going to enjoy that, never mind anyone else?'

So if they were batting he wanted runs, if they were bowling he wanted wickets, and if they were fielding he wanted them shying at the stumps every chance they got. In short, when these Australians said they wanted to enjoy their cricket, what they meant was, they wanted to play out of their skins every time, and trash everyone they came up against in the process. As a result, they were terrific to watch – and so good that gender simply stopped being an issue.

At the 2nd Women's Football World Cup in Sweden in 1995, the Germans handed England an ignominious 3–0 thrashing in the quarter-final – the scoreline doesn't even begin to suggest the dominance they enjoyed in that game – and afterwards their coach told me, 'In Germany it's not women's football, men's football. It's just football.'

The same thinking applied to these Australians. When you watched them play, you forgot about their sex. You just thought, That's a bloody good cricket team.

Come the lunchbreak at Eden Gardens, the one thing we didn't know about Australia was how good their batting was. We knew Belinda Clark was outstanding – but as a batting side overall, they'd barely had to do any. They'd been rained off against Ireland, set that laughable target of 28 by Pakistan, and a not exactly daunting one of 96 by England. When they batted first against Denmark, Clark ran riot to get her 229 off 157 balls – but as far as the rest of the batting went, Denmark hardly constituted a test, and they lost only three wickets.

South Africa gave them something to aim at, scoring 163 – so they passed it without dropping a wicket inside twenty-nine overs. Against the Dutch they got 223 for 4, but again, it's hard to know how much of a test that was; Jet van Noortwijk, who plays for Yorkshire, is a pretty handy bowler, and she went for four an over, but whether the rest were any good or not I can't say. What we did know is that they got wrapped in a few knots against the Indian spinners – so if there was a question about

Australia, if they had a weakness, maybe it was in the batting. Maybe, if you got rid of Clark, you could start working through the rest of them.

Forget it. Their pursuit of the total was as composed and well paced as New Zealand's bowling was modest; the foundation was laid with 52 runs from 81 balls by Belinda Clark, and all the top five bats made double figures. It was Clark's eleventh half-century in forty international one-day innings; it took her to 1,868 one-day runs at an average of 54.94, and given that she's only twenty-seven years old, you can expect her to get plenty more.

She went about it steadily; she and Joanne Broadbent played themselves in against Withers and Nicholson, content to let the maidens go by, to take the singles here and there, to punch any rubbish across the boundary when it came, and to wait patiently on the lesser bowlers.

They took 25 off the first ten overs – then Kelly Brown came on, got bashed for ten off one over, and was promptly taken off again. Kathryn Ramel replaced her, and had better luck; her second ball was a full toss, Broadbent swiped it to cover, and Maia Lewis took a fine catch low down in front of her. Broadbent had made 15; Australia were 36 for 1.

Michelle Goszko came in to bat with dash and fire; Clark played the anchor, sharp between the wickets, flawless at the crease. As Goszko caught up to Clark's score, their fifty partnership came up off 70 balls; Australia passed the hundred mark in the twenty-seventh over, and looked to be cruising.

Two overs later, Goszko played an uncharacteristically horrid swipe through a straight one from Withers that took out middle and off; she left the field with 37 runs from 54 balls, and Australia were 107 for 2. The partnership was worth 71 runs; Harmer said later he'd always thought they'd win, once those two had built the base.

Clark fell in the thirty-fourth over, victim of an outstanding caught & bowled by Catherine Campbell; Melanie Jones came in to join Karen Rolton with the score on 117 for 3, and all they had to do now was stay sensible. They needed three an over, and proved readily capable of getting it; in the ten overs they were together, they put on 36 runs. The difference between the two sides was summed up in the moment when the ball came back to the top of the stumps from point to Withers at the bowler's end, with Rolton miles out of her ground – and Withers dropped it.

In the forty-fourth over, Withers took out Jones' off stump; she'd made 17 off 37 balls, with three 4s, and Australia were twelve runs from victory. With five overs remaining, they needed just nine runs – so the hapless Kathryn Ramel stepped up and bowled two wides. Before it was over, Rolton slashed a top edge high for Kelly Brown to take at short backward square with the score on 160 – so Bronwyn Calver crunched four through the covers, tapped away a single, and that was that.

Australia won by five wickets, with two overs and two balls to spare; they looked comfortable all the way. It wasn't much of a contest, but that didn't greatly matter; before an enormous crowd in a festive Eden Gardens, by far the most complete outfit in the tournament had done the job they needed to do without scares or nerves. They were cool-headed with the bat, razor-sharp in the field, tight and aggressive in their bolling bolling – and, for the fourth time, they were world champions.

A vast number of policemen in khaki tin hats, soldiers in extremely fetching marbled aquamarine camouflage outfits, and dancing girls in Indian 50th anniversary T-shirts spilled onto the field, accompanied by a major outbreak of pop music. In front of the dressing rooms, musicians with electric keyboards, guitars and an accordion made ready to make merry; a pack of seriously grim-visaged military types jogged past them toting sten guns, and the Chief Minister of West Bengal appeared amid a ruck of other worthies.

The security was brilliant. At the top of the day they hadn't even wanted to let Thrasy in the stadium; at the end of it, he and I were now standing unauthorised on the boundary, just yards from the folk all the weaponed-up jowlies were supposed to protect. Still, I'm not quibbling about stuff like that any more; the atmosphere was great, really bubbling, and when the two teams started dancing among the choreographed hordes of schoolgirls, it got even brighter. Someone was crying out on the PA about the crowd, 'Mobilised by the government of West Bengal – look at that, ladies and gentlemen! We have never seen that in all the world!'

Clark collected the trophy, Hockley was Eve of the Match, and the sun dropped low behind the giant stands, an orange disc in the rank grey sky. But it was blue overhead, the stadium was heaving with throngs of happy women, and the PA crackled with the busy sound of many esteemed and honourable types outdoing each other in praise for the day that the day truly merited.

It was a fine way to end an experience that was, ultimately, as enjoyable as it was exhausting. Before it all began, India's coach Srirupa Bose had said, 'This World Cup will make or break women's cricket in India.' I suspect that's overstating it – but I'd certainly like to think that this tournament did a lot more making than breaking.

18

Next Up

I went back to the Oberoi to file. Mihir Bose was filing some-where too – a piece in which he called the Australian captain Debbie Clark, and said that Hockley's six was the only one of the tournament. It wasn't – BB got one in Vijayawada against Pakistan, and Shaiza Khan hit three of them. Still, we all make mistakes, eh?

From the confusion at the start of the day, when they wouldn't let us in the press box, arose my own little glip in the *Independent* where I wrote that Emily Drumm was lbw to Calver, not bowled. I don't know why that happened – I'd *seen* the woman bowled – but like I say, we all make mistakes.

Rodents being sloppy is one thing. Other rodents can be snide, malicious, or downright fictitious, so it's no surprise that a few members of the England touring party should have turned out so wary of the media. Their *bête noire* is Carol Salmon, who writes about the women's game in the *Cricketer*; they felt she forever did them down, digging and carping. In her end-of-tournament review, what little space she gave England did indeed snipe about the batting order, and made no mention of what England actually went through to get as far as they did. But then, Salmon didn't go through it either.

What irks them is a feeling that Salmon ought to be on their side – she is, after all, an officer of the WCA – and if you can't count on your own people to give you at least a little credit, who can you count on? The way the players feel is best summed up by the reaction of one of them, on hearing gossip in Calcutta that Salmon had been relieved of 600 rupees (the best part of a tenner) by a canny shoeshine boy. 'I'd like,' she said firmly, 'to shake that shoeshine boy by the hand.'

Little squabbles inside the private world of an amateur game, however, pale into insignificance beside what can happen when the tabloids go to work. During the South Africa series last summer, England were practising at Lord's when Mike Atherton dropped in for a net ahead of the final Test against Australia at the Oval. Scenting a PR chance, the Vodafone people got a picture of him and Smithies together, then wired it round the papers.

The picture appeared on the back page of the *Mirror* the following day. One captain, said the copy, was a world champion, leader of the most successful English cricket side in modern times; the other was Mike Atherton. Smithies, they said, had dropped in at the Oval (not true, the picture was taken at Lord's) to give Atherton a few tips on how to beat the Aussies. This left the women understandably embarrassed. Sure, they were glad to see their captain on the back page, in company with the men's captain – but to be used as a stick to beat the men with, in a story cooked up out of absolutely nothing, was something they didn't want or need.

So caution in the matter of rodents is justified and understandable. That caution is further intensified by a strong sense among the players of gratitude and responsibility to their sponsors; after long years without backing of any kind, they're frankly petrified of anything that might jeopardise this new-found support. The notion of a rodent creeping in on them and (for example) blowing one pint of beer into a foul-mouthed orgy weighs, therefore, more than somewhat on some of their minds.

None the less, England's women are going to have to learn how to cope with the press whether they like it or not – not least because getting in the press is what Vodafone are paying for – and when Australia turn up in the summer, I'd guess there'll be a fair few media folk about. The best advice I've heard on this score came from Neil Hamilton's beleaguered agent in Tatton during the general election: 'Always deal with the national press pleasantly, as though they were real human beings.'

Not for the first time, Barbara Daniels had the sensible approach. The notion that Thrasy and I might be 'media pressure' made her laugh; given that they were world champions playing for their country at a World Cup, she'd have liked a bit more media pressure. But at least nowadays, she said, when they played at home, 'Decent papers do send decent journalists. So I've said to the players that they have to accept that those people won't always write nice things. If they think we've played a load of crap, then however eloquently they're going to say that, they have to be free to do so. Equally, if we play some stunning cricket, I'd hope they'd say that too.'

When I got back to the Oberoi, England were boarding their bus for the airport and home. As she went up the steps Shirley said sadly, 'You'll have a great party tonight. Just not with us.'

England should not, however, be disappointed in what they did. There are four good women's cricket teams in the world (South Africa will pretty soon make that five) and England solidly confirmed that they're one of them. Moreover, no one could have foreseen Australia turning up so able and positive, so focused, so intensively well prepared; just to give one example, John Harmer made videos of each of his bowlers' performances for them to go back and watch in their rooms, with his own comments inset onto the screen. He said, 'If they didn't run so many singles so I had to keep on changing the tape, I'd do it for the batters too.'

I therefore doubt, had England made it to the final, that they'd have fared any better than the Kiwis. I'm pretty sure they'd have done better than they did in Nagpur – but I'm pretty sure as well that the Australians, on that form at that time, would have won. As for losing the semi, of course it was disheartening, but England are not a worse side than New Zealand. After bowling and fielding as well as they did, they shouldn't have let Withers and Ramel get so many runs in the last five overs – but on nine other days out of ten, you'd back their batting to make that total anyway.

Why they didn't, on that particular Boxing Day, I don't know. Inexperience in chasing totals in pressure situations may be part of it; by the looks of it, that's a common failing in women's teams, as only Australia pulled off chasing totals of any size against decent opposition. Otherwise, not one player raised this as an excuse after the event – but I think it's fair to say that by the time they reached Madras, it was a miracle England were still standing up, never mind playing cricket.

Of course there were blemishes; no one can be perfect across seven games of World Cup cricket. The bowling and fielding against Pakistan was indolent, and against Denmark it wasn't massively better – but England came into the competition out of season, and they steadily improved on both fronts despite the most trying of circumstances. It didn't help losing the Lengster's foot down a pothole in the Hyderabad outfield before the opening game, either – that threw our efforts to find the best bowling attack out of kilter, and ended up resulting in the only real huff of the month. Given what that month was like, to have had only one huff seems to me evidence of pretty exceptional good humour.

On balance, there was far more good about them than bad; some phenomenal batting, some big-hearted performances with the ball and, when it mattered, a lot of good work in the field. They should be proud of themselves – and it's also important to note that they were a pleasure to travel with. These people tackled an itinerary that the men would have turned down flat – tackled it for the simple reason that they all just wanted very badly to play cricket for their country. And that's why writing about people who play for love instead of money will always be more fun.

The 7th Women's Cricket World Cup will be a Millennium affair. It takes place in New Zealand during December 2000, and it will have only eight teams in it – the eight quarter-finalists from India. For the following tournament in South Africa in 2004, the top six finishers from New Zealand will be joined by the two winners of a qualifying tournament involving the two sides who come last in New Zealand, plus Pakistan, Denmark, the West Indies, and one or more from Canada, Bangladesh, and Japan.

This is a more sensible way to do it; India's World Cup ended well, but along the way it was crazy. Eleven sides taking part was too much; top sides playing the minnows resulted in little more than pointless slaughter, and new sides like Pakistan will learn more if they play in what would, effectively, be a second division – if they get more meaningful competition against a set of teams more balanced in ability.

Before all that, meanwhile – next up, and more pressing for England altogether – comes the visit of Australia this summer. Despite what I've said about the Australians so far, however, no one should think for a minute that the result is a foregone conclusion. In India, they weren't really tested – and since at least a part of their success relies on bravura, it'll be interesting to see how they fare if England put them under pressure. England can certainly play well enough to do that, especially at home – and then we might find, I suspect, that the new world champions have a brittle element or two. It will, whatever happens, be a fascinating summer; if there's a game near you, you should go.

One who'll be playing (if selected) is Barbara Daniels. A fortnight after we got back she told me, 'I've revised my decision to retire. When we get to the middle of the series with Australia, I might regret that in terms of my personal life or my sanity – but I thought I played quite well in India, I hate to see the Australians win at anything, and I want another go at them. I want to beat the world champions, and I want to match what they've done. They've obviously worked really hard, and in India they were head and shoulders above everyone else – but I think we can beat them, and I'm going to go on playing because I want to have a go at it.'

On Sunday 25 January, I went to the Yorkshire Cricket School at Headingley. In the indoor nets, eight of the players who'd been to India the month before were working, among other Yorkshire players, with Megan and two other coaches. One of these, a senior ECB coach called Ralph Middlebrook, was working the bowling machine, with one after another of England's batsmen facing him. The machine was set on fast.

Appendix:

Australia in England, Summer 1998

July

Sun 5	England U-21 v Australia (1 day)	Finchley, Middx
Tue 7	South of England v Australia (1 day)	Shenley, Herts
Thur 9	North of England v Australia (1 day)	Oxton, Wirral
Sun 12	ENGLAND v AUSTRALIA 1st one-day international	Scarborough
Wed 15	ENGLAND v AUSTRALIA 2nd one-day international	Derby
Sat 18	ENGLAND v AUSTRALIA 3rd one-day international	Hove
Sun 19	ENGLAND v AUSTRALIA 4th one-day international	Southampton
Tue 21	ENGLAND v AUSTRALIA 5th one-day international	Lord's
Wed 22/29	Australian team to Ireland	
Fri 31	England A v Australia (3 days)	Gore Court CC Sittingbourne, Kent

August

Wed 5	ENGLAND V AUSTRALIA	
	1st Test match (4 days)	Guildford
Tue 11	ENGLAND V AUSTRALIA	
	2nd Test match (4 days)	Harrogate
Mon 17	President's XI v Australia	Littleborough,
	(3 days)	Rochdale
Fri 21	ENGLAND V AUSTRALIA	
	3rd Test match (4 days)	Worcester CCC

Acknowledgements

I am grateful to my publisher Richard Beswick and my agent Rachel Calder for believing that this story was worth telling, and to all at the sports desk of the *Independent* for giving England's progress the space it deserved.

Thanks are due to Joce Brooks for keeping me going with her Chinese potions, and to Selena Colmer and Thrasy Petropoulos for getting the beers in on Christmas Eve. Thrasy read the manuscript, too – but if there are any mistakes, they're mine.

I would also like to thank Sandeep Singh Nakai for his hospitality in Delhi, and the good people at Gulf Air who made what could have been a nightmare journey home into a thoroughly enjoyable experience.

Finally, thanks to Rebecca, Joe, and Megan for putting up with me going away over Christmas, and for putting up with the state I was in when I got back.